Business D

Palgrave Study Skills

Authoring a PhD
Business Degree Success
Career Skills
Critical Thinking Skills
e-Learning Skills (2nd edn)
Effective Communication for
  Arts and Humanities Students
Effective Communication for
  Science and Technology
The Exam Skills Handbook
The Foundations of Research
The Good Supervisor
How to Manage your Arts, Humanities and
  Social Science Degree
How to Manage your Distance and
  Open Learning Course
How to Manage your postgraduate Course
How to Manage your Science and
  Technology Degree
How to Study Foreign Languages
How to Write Better Essays (2nd edn)
IT Skills for Successful Study
The International Student Handbook
Making Sense of Statistics
The Mature Student's Guide to Writing (2nd edn)
The Personal Tutor's Handbook
The Postgraduate Research Handbook (2nd edn)

Presentation Skills for Students
The Principles of Writing in Psychology
Professional Writing (2nd edn)
Researching Online
Research Using IT
Skills for Success
The Study Abroad Handbook
The Student's Guide to Writing (2nd edn)
The Student Life Handbook
The Study Skills Handbook (3rd edn)
Study Skills for Speakers of English as
  a Second Language
Studying the Built Environment
Studying Business at MBA and Masters Level
Studying Economics
Studying History (3rd edn)
Studying Law (2nd edn)
Studying Mathematics and its Applications
Studying Modern Drama (2nd edn)
Studying Physics
Studying Programming
Studying Psychology (2nd edn)
Teaching Study Skills and Supporting Learning
Work Placements – A Survival Guide for Students
Working for Nursing and Midwifery Students
Write it Right
Writing for Engineers (3rd edn)

Palgrave Study Skills: Literature

General Editors: John Peck and Martin Coyle

How to Being Studying English Literature
  (3rd edn)
How to Study a Jane Austen Novel (2nd edn)
How to Study a Charles Dickens Novel
How to Study Chaucer (2nd edn)
How to Study an E. M. Forster Novel
How to Study James Joyce
How to Study Linguistics (2nd edn)

How to Study Modern Poetry
How to Study a Novel (2nd edn)
How to Study a Poet
How to Study a Renaissance Play
How to Study Romantic Poetry (2nd edn)
How to Study a Shakespeare Play (2nd edn)
How to Study Television
Practical Criticism

Business Degree Success

A Practical Study Guide for Business Students at College and University

Jonathan Groucutt

1/09

palgrave
macmillan

Published by
PALGRAVE MACMILLAN
Houndmills, Basingstoke, Hampshire RG21 6XS and
175 Fifth Avenue, New York, N.Y. 10010
Companies and representatives throughout the world

PALGRAVE MACMILLAN is the global academic imprint of the Palgrave Macmillan division of St. Martin's Press, LLC and of Palgrave Macmillan Ltd. Macmillan® is a registered trademark in the United States, United Kingdom and other countries. Palgrave is a registered trademark in the European Union and other countries.

ISBN-13: 978–0–230–50645–9
ISBN-10: 0–230–50645–3

This book is printed on paper suitable for recycling and made from fully managed and sustained forest sources. Logging, pulping and manufacturing processes are expected to conform to the environmental regulations of the country of origin.

A catalogue record for this book is available from the British Library.

Library of Congress Cataloging-in-Publication Data

Groucutt, Jon.
    Business degree success / Jonathan Groucutt.
        p. cm. — (Palgrave study guides)
    Includes bibliographical references and index.
    ISBN 0–230–50645–3 (alk. paper)
    1. College students.   2. Business education.   3. Study skills.
        4. Learning strategies.   5. Success.   I. Title.
LB3605.G74 2008
650.071′1—dc22   2008016313

10   9   8   7   6   5   4   3   2   1
17   16   15   14   13   12   11   10   09   08

Printed in China

This book is dedicated to the memory of my loving and caring partner

Shereen Baig (1958–2007)

who enriched so many lives through her knowledge, warmth, generosity, love and humanity. The world is so much poorer without her.

Contents

List of Figures, Tables, Examples, Slides, Illustrations and Scenarios   xi
Preface   xiii
Acknowledgements   xvii
Note on the Author   xviii

1   Introduction   **1**
  What is a business school?   1
  What constitutes the meaning of the world 'business'?   2
  What do you seek from reading for a business degree?   2
  The purpose of studying for a business degree   3
  Before your arrival at business school   4
  Creating documentary folders   8
  Expectations – students and staff   9
  Your motivation   10
  Events that are beyond your control   10
  Reflection zone   11

2   Important First Steps to Success   **12**
  Why study?   12
  When should you start studying?   12
  What are your reasons for undertaking this programme of study?   12
  Day 1 – semester/term 1 – year 1   13
  So, what is your previous experience of studying?   14
  'There's plenty of time – I do not need to start studying yet'   18
  Important first steps to success   18
  Understanding your programme   19
  What are your language capabilities?   21
  The role of your tutors   22
  Business myths and realities   23
  Lectures and lecture handouts   26
  Seminars/workshops   27
  Types of assessment   33
  When do you take time to study?   35
  Know the regulations   36
  Learning resources   36
  The knowledge triangle   40
  Leisure and relaxation – balancing work and social time   40
  Reflection zone   41

3   **Getting to Know Your Tutors and the Administrative Staff**   **43**
     Introduction   43
     Managing expectations   43
     Different types of faculty   44
     The administrative team   45
     Understanding the role of your tutors   45
     Communicating with your tutors   46
     Tapping into their wealth of knowledge   48
     Reflection zone   48

4   **Preparing for Study**   **49**
     Introduction   49
     Your personal exploration   49
     Making the connections   51
     Thinking critically   58
     Your physical environment   60
     When do you study?   61
     Staying focused   61
     Group/team discussions   61
     The high-risk approach to studying   62
     What is the purpose of a module guide or workbook?   62
     Lecture and workshop skills   66
     Your approach to research   68
     Using textbooks and other resources   70
     Key points for designing a successful study timetable   75
     Reflection zone   78
     Further reading   78

5   **So, Who Marks Your Work?**   **79**
     Introduction   79
     What do markers seek from your work?   79
     Processes   80
     Reflection zone   82

6   **Cheating: Copying, Collusion and Plagiarism**   **83**
     Introduction   83
     Forms of cheating   84
     Why do some students cheat?   87
     Detection   88
     Consequences   88
     The potential wider impact of cheating   91
     Seeking guidance   91
     Reflection zone   92

7   **A Brief Guide to Referencing**   **93**
     Introduction   93
     Referencing styles   94
     Potential difficulties   98
     The difference between a reference list and a bibliography   99

A few general thoughts   99
Reflection zone   99

8   When Things Go Wrong – You Are Not Alone   **100**
Introduction   100
Focusing on underlying issues   101
Reflection zone   103

9   Assignments   **104**
Introduction   104
Why assignments are used as a method of assessment   105
Assignments and the business perspective   105
Group and individual assignments   106
Assignment formats   108
Examining a case study   110
Peer review   113
Presentation of assignments   117
A word on getting started and writer's block   119
The purpose and value of feedback   122
Using feedback effectively   123
Making deadlines work for you   126
Reflection zone   130
Further reading   130

10   Team Working   **131**
Introduction   131
Why is team working often integrated into business programmes?   132
Why is team working important to your future?   134
Necessary skill development   135
Creating a team work agreement   136
Reflection zone   138

11   Presentation Skills   **139**
Introduction   139
Developing your mindset   139
Organization of your materials   140
Creating a format   140
Creating visuals   141
Prompts or cues   143
You!   145
Issues for your next presentation   147
Reflection zone   148

12   Examinations   **149**
Introduction   149
Why examinations?   149
Types of examinations   149
Planning your revision   153
Examination week   156
What to do the night before the examinations   156

The day of the examination   157
Examinations – frequently asked questions   163
Common examination mistakes   164
What makes a good answer?   165
Post-examination   173
What should I do if I fail?   173
Reflection zone   174
Further information   174

13 **Managing Dissertations**   **175**
Introduction   175
Using previous experiences   175
What is a dissertation?   176
Structure of a dissertation   176
Opportunities presented by dissertations   179
A few thoughts to help your approach   180
Working with your supervisor   184
Your dissertation proposal   189
Feedback and progress logs   192
Reflection zone   193
Additional resource   193

14 **What's Next for You?**   **194**
Introduction   194
What do you want to do?   195
Your *curriculum vitae*   196
Advice on references   197
What will business seek from you?   197
Staying in touch – *alumni*   198
Further reading   198

Appendix   199
References   208
Index   211

List of Figures, Tables, Examples, Slides, Illustrations and Scenarios

Figures

2.1	The knowledge triangle	40
4.1	Silos of knowledge	51
4.2	A vertical slice of the main silo	52
4.3	The interlinking of the silos to create a relational architecture	52
4.4	A semester plan synopsis	64
4.5	An example of a basic mind map	68
4.6	A format for making notes from a textbook	73
4.7	An example of a study timetable	77
9.1	An example of an assignment grid based upon grids used by the Business School, Oxford Brookes University	120
11.1	Clear and functional slides	142
11.2	Cluttered slide presentation	143
11.3	Readable slide presentation	143
11.4	Clear methods of presentation	144
11.5	Critical review	144
11.6	Referencing	145
11.7	Images as prompts	145
12.1	Example timing break-down of an examination	161
12.2	Identification of key issues by brainstorming	162
13.1	An Illustration of a Gantt chart	191
13.2	Progress log	192

Tables

2.1	An adaptation of Bloom's taxonomy	16
2.2	Business subjects	20
2.3	Key assessments	34
9.1	The DOs and DON'Ts of deadlines	127

Examples

2.1	A practical exercise undertaken by first-year business undergraduates	33
4.1	Mini case: an example of connectivity – an international airline	54
4.2	Mini case: Republic of Zimbabwe PESTLE factors	56
9.1	How to work with a case study	111

9.2   Peer review questionnaire   115
9.3   Student feedback portfolio: log 1   124
9.4   Student feedback portfolio: log 2   126
10.1   Student group working agreement   137
12.1   Case study: Crisis in the European Airline Industry (in Brennan *et al.* 2003)   152
13.1   Outline of a dissertation proposal   189

Slides

2.1   Tools and techniques   28
2.2   Learning outcomes   28
2.3   The role of the marketer   29
2.4   Strategy   30
2.5   Strategy requirements   30
2.6   Strategy levels   31
2.7   Marketing audit   31
2.8   Referencing   31
2.9   Next session   32

Illustrations

1.1   Making notes on your vacation   8
2.1   Friends enjoying quality time together in the peaceful setting
       of a botanical garden in Washington State, USA.   41

Scenario

6.1   Cheating: the aftermath   90

Preface

● The aims of this book

> '*Curiously enough, one cannot* read *a book: one can only re-read it.*
> *A good reader, a major reader, an active and creative reader is a re-reader.*'
>
> Lectures on Literature (1980)
> Vladimir Nabokov, 1899–1977, Russian novelist

As the main title suggests, the overall aim of this book is to create success – *your* success – in achieving a business degree. The content of this book is equally applicable whether you are studying in Budapest, Hong Kong, Karachi, Melbourne, Oxford, Pune or Singapore. This book is aimed at an international audience and it is applicable to foundation, undergraduate and postgraduate students. Moreover, you may be studying at a private college (working in collaboration with a degree-awarding organization), a private or state/government accredited university.

Effective studying is assisted by a strong sense of purpose, knowing what you hope to achieve and why you hope to achieve it. In order to succeed in your objectives, you need to become an active participant within the learning process.

This book interweaves both the study and reality of business. The idea is that you start preparing yourself for a business world while you are at college and university. As you read through this book, you will see direct comparisons with *real* business. If you really want to succeed within the highly competitive business world, then you need to think *business* (and everything that entails) from Day 1 of your studies.

What this book is and is not

Unless you consider specific literary classics by such renowned and gifted authors as Dickens, Kafka and Tolstoy, there is, perhaps, no such thing as a perfect book. It is always a difficulty for an author to know what to include and what to exclude. My aim was to create an accessible and useful text of approximately 70,000 words. Moreover, I know how expensive academic books can be and thus wanted a text that would command an affordable price.

In order to achieve this balance, there may be omissions and, perhaps, greater brevity in a few places than one would have wished. However, further information (ideas, concepts, useful tools and points of view) and downloadable forms are available via the website: www.palgrave.com/studyskills/groucutt.

The objective of this book is to provide a *one-to-one guide* on how to achieve practical day-to-day success in your business degree.

This book is not an analysis of teaching and learning styles. If you are interested in knowing more about your learning style, then additional reading sources are provided (see Appendix 1).

This is not a textbook – this is a *guide* to help you through your business degree.

Learning – and, therefore, studying – is a very personal matter. Different people tend to learn in various ways. I recommend that you take the time at the beginning of your programme (when things are usually less hectic) to read this guide, and plan your studying.

As the quote from the Russian novelist Nabokov stated above suggests, I recommend that you:

- Read this guide at least twice when you first purchase it and then use it throughout the length of your programme. Read and re-read sections as appropriate to reinforce your understanding and guide you through your assessments. It will become an indispensable resource to your future success.
- Read this guide in conjunction with the individual module/unit descriptors within your programme handbook. These should provide you with detailed descriptions of the module/unit with the appropriate learning outcomes and topics to be covered.

Many of you may already be familiar with some of the points in this guide. However, I strongly urge you to read this guide carefully. This guide has been written to help you succeed. However, it is *your* responsibility to develop your study skills, so that you do achieve success. Learning is a constant journey of discovery.

ASSUME the role of a business executive

I have placed particular emphasis of the word 'assume' in the title of this section for a particular reason. As stated in Chapter 2, I suggest that you adopt the mindset of someone in business while undertaking your business degree. I would equally suggest that a student studying a degree in music adopt the mindset of a composer and/or performer. Your real aim is to get under the skin of the subject. Therefore, why should the student studying classical music not think of themselves as the next generation of composers, such as John Barry, Ennio Morricione or John Towner Williams? Therefore, why should you not think of yourself as the next Luciano Benetton, Richard Branson, Viceca Chan, W.L. Gore, Kiran Mazumdar Shaw, Akio Morita, Marjorie Scardino or Ricardo Semler? There are new businesses still to be created – and you could be the person who is the creator.

Writing style

I have written this book in the first person, as I want to have a conversation directly with you. So often business books and academic textbooks are written in a very detached way, where the writer is seen as remote. I am as guilty as anyone of this approach, although I have attempted on previous occasions to have a one-to-one conversation with the reader. Through the use of the first person, I do hope that I am able to connect with you and thus help you in your endeavours to successfully achieve a business degree.

A brief word on terminology

Within universities there are a myriad of titles – Associate Lecturers, Lecturers, Senior Lecturers, Readers, Professors and so on. For simplicity I have adopted the all-encompassing word 'tutor'.

Throughout the book I refer to business terminology. Some of these terms may be unfamiliar to you, in which case I suggest that you check out their meaning using a business dictionary. Both Collins and Oxford University Press publish very good and reasonably priced business dictionaries.

Structure

Chapter ordering

The chapters are ordered to help you maximize your understanding of both the processes and the subject material over the length of your programme. Although there is some chronology it is advisable, as stated earlier, to read through and then re-read, as and when appropriate.

Connections

From time to time the word 'connections' will appear. This is a signpost that alerts you to the fact that there is a major link to another section and/or chapter. Business is a series of interrelated events or subjects. Your business programmes comprise a series of modules. Each module covers a particular disciplinary strand – for example, Introductory Accounting. However, these modules do not operate in isolation – as in the real world, they are linked. Equally, each chapter of this book should be considered as interrelated. There are signposts throughout that help you to see the connections. However, it is equally important for you to make those connections in relation to your own particular studies.

Reflection zone

At the end of each chapter are brief reflection zones. This is where you are asked to stop and think about the key issues and relate them to your own work.

References

This book is not heavily referenced – as stated earlier: this is not a textbook as such but, rather, a guide. However, I have included references where appropriate. In addition, several texts and web resources are given in Appendix 1.

Additional resources

At the end of several chapters, there are additional resources that may be helpful.

Online resources

There is a website that accompanies this text that features:

- Further comments and thoughts
- Information on additional resources and links
- Useful templates for you to download.

The importance of reading

The literary critic and scholar Harold Bloom wrote:

> It matters, if individuals are to retain any capacity to form their own judgements and opinions, that they continue to read for themselves. How they read, well or badly, and what they read, cannot depend wholly upon themselves, but why they read must be for and in their own interests (Bloom, 2000).

Even in our 'virtual speed of light' society, 'the word' remains fundamental to our very existence. Whether spoken or written, 'the word' is our light on the world. If you believe that you do not have to read for a degree or, indeed, for your future, then you are living on a falsehood. The key to your future is reading. Whether it is the work of academics such as Frances Brassington or literary writers of the calibre of Annie Proulx, your future is bound by 'the word'. Embrace reading, read widely, re-read, and you will open vistas to your life that you never imagined.

Acknowledgements

First, I would like to acknowledge the economist Dr John Kissin for being an inspirational and supportive personal tutor when I was a young undergraduate so many years ago. Second, Simon Williams (1952–2005), former Dean of Oxford Brookes Business School, who was supportive, encouraging and generous.

No book is written totally in isolation. I would therefore like to thank those who have given their time, enthusiasm and emotional support. Some have read the text and made critical comments that have enhanced this work beyond my original ideas. Shereen Baig (as always, a very special thank you), Chris Blackburn, Michael Brown, Elizabeth Brown, Suzannah Burywood, Susan Dailey, Camille Davis, Liz Dembina, Christine Ewers, Paul Griseri, Colin Horner, Alex Johnson, Wilf Jones, Bridget Latimer-Jones, John Muir, Shona Muir, Wendy Muir, the reviewers for their comments and colleagues at Oxford Brookes University Business School.

A thank you must also go to the undergraduate and postgraduate students who, over the years, have shared their concerns and thoughts on the subject of studying for a business degree.

Final thoughts

'The real voyage of discovery consists not of seeking
new landscapes, but having new eyes'
Marcel Proust, 1871–1922, French novelist

If you achieve your goals by reading this book, then I will have achieved mine.

JONATHAN GROUCUTT
London

Note on the Author

Jonathan Groucutt is a Principal Lecturer at the Business School, Oxford Brookes University, England where he teaches both undergraduate and postgraduate students. In addition to teaching, he has contributed to module and programme development, both in the UK and overseas. He has extensive experience of teaching international students.

Jonathan holds Fellowships to the Royal Society of Arts and the Royal Geographical Society, as well as memberships to various institutes and organizations.

He is author/co-author of several books including *Foundations of Marketing* and *Mastering e-Business* (with Paul Griseri) both from Palgrave Macmillan.

1 Introduction

'Learning without thought is labour lost;
thought without learning is perilous.'

K'ung Fu-Tzu (Confucius), 551–479 BCE,
Chinese philosopher

Contents

► What is a business school?
► What constitutes the meaning of the word 'business'?
► What do you seek from reading for a business degree?
► The purpose of studying for a business degree
► Before your arrival at business school
► Creating documentary folders
► Expectations – students and staff
► Your motivation
► Events that are beyond your control
► Reflection zone

● What is a business school?

While it is beyond the scope of this book to examine fully the role and purpose of a business school, it is nonetheless worthwhile briefly exploring the concept. The aim is to provide you with an understanding of the world you are now entering.

Perhaps, contrary to popular belief or myth, the development of business and management knowledge did not start in the United States (Antunes and Thomas, 2007). During the 19th century, several schools of commerce were established across Europe. In fact, it was not until the late 19th century that US business schools were established. As Antunes and Thomas (2007) state, the now famous Wharton Business School launched its Bachelors Degree in business in 1881, while in 1900 Dartmouth offered the first US Masters Degree in business. Compare these events with the study of classics that date back centuries. So, business as a subject is, relatively, the 'new kid on the block'.

Business schools and their students though have their own set of issues of which you need to be aware:

- Increasingly, they operate within highly competitive global environments, both for recruiting students and reputation. No longer is it competition with other universities within a particular home region or a state. Universities as geographically separate as the UK and Australia are often competing for similar student groups. Psychic distance (perceived physical distance from one place to another) is no longer a barrier to market entrants. Students today (and in the future) increasingly venture across regions in search of their educational goals.
- Good business schools have very strong links to industry. This is often achieved through placements (internships), work-based learning schemes and executives contributing to business school advisory boards. Such activities contribute significantly to providing you with the learning and understanding that 'fits' with business, both today and tomorrow.
- Business schools, as with universities as a whole, have to be generators of revenue and financial surplus. While academic learning is an important concept, so

too is the combination of financial stability and growth. In many ways they are no different to numerous other companies and organizations.

- They are often either the rising stars or the cash cows for the university (see your studies on the BCG or Boston Consulting Group Matrix). However, that does not mean that they have priorities in terms of, for example, building requirements. You might still find yourself in poor teaching room accommodation.
- Occasionally, business schools operate independently of a university, either with their own powers to award degrees or in a collaborative provision with another.
- According to various surveys, over recent years, 'business studies' has usually been in the top three of most chosen courses. This trend is likely to continue as industry, commerce, government and non-governmental organizations seek graduates with an understanding of business techniques.

● What constitutes the meaning of the word 'business'?

This is more than you buying a CD from a music store. There is a whole chain of interrelationships across subject disciplines, ranging from accounting through to warehousing (both electronic and physical). Moreover, a business does not have to exist purely for the creation of profit. Consider, for instance, the role of charities. Although these are not-for-profit organizations, they are still involved in business. For example, they have to purchase goods and services, whether it is for those who directly benefit from the charity or those who might support the charity by purchasing merchandise. An example would be greeting cards from the international charity Save the Children Fund.

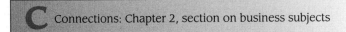

C Connections: Chapter 2, section on business subjects

Business is an all-encompassing activity that influences all our lives, no matter where we live in the world.

● What do you seek from reading for a business degree?

Here are just a few thoughts on what you personally might seek from undertaking a business degree. Rather than thinking of these as mutually exclusive, consider them more as nodes that are linked to form a network.

The ability to:

- Gain knowledge of how businesses (both for-profit and not-for-profit) actually operate.

- Develop your own ability to think rationally and critically.
- Enhance your ability to gather evidence (information), review it and critically deconstruct it. Then use this knowledge to build a case either for or against an idea or action.
- Gain experience of team working and knowledge of team-working skills within a 'protective' environment. In other words work in an environment where you have greater flexibility to make mistakes. Such flexibility might not be afforded you within an actual organization, especially where substantial financial investment is involved.
- Enhance your understanding of and appreciation for other people's points of view. This might be especially true if you are studying within a multi-cultural environment.
- Build your confidence prior to entering a working environment.

The purpose of studying for a business degree

As already suggested – business surrounds you! Everywhere you go, you are faced with some aspect of business – be it the advertising billboards, products in your local store, the ticket for your bus journey or even where to buy your lunch!

Business is also about exploring the world around you!

This book is for everyone who is studying for a business degree – you might be young or not so young (age is relative). Whoever you are, and whatever age, you must remember that we learn more over time. Learning is an ongoing process. We are continually learning, and learning continues long beyond the completion of our studies. Studying, on the other hand, is very much a skill that needs to be practised and self-assessed (gauging your own standards and level of development).

You might wish to study for a business degree for a variety of reasons. These might include the following:

- You have decided that you want to make a career within a certain aspect of business; for example, accounting or logistics.
- You have aspirations of being an entrepreneur and developing your own business, and thus need to understand how businesses operate.
- Your family owns a business and you are being educated to take the company to the next level of success.
- You have no career plan; however, the subjects in the business degree appear interesting.
- You might be undertaking a joint degree; for example, music and business. Music might be your passion and you have aspirations of working for a music company. To compliment your musical knowledge, you have chosen business studies. Music might well be an art form; however, anyone engaged within the music industry (from composers through to publishers and orchestras) also knows that it is a business that must be run on commercial principles.

Your approach – be objective!

On any programme, especially at university level, you will find that there are many different activities competing for your time. This guide has been devised to help you plan your studies effectively and efficiently. Thus it helps you to maximize your time – not only to learn – but also to enjoy life as well.

It is important that during your programme you adapt to different methods of learning and studying. For example, you will be required to undertake independent study (where you spend time reading around the subject area or researching a dissertation).

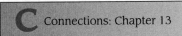

Connections: Chapter 13

Another skill is developing your ability to be critical of information, rather than simply repeating one fact after another.

Do not forget that the different subjects within your programme comprise a course of study, so do not look at each subject in isolation. It is important that you explore across the boundaries of the modules/subjects studies.

Ask yourself:

- How does your programme of study fit together?
- What are the reasons for these subjects being put together in that particular way?
- Where are the linkages and crossover points? In today's dynamic business environment, each subject cannot be considered in isolation – everything is interlinked. Business is holistic.

● Before your arrival at business school

As stated earlier, business is all around you and, more so than with many subjects, it is easily accessible. Therefore, use this accessibility to your advantage. Here are a few suggestions to help you prepare for your future studies:

- Find out about the location of your chosen college or university. This is particularly important if you are studying in another country. The institution will supply you with general information; however, undertake an online or library search to find out more on the country and locality. This will help you in terms of cultural understanding and sensitivity. Equally, it will help you to gain an understanding of the local and regional businesses; for example, agriculture. Local industry and commerce might feature in your studies. If you were studying in Seattle, for instance, you would have the aircraft manufacturer Boeing and the headquarters of the coffee shop franchise Starbucks nearby.

- If you are studying in a second language, take every opportunity to practice that second language before you arrive.
- Check out available resources. If you do not already, watch television news programmes, read quality newspapers and business magazines, and check online business resources. Now is the time to start. Become familiar with these sources of information because they will be a necessary adjunct to your studies. You need to be aware of what is happening now – the breaking news – and how it can affect a company or an industry.
- Specific module reading lists might not always be available in advance. Often, the reason for this is that the module leader might decide to revise the reading list, especially if he or she has discovered a more suitable core text. Even if a specific reading list for your chosen module is not available, you can still ask for the titles of suitable texts. You might be able to borrow these from your local library, a friend or, indeed, purchase them as supplementary reading. One of the positive aspects of studying business is that there is a plethora of books available.

    Your tutors will expect you to use the latest sources (journal articles, textbooks, quality business magazines and newspapers). However, do not neglect older sources as these might provide you with an interesting historical perspective and/or the origin of a specific theory or concept. This latter point is specifically relevant (a) in order to understand the original thinking behind the theory/concept; (b) to understand the development and/or criticism of the theory over time; and (c) to 'correct' any errors or misconceptions regarding the theory that might have occurred over time. As statements are handed down through time, there is occasionally the tendency for them to be misinterpreted.

- Buy a good English language dictionary: The vast majority of business degrees are taught in English, in part if not in full. Even if your first language is English, it is advisable that you have a dictionary to enhance your skills. Online spelling and grammar checkers are useful – however, they are not always accurate.

> **C** Connections: Appendix

- Buy a general business dictionary. If you do not already possess a high-quality business dictionary, consider buying one. Both Oxford University Press and Collins publish business dictionaries. A business dictionary will not provide you with all the answers; it will however help you understand key terminology. At a later stage, you might decide to supplement this with more specialist dictionaries (for example, in relation to accounting or economics).

> **C** Connections: Preface and Appendix

- Be objective and explore. Business, in all its forms both positive and negative, envelops every waking moment of our lives. The vast majority of us are oblivious to this as we go about our daily activities, whether buying groceries, catching the bus or even buying a lunchtime snack. Yet, all these activities involve several businesses, many acting together to provide you with a product and/or service. Rather than undertaking these activities simply because they have become routine, try looking at them from a different perspective. For instance, where do all the products originate from that adorn your local grocery store? How did the movie you watched last night actually get made? What about the clothes you wear – how did you get to wear them? These questions are not as simple as you might at first think. That is why you need to be objective in your exploration of the subject.
- While it might be early days into your programme of study, you are advised not to consider selling your textbooks at the end of the term/semester. Even when completing your dissertation or related projects (year 3 or 4 of your programme), you might well find these very same textbooks of immense value.

Making the connections

Exploration should extend beyond the words on a page or images on a television screen. Exploration also means what you experience. For example, any travelling that you undertake, such as from your home country to the host country of the university. There are processes involved – from the acquisition of the ticket, the management of the operations, customer services and marketing.

Also, do not always focus on the large-scale issues. Your focus should also be on the range of organizations, from the well established (such as Qantas, Unilever, Tata and Cadbury) to the new entrepreneurs, those at the cutting edge of business. Each organization faces its own specific range of challenges (both internal and external).

Some of you will have part-time jobs in the evening or at weekends. Such activities should not be purely concerned with gaining additional, often necessary, income. Whether you are working in a hotel, a supermarket or an office, use the experience to observe the very function of business. You might, for instance, consider the following questions:

- What does the organization do – manufacturing, service provision, product distribution, operate as a non-governmental organization (NGO), a charity, government department or something else?
- Who are the stakeholders? Remember, these are more than just the shareholders of a business – those who invest into the organization. Stakeholders can be many and varied in their composition and have significant influence. They range from the employees to members of the local community.
- Does it operate locally, regionally, internationally and/or globally?
- How many tiers of management does it have?
- How does the organization operate?
- What is the scale of operation?
- In which markets does it operate?

- Is it a micro business or a multinational? What is the difference?
- Does it have any specific Human Resource Management issues (for example, seasonal or part-time workers)?
- What is the breadth and depth of the media coverage on the company? For example, are there comments/analyses regarding share price, financial stability, quality of operations and growth potential? Is it a potential take-over target or, indeed, able to take over other companies?

Whether it is a micro business or a multinational, you can compare and contrast what you have learnt within the lecture room with your very own personal case study. You might discover that issues discussed within the lecture room match perfectly well with your experiences. However, in other cases they might not. Ask yourself the question: Why?

Observation

We can gain a sense and an understanding of business through observation. Observation is twofold:

- Observing through doing – this is work-related. You might be working in a supermarket or local store. Consider the work you do and how that fits with the overall operation and success of that business.
- Pure observation of situations and activities. You can observe business operations at any time, for example, when visiting:
  - CD stores
  - Clothing outlets
  - Fast food outlets
  - Stationery outlets
  - Supermarkets
  - Your college or university
    or
  - Using transportation services (buses, coaches, trains and planes)

To help you in your observation of business here are a few hints:

- Carry a small note pad. Whether you are on public transport or in a café, you might have an idea. If so, just jot it down.
- Place a note pad by the TV and radio. Often, on news, documentaries or other specialist programmes there are issues relevant to your studies. Make a note of them. You might be able to follow up on the programme via the broadcasters' websites (for example, the BBC and CNN) where additional information might be available. The topical issues raised within the programmes might be useful for current and future modules. Indeed, they might be relevant to your dissertation.
- Vacation. While you are a student, a vacation is more than a holiday. It is an opportunity for you to observe how businesses operate. That can be everything from a local restaurant to an extreme sports venue. What is important, though, is

Illustration 1.1   Making notes on your vacation
© Jonathan Groucutt 2006

that you take the opportunity to make a note of how it links back to your studies. Illustration 1.1 is an example of where notes were being taken, while on vacation, for a particular book. Inspiration can arrive from any number of sources. What is important is that you are receptive to such sources. This will not only be of value to you as a student of business, but also later when you enter the commercial world. However, it is not suggested that you spend all your time observing businesses in operation. Enjoyment and pleasure should be the focus of any vacation.

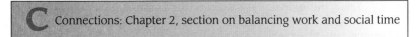

Connections: Chapter 2, section on balancing work and social time

Creating documentary folders

At this early stage, it is worth considering the idea of documentary folders for each of your subject areas; for example, 'Business strategy' or 'Introduction to business'. The aim is to create a system whereby you can collate information from a variety of sources.

The contents could include:

- Articles from quality regional and international newspapers; for example, *The Asian Times*, The *Budapest Business Journal (Hungary)*, *Business Daily* (South Africa), *Business Times* (Singapore) *China Daily*, *Corriere della Sera* (Italy), *Les Échoes* (France), *The Financial Times* (UK), *Il Sole 24 Ore* (Italy), *International*

Herald Tribune (US), *Kommersant* (Russia), *The Melbourne Age* (Australia), *The Seattle Times* (US), *The Standard (Hong Kong), The Times of India* and so on. Many newspapers now have associated websites where you can access material. Some websites are on a subscription/registration only basis.

- Articles from quality regional and international magazines; for example, *The Economist, African Times, Business Week, Fortune* and so on. Many business magazines have associated websites.
- Copies of journal articles; for example, Wu and Pangarkar (2006) Rising to the global challenge: Strategies for firms in emerging markets, *Long Range Planning*, 39 (3), June pp: 295–313. (This is the journal of the Strategic Planning Society – UK.)
- Your own notes; for example, you can include lecture notes, additional notes that you have made from your reading (see later section in this chapter) or from your own observations (see later notes in this chapter).

The value of the documentary folder

Such a folder will help you to:

- Collate all the material that is relevant to a particular subject.
- Explore the topic area. It will expand your knowledge base, often beyond the realms of business itself (this could encompass the arts, politics and history).
- Prepare for the assignments and other coursework, including, towards the end of your programme, your dissertation.

[*Note*: Newspaper, magazine and journal articles might well be available via your college or university's online library resources. It is important that you check out these resources within a few days of your arrival.]

> **C** Connections: Chapter 2 and Appendix, websites

● Expectations – students and staff

Everyone has expectations. After all, you have become a student at a university and you will have expectations of both the university and the staff. Equally the staff (administrative and academic) will have expectations of you. These expectations are usually written down in the module/programme handbook or explained to you in your induction or first lecture.

> **C** Connections: Chapter 3

● Your motivation

Motivation comes from within. You are the driver of your own motivation. It is our responsibility, as tutors, to create a stimulating and motivational environment in which you can learn and develop.

You must be committed to succeed. Self-confidence is vital here. There might be times when you find the course difficult; for example, working on a particular assignment. This is when you must draw on your commitment and self-confidence to help you achieve success. What is important to remember is that you are not alone – everyone, whether student or tutor, suffers difficult times (please refer to the Mentoring section).

Be prepared for setbacks. If you fail an assignment/examination, learn from the experience. Prepare carefully for the re-sit and be confident of success.

Your role in the learning process

Ask students at different universities what they are studying and they reply 'reading law' or 'reading chemistry' and so on. This statement underlines the action the student is participating in. At university level, students have a responsibility to themselves to *read relevant literature* associated with the module/programme/course of study. By reading widely, you gain more knowledge and insight about the subject. Remember that not everything on a subject can be fully contained within *one* textbook.

In order for you to be successful you will have to take ownership for your own success.

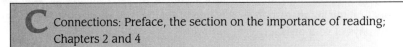

C   Connections: Preface, the section on the importance of reading; Chapters 2 and 4

● Events that are beyond your control

Illness, bereavement, family problems, personal issues, accommodation and financial difficulties – these affect everyone in their life. These events can affect your study time, meeting assignment deadlines and your examinations.

If you have any problems, academic and/or personal, you are strongly advised to seek out your personal tutor. They, depending upon the nature of the problem, might or might not be able to provide you with a direct solution. However, they have a duty of care to place you in touch with the appropriate college/university support teams; for example, counselling.

If you have a problem, it is in your own best interest to seek guidance. Otherwise, through no fault of your own, you might actually jeopardize the success of your degree.

Reflection zone

Here are a few key summary points for you to reflect upon:

- Explore the business world that surrounds you via your own experiences and documented sources. Seek to understand how businesses operate locally, regionally and internationally.
- Be observant.
- Adopt a business mindset.
- Examine how your programme fits together – where are the connections? Think of your programme holistically.
- Create documentary folders that will help you collate relevant information.
- Seek to monitor expectations and your own motivation – think *Success*.

2 Important First Steps to Success

'Our goals can only be reached through a vehicle of a plan, in which we must fervently believe, and upon which we must vigorously act. There is no other route to success.'

Pablo Picasso, 1881–1973, Spanish painter and sculptor

Contents

- ► Why study?
- ► When should you start studying?
- ► What are your reasons for undertaking this programme of study?
- ► Day 1 – semester/ term 1 – year 1
- ► So, what is your previous experience of studying?
- ► 'There's plenty of time – I do not need to start studying yet'
- ► Important first steps to success
- ► Understanding your programme
- ► What are your language capabilities?
- ► The role of your tutors
- ► Business myths and realities
- ► Lectures and lecture handouts
- ► Seminars/workshops
- ► Types of assessment
- ► When do you take time to study?
- ► Know the regulations
- ► Learning resources
- ► The knowledge triangle
- ► Leisure and relaxation – balancing work and social time
- ► Reflection zone

Why study?

Effective studying is assisted by a strong sense of purpose, knowing what you are hoping to achieve, why you are hoping to achieve it, and how the subject holds together. If you can grasp hold of these ideas, you will find studying much easier. You become an active participant within the learning process. Just sitting back, reading a few notes, listening to a few lectures, and hoping that you understand usually has one outcome – *failure.*

When should you start studying?

Start today!

If you have the programme/module descriptors for this semester/ term, you are advised to read through these to get a feel for the topic areas. Once you have obtained a copy of the core text(s), you can match the topics to the relevant chapters. Later in this book you will find advice on how to read critically and make appropriate notes.

Do not procrastinate!

What are your reasons for undertaking this programme of study?

You have made a series of decisions that led you to undertake this programme of study. The decision to undertake and apply for this programme was yours. You were motivated by many personal factors – a desire to achieve, to be successful, to be with your peers, perhaps to become wealthy. These factors will form the basis of your motivation to complete this programme of study successfully.

The objective of studying at college/university is to increase your:

- Knowledge of the subject.
- Critical thinking ability.
- Retention and recall of ideas and concepts.
- Application of ideas and concepts.
- Ability to evaluate and synthesize various forms of information, ideas and concepts.
- Ability to make valued and realistic recommendations.
- Ability to draw thoughtful conclusions.

If you think that this is a lecture, then I want you to think again. This is about you gaining a university degree in business studies. If you have straight 'A's and you think university will be a pushover, I want you to think again. Life at university is *very* different to anything you might have previously experienced.

You are planning a career in business – so prepare for one. As suggested in the Preface, start thinking like a business person. Therefore, start thinking about:

- Your ideas.
- Your ideas supported with a rationale.
- How to present your ideas effectively and efficiently.
- Deadlines.

This is your starting point. The really great thing about university is that you can experiment with ideas, test them out before you get into the real world.

● Day 1 – semester/term 1 – year 1

Welcome to university.

For many of you, this is the first time away from home. An adventure awaits – one that contains a multitude of hurdles for you to cross. Perhaps a daunting task, but one that I can assure you will help to prepare you for the 'madness' of the real world that lies beyond the gates of the university. But, if you do not understand that 'madness', you will not survive within the business community.

Let's be direct – unless you have had some previous experience of university, you will not know what studying at business school is really all about. So what is the first thing you need to do? That is relatively simple – start afresh!

Puzzled?

Then welcome to university life!

Whilst what you have learnt prior to university has great value in underpinning knowledge, university life is very different. Moreover, you *have* to get used to the idea that life is very different.

In this chapter we explore together some fundamentals about starting a business degree at university.

OK . . . I hear muttering voices . . . 'it will be the same as at college or wherever, so what is he going on about . . .' NO! It will be very different . . . so much will be down to you and you alone – if you do not grasp that, then you will most likely have problems.

Now, welcome to the real world!

The whole purpose of a business degree is to provide you with the knowledge and the skills to succeed. It is very much up to you how you grasp the knowledge and skills, and how you use them. As stated in the Preface, the objective is to help you gain the necessary skills in order to be successful in obtaining your business degree. Moreover, these skills will benefit you within your working environment.

● So, what is your previous experience of studying?

Your previous experience prior to entering university might have been a mixture of the following:

- Your previous tutors might have dictated copious notes during your lectures. You probably wrote them down, as best you could, word for word.
- Use of only one (adopted) textbook. You were discouraged from reading wider than the set textbooks or notes provided.
- You were taught not to question the author's or, indeed, the tutor's views.
- Little or no open discussion of topics or issues.
- During assessments you were expected to repeat 'exactly' the words and phrases as dictated by your tutor, or from the textbook.
- You thought the teacher was a 'god' and thus you needed to repeat everything they said – word-for-word. While having respect for tutors is a commendable trait, they should not be viewed as having a god-like status.

or

- You were taught to explore every avenue in order to gain a depth and breadth of knowledge.
- You were taught to question – whether they be opinions, facts or concepts.
- You were taught to debate ideas with both your contemporaries and your tutors.
- You were encouraged to have your own points of view as long as you could support them with evidence.

Students who embark upon undergraduate and postgraduate programmes come from a diverse range of backgrounds and learning experiences.

The teaching and learning approaches taken at most universities can be very different from your previous experiences. Teaching sessions can be a much more interactive experience. At university, you must take a considerable level of personal responsibility for studying, researching assignments and preparing for examinations. Therefore, reading and appraising work critically is valuable to your success.

University is about:

- Independent thinking.
- Being critical in your thinking (there is more on Critical Thinking and what it means in Chapter 4).
- Being an independent person.
- Exploring ideas.
- Challenging ideas.
- Reading around the topic and subject areas.
- Developing your own character.

Overall it is about your intellectual, analytical and personal self-development.

I stated in the Preface that this book would not be full of academic literature on teaching and learning – that remains true. However, it is important to refer to one particular taxonomy (or classification/structure) as a means of demonstrating the difference between your previous studying experiences and the one you will face at university. In the late 1950s and early 1960s, the American educational psychologist Benjamin Bloom (1913–99), together with his colleagues, created a structure to classify a series of 'educational goals and objectives'. This was to become known as Bloom's Taxonomy of Cognitive Domain (Bloom, Englehart, Furst, Hill and Krathwohl, 1956). What has become generally known as Bloom's Taxonomy (or classification) can be used to separate your pre-university and university learning objectives.

Table 2.1 is an adaptation of Bloom's Taxonomy. The level refers to what you can achieve or attain. As you can see, I have highlighted the view that certain levels of attainment should have been achieved prior to university. However, it is recognized that these skills are more developed in some students than others. The definition provides an explanation of the various skill levels. However, questions and cues provide us with the types of adjectives that are often present in assignment or examination questions.

You will be able to relate Table 2.1 to both your learning outcomes, as depicted within your module/student guide. Moreover, the sample marking grid provided in Chapter 9 also illustrates how Bloom's Taxonomy can be related to your various assessments, especially when considering assignments and projects such as dissertations.

Stage	Level	Definition	Key words for Questions
Pre-university	Knowledge	At this level, you will normally recall or recognize information, ideas, concepts and principles. Usually it will be in the form learnt from a lecture or a book. For example, you will be able to demonstrate knowledge of who are the key writers on leadership, including: Blanchard, Kotter and Bennis.	For example, questions will use such words as list, describe, identify, show, collect, examine, state and define.
	Comprehension	At this stage, you will translate, comprehend or interpret information based upon your prior learning. In other words, you can demonstrate an understanding of information and be able to group information together in a logical format. You will also be able to interpret information and thus compare and contrast ideas and concepts. (As will be seen later in this book, this is vital in terms of both your assignments and your dissertation.)	For example, questions will use such words as summarize, interpret, contrast, predict, discuss, distinguish and differentiate.
Pre-university	Application	This is the use of infor-mation, ideas, concepts, theories and models. For example, it is a straightforward exercise to reproduce Porter's Five Forces model directly from the textbook (Porter, 1985). This is a model used for analyzing an industry's environment.However, it is the 'application' of the model that your tutors will be seeking. So, for example, how could you apply Porter's Five Force model to the airline industry within your own geographical region?	For example, the questions will use such words as apply, demonstrate, illustrate, develop and operationalize.

Table 2.1   An adaptation of Bloom's taxonomy

Stage	Level	Definition	Key words for Questions
University	Analysis	This is where you deconstruct information into its different elements or constituent parts. You then examine these elements in order to understand any emerging patterns. This allows you to identify motives and/or causes behind certain actions. For example, you may be analyzing the reasons why a company seeks to divest certain products from its portfolio. This may be because they are no longer profitable and/or strategically fit the company's longer-term vision.	For example, the questions will use such words as explain, infer, outline, recognize, prioritize, correlate, compare and contrast.
	Synthesis	This is where you bring together information from different sources and areas to draw conclusions and/or create a plan or proposal. For example, you might be asked to examine a company's business performance. You would draw upon several performance indicators from the fields of, for instance, accounting and marketing. You would bring the information together (or synthesize) to draw a conclusion on how well the company had done, and perhaps how it might do in the future.	For example, the questions will use such words as combine, integrate, re-arrange, formulate and reconstruct (bring ideas/ concepts together and fuse them together in your own words.)
	Evaluation	This is where you assess the value of theories, ideas, concepts and models. Although there will be some subjectivity, the aim is to be objective in your evaluation. Throughout your degree programme you will be asked to evaluate theories and models – this may be one theory or view against another or, indeed, assessing the value of a model within a real-world context. What is important it that you support the evaluation with evidence. In other words – WHY?	For example, the questions would use such words as judge, recommend and critique.

Table 2.1 Continued

● 'There's plenty of time – I do not need to start studying yet'

This is a BIG PROBLEM! . . . but why?

Yes, it is so easy to say, for instance, that you should start preparing your assignment today . . . this evening . . . tonight . . .! You might think 'Well, there is plenty of time before the Week 9 deadline.'

BUT, in reality, there isn't. There will be other assignments, seminar preparation and general reading to undertake.

The pressure is on:

- You start the assignments late, you are trying to read the various journal articles, the textbook and keep up with the reading for the seminars.
- You pray that you will not be picked to comment on this week's reading for the seminar.

Welcome to university life . . .

This is the very reason why you should start working on the assignment the very day that you receive it. In Chapter 9, we will explore assignments in more detail. Suffice it to say, please do not leave it to the last minute before you start work. Unless you are a brilliant individual, you risk failing both the assignment and the module!

● Important first steps to success

It is important that you:

- Attend *all* lectures (let your tutor know if you cannot make the lecture and the reasons why – illness, placement interview and so on). As well as being a basic courtesy, the tutor might be able to meet with you and discuss any critical issues that were raised within the lecture/seminar). Overall, if you miss a lecture, it is your responsibility to collect/copy notes, read the relevant section(s) in the textbooks and make additional notes.
- Be on time for all your lectures. Some institutions have a policy that, if you are more than five minutes late, you are not permitted to enter the lecture room. Being late is (a) a sign of poor manners and disrespect; and (b) disturbs those students who have sought to be in the lecture room on time.
- Take notes during the lecture.

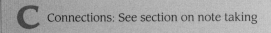
C   Connections: See section on note taking

- After the lecture (while the subject is still clear and fresh in your mind), make additional notes. This will help increase your retention of the topic area.
- Ask questions. If you are unsure about a particular point, ask the lecturer questions. If you do not want to ask questions in class, discuss this with the tutor at break or after the class. Alternatively, make an appointment to see or email the tutor.

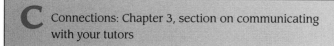

C Connections: Chapter 3, section on communicating
   with your tutors

- Discuss and debate the issues/ideas with your friends and colleagues. Again, this helps you to gain different perspectives on issues and increase your retention of the topic. Such discussions can take place over the telephone, by email or face-to-face.

Business subjects

There are many and varied business subjects. However, it might be useful to state some of the subjects that appear common to most business-related degrees (see Table 2.2). You might wonder why you study some of these subjects – for example, 'Ethics in Business'. However, without an informed understanding of ethics within a business context how do you know whether you are behaving morally in relation to employees, suppliers and your customers? You might, for instance, believe that business is purely profit driven and question why ethics should play a part. However, if you seek to gain profit at any cost, then your profits might be very short-lived. Indeed, you might well find that you have no business at all and are declared bankrupt (a position that is more severe in some countries than others). Therefore, consider all your business subjects important and interlinked – there is no business subject that is not related to another (a point that is often referred to throughout this book).

● Understanding your programme

Degree programmes come in various shapes and sizes: modular; linear; two-, three- and four-year. It is important that you have some understanding of your (potential) programme prior to enrolling. The following is a very brief summary of some of the issues that you might encounter.

Linear programmes

This is where the student studies a set programme of modules, especially over the first two/three years of the programme. In their final year, they might have the choice of one/two electives in addition to their final dissertation.

Modular programmes

This type of programme varies from university to university. Typically, the modular system provides students with the opportunity to study a range of subjects as well as undertake a joint honours programme. While there will be compulsory subjects to take, such a system does provide a level of flexibility that allows a student to experiment with module combinations. For example, you might combine psychology, language and business modules within your first year of study.

However, what you must ensure is that you will have the correct pre-requisites, if there are certain modules that you wish to undertake in years two and three. For example, there might be a module on 'Business aspects of management accounting'. In order to take this you might have needed to take a module on 'Foundations of management accounting', as one develops logically out of the other.

Accounting	Macroeconomics
Audit practice	Management accounting
Banking	Management information systems
Business-to-business marketing	Managing business projects
Business history	Marketing
Business law	Marketing communications
Critical thinking	Marketing research
Economics and society	Marketing strategy
Entrepreneurship	Microeconomics
Ethics	Non-profit organizations
Finance	Organizational behaviour
Financial management	Personal development
Globalization	Purchasing and supply management
Human resources	Retail buying and supply management
Innovation and design	Retail operations
International accounting	Retail store design
International business law	Strategy
International marketing	Strategic logistics and operations
International trade	Strategic management
Introduction to business	Sustainability
e-business	Taxation
e-commerce	Tourism
Hospitality management	Transport economics
Knowledge management	Trade agreements
Logistics	Travel trade

Table 2.2   Business subjects

Two–four year programmes

The length of a business degree programme, especially, can vary from two to four years. Two-year degree programmes (also known as fast-track degrees) are usually based upon three intensive terms or semesters of eight–twelve weeks over the two years. There is normally very little vacation period between the terms/semesters.

Four-year programmes can be either a:

- Formal programme structure – degrees awarded by Scottish universities tend to be of four-year duration.
- Placement year – some universities offer students the opportunity to undertake a placement (or internship) year with companies. This is, in effect, a year in industry where the company employs you on a salary. Typically, you have no classes to take. However, you are expected to use the experience gained in your placement during your final year of study at your university. For example, if you worked within the finance department of a multinational company, it is expected that you will have gained useful knowledge in terms of accountancy and financial management practices that you can incorporate within the seminars, your coursework and examinations.

● What are your language capabilities?

In the study of business, three vital elements are often overlooked:

1   In today's globalized world, many students study business in a second language, most often English. While understanding the complexities of the English language, you also have to appreciate the nuances and complexities of business English as well. This is often a double difficulty to master. Computerized language translators will help. However, they are not the solution if your comprehension of the language is insufficient to understand either a lecture or seminar presentation. Moreover, such devices are usually not permitted in an examination as they can often store far more than language translations. If you experience difficulties, I would suggest that you seek help from your tutors. Many colleges and universities provide additional language support services.

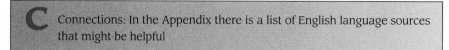

C   Connections: In the Appendix there is a list of English language sources that might be helpful

2   Some textbooks lack a distinct clarity in their use of language. It is almost as if the author(s) sought to write in the most convoluted way possible. Contrary to popular belief, the use of complex language is not necessarily the sign of a superior intellect. Perhaps it is more a case of someone who thinks that they have one! That said, from time to time, within your course of study you will be recommended

textbooks and journal articles that seem totally impenetrable in terms of their understanding. If this is the case, consider the following actions:

- Give yourself time to read the article/chapter carefully. Do not leave it until the night before your seminar.
- Discuss the article with your friends and colleagues. What is their view and why have they formed that opinion?
- If you still do not understand it, make an appointment to see either the module leader or seminar leader for that particular module. Ask them to explain or outline the key issues and explain to them why you have found it particularly difficult.
- If the problem is with a particular textbook on the subject, then seek out another that you find more easily accessible. Often module leaders will recommend several core texts – therefore choose from the recommended list the text that best helps your understanding. If only one book is recommended, check out the texts within the library. You might well find one that either complements the recommended text or can be used as an alternative. It is important that you find the text that helps you in your understanding of the subject, even if it is only a secondary source.

3 Take every opportunity to practice your English. It is very easy, once you have achieved your required IELTs score, to relax. Achieving your IELTs is just the beginning. When you are either socializing or working with a group of friends from your own country, resist talking in your native language. By continually practicing your English, you will improve your skills. Otherwise, there might be a tendency to fall below the skill level required to complete your course successfully. As we will see later, the dissertation comes at the end of your programme. In order to succeed at your dissertation you need to have a high level of reading and comprehension skills.

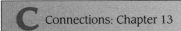

C Connections: Chapter 13

● The role of your tutors

Your tutors usually undertake several roles in providing you with the necessary motivational environment.

They act as:

1 A guide/facilitator – to explain and develop ideas and thoughts on the subject.
2 A questioner – to ask you relevant questions that will help you understand the subject, and develop your critical thinking and analytical skills.
3 A supporter – to provide support to you, which might be through listening to your concerns or providing you with extra reading in areas where you might feel weak.
4 An encourager – to provide you with encouragement to undertake the various assessments and enjoy the programme.

C   Connections: Chapters 1, 3 and 13

● Business myths and realities

Prior to starting your business degree programme, it is worth considering a few of the myths and realities that pervade the subject. Understanding these from the outset will help you to place business in a proper international context.

Myth: America invented business, commerce and trade.

There is often a mindset that these three functions emanated from America. On the contrary, business, commerce and trade operated long before the European discovery of America. Indeed, its very discovery was born out of trading nations (namely Britain, France, Spain, Italy and the Netherlands) seeking raw materials and land to colonize. Moreover, we can link these three functions back to the Roman and Greek civilizations.

Reality: What the Americans did was introduce mass production on a scale that had not been previously achieved elsewhere.

It was the American entrepreneur and industrialist Henry Ford (1863–1947) who mechanized the conveyor belt process, allowing him to create economies of scale in production. This, in turn, allowed him to sell an affordable automobile (the Model-T Ford). However, this was only one part of his contribution to mass production. By owning rubber plantations in Malaysia, steel mills and his own railway company, he was able to control his supply chain. In terms of his workforce, he introduced revolutionary practices for the time (based on the work of Frederick Taylor).

C   Connections: Chapter 4

Reality: So there was the basis of mass production; however, how could the public be persuaded to purchase?

The new age of mass production was converted into the new age of mass consumption by the like of the Public Relations Practitioner Edward Bernays (1891–1995). A nephew of psychoanalyst Sigmund Freud (1856–1939), Bernays used techniques developed by his uncle and others to persuade people to become consumers of the new products. Bernays and his contemporaries used psychology to change attitudes and practices, whether it was 'cool' for women to smoke or involving the whole family in purchasing a new car. The combination of mass production and psychology helped convert America into a mass consumption society. Much of the rest of the world has since followed this mass consumption approach.

Myth: Large companies only exist in America and Western Europe.

Yes, there is a large concentration of sizeable corporations within these regions. However, do not forget other economies. Consider, for example, the following very brief selection:

- Argentina: Grupo Arcor, Organización Techint, Tenaris
- Australia: Coles Myer, Macquaire Bank, Telstra, Westpac, Woodside Petroleum
- Brazil: CSN, Embraer, Petrobras, Semco
- Chile: Enersis, SACI Falabella
- China: Lenovo , PetroChina, Qingdao Haier
- Hong Kong: Cheung Kong (Holdings), China Unicom, Hutchinson Whampoa and Swire Pacific Group
- Hungary: Graphisoft, Hungarian Telekom, MOL, OTP and TVK
- India: Aditya Birla Group, Jet Airways, Tata Group, The Times Group
- Japan: Aeon, Honda, Sony, Sumitomo Metal Industries, Toshiba and Toyota
- Malaysia: Malaysian International Airlines, Petronas, Proton Holdings, Royal Selangor, Sunway Holdings and Supermax
- Mexico: Cemex, FEMSA, Grupo Carso and Grupo Televisa
- Russia: Aeroflot, Gazprom, Rosneft, Sukhos Corporation
- Saudi Arabia: SAVOLA Group, Saudi Basic Industries Corporation, Sahara Petrochemical Company
- Singapore: DBS Group Holdings, Singapore Airlines and United Overseas Bank
- South Africa: Harmony Gold, South African Airways
- South Korea: LG Group, Hyundai, Samsung and SK Telecom
- Switzerland: ABB, Nestlé, Swatch Group
- Taiwan: Acer Computers, Formosa Plastics Corporation
- UAE: Emaar Properties, Emirates Telecommunications Corporation.

Myth: Entrepreneurship is limited to America.

Since the very first transaction, there has been entrepreneurship. It is fair to say that the core of all the businesses that we call global started out as single idea in someone's mind. For instance, Unilever, an Anglo-Dutch company with a market value of over US$60 billion (Unilever, 2006), started life as a small soap company in the Liverpool area of England in 1884. Today's micro business might become a global player tomorrow – that is why business is so dynamic.

A case in point is the Taiwanese company Acer. Established in 1976, under the name Multitech, Acer has gone from being a relatively small component manufacturer to a global business. In 2006, Acer had achieved the number three position for notebooks and was number four for desktop brands worldwide, delivering revenues of US$11.32 billion (Acer, 2007).

Clearly, entrepreneurship is championed in America where failure is not stigmatized as in some other nations. So, there is a very positive cultural angle taken. This reinforces the view that America, as a nation, has been built by the courage of risk takers. This is true, however, the vast proportion of the world's commercial operations comprise micro and small to medium-sized enterprises. Indeed, many of these are family owned, often with three generations actively participating.

The scale of such entrepreneurial activity cannot be underestimated in terms of the wealth generated within a nation state. When, in the 1970s, dictator Idi Amin expelled the Asian community from Uganda, in one stroke of the pen he destroyed the Ugandan economy. Many of these displaced people, with just a suitcase, made their homes in the UK and Canada. Having lost everything, they rebuilt their lives and created new entrepreneurial activities, thus making a significant contribution to the respective economies.

The Ugandan example also highlights how the macro or external factors are linked to the micro factors of business and commerce.

Myth: Companies must focus only on the young. That is where the real market exists.

This is only partly true. You must consider the baby boomers who are in their 50s and early 60s (as of 2006/2007). Generally, in countries such as America, Canada, parts of Europe, Australia, New Zealand and regions of Asia and the Pacific Rim, these form the greater proportion with disposable income. True, they might not seek the latest gadgets. However, collectively they have significantly more spending power and influence than the young. Companies therefore ignore them at their peril. Will the next generation have as much spending power? Well, that is probably dependant upon the expanding levels of personal debt (just examine the UK and the United States, for instance), global conflict (this will impact upon the economies of such nations as the UK and the United States) and global warming (the impact upon households, governments and industry) to name but a few problems.

In terms of the here and now – it is not the young with the financial power in many countries.

Myth: Every business operates in exactly the same way no matter where it is located.

This is an ethnocentric view of life. Although a business might operate within the same marketplace, be governed by the same legal frameworks (for instance, accountancy procedures), the culture and operational methods can vary enormously from those of a competitor. This might be imbued within the defined culture of the business.

This leads to the fact that you cannot copy a business like-for-like. Yes, the two companies can be rivals and have similar manufacturing capabilities (and indeed competencies) to produce similar products. However, it is often the skills of the people and the culture of the organization that differentiate it from the competitors. In other words, these factors can determine the uniqueness in terms of the company itself – not necessarily the products they produce or the services that they provide. This is about talent – choosing the right people and creating the right culture so that, as a business, it 'works', and works well.

Think of it this way. How did you choose your college or university? Bricks and mortars are just that. Most universities are similar – perhaps some with better designed buildings than others. Yes, it might have been the programme of study. However, there is a chance that you chose it on the people, the culture – the atmosphere you felt as you walked around before making your decision. Equally, what makes a 5-star hotel really shine amongst the rest of the 5-star hotels? Usually it is the people who deliver the service – both individually and collectively. Such service is dependent upon leadership and the culture of the organization.

So what do these myths and realities really mean for you? Well, in order to both study and be successful in business your need to:

- Have an open mind.
- Explore the world – be ever questioning.
- Explore business – both from a micro and macro perspective.
- Seek to understand different perspectives.
- Focus on a range of companies not purely on the large global companies or corporations.
- Refuse to take anything for granted – business is full of surprises.
- Think about people – and how individual and group actions affect people, both positively and negatively. You need to place yourself in the other person's shoes. How will they feel to you? A company, for instance, might have a great product. However, if the employees are poorly trained and de-motivated, the product – and, hence, the company – might fail.

Lectures and lecture handouts

The purpose of lectures

Everyone will have his or her own different experiences of lectures prior to arriving at college or university. For many of you, the approach at university will be very different from your previous experiences.

It is important to realize that lectures are not 'the whole thing'. They provide (as do lecture notes) a snapshot of the key issues, especially as they are normally only one hour in duration. In order to benefit fully from the lecture, you should have conducted pre-reading on the topic area.

Generally lectures present a range of issues/ideas including:

- Learning outcomes for the topic – this will include your reading around the topic area.
- Definitions – for example, the meaning of the term 'depreciation' in accounting.
- Key words and phrases – these can be useful links to help you explore the topic further.
- Models – for example, Porter's Five Forces or the equilibrium point of a demand and supply curve in economics.

- Areas of dispute – this can range from definitions to how models perform under certain conditions. It is important to realize that even the most established models or theories can be challenged.
- Mini cases – a tutor might use a mini-case to illustrate how a model or theory operates. The mini-case might be theoretical or based upon a real organization.
- Further reading – at the end of a session, the tutor might present you with further reading. This might already be cited in your module guide or could be additional. What is important, though, is that you engage in reading around the topic area. It is only by exploring the topic that you will be able to enhance your knowledge and understanding.

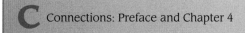

C   Connections: Preface and Chapter 4

How to use lecture notes

It is important to understand the role of lecture handouts as part of your study process. Normally, you will receive a handout that illustrates all or some of the slides that form your tutor's presentation.

As with lectures, there is often a misconception that lecture notes are all inclusive – in other words, lecture notes alone will get you through your module and, hence, your programme. This is a mistaken view. Lecture notes simply provide an overview or snapshot of the key issues of the lecture session. It is your responsibility to develop the lecture notes further. This can be achieved through reading around the subject area – for example, a combination of books, journal articles and quality business magazine articles.

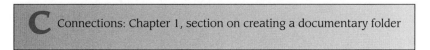

C   Connections: Chapter 1, section on creating a documentary folder

Slides 2.1 to 2.9 are from the lecturer slide pack for Groucutt (2006).

● Seminars/workshops

These are designed:

1   To follow on from the key themes discussed within the lecture with a practically-oriented exercise (it is not another lecture); and/or
2   As an exercise that is part of an ongoing activity. For instance, it can be another 'instalment' based upon your previous knowledge in the understanding of a particular case study problem. This might be the case study that will be presented to you in the examination. Thus, the seminar is helping you gear up, in terms of your knowledge base, for the examination.

Slide 2.1   Tools and techniques

Part 2
Tools and Techniques

Chapter 6
Strategy in Marketing

© Jonathan Groucutt 2006
Foundations of Marketing

Slide 2.2   Learning outcomes

Learning Outcomes

- Discuss the relevance of strategy to marketing.
- Explain the role of the marketing audit in relation to meeting the organization's overriding objectives.
- Debate how various strategic tools or techniques can assist marketers to meet both marketing and corporate objectives.
- Explain how organizations can gain and defend market share within turbulent markets.

© Jonathan Groucutt 2006
Foundations of Marketing

These should express what you should gain by the beginning of the next session – that is, by attending this lecture, the following seminars and your additional reading. If you have completed these basic activities, you should have achieved the learning outcomes.

Slide 2.3   The role of the marketer

The Role of the Marketer

- Analyse both the micro and macro environments using appropriate tools and techniques.
- Continually refine this analysis in relation to changing environmental conditions.
- Continually analyse competitive actions and be able to either pre-empt or react to such actions.
- Link marketing to the overall ambitions of the organization (the corporate strategy) but with a need for flexibility.
- Marshall or group resources and core competencies to compete within the marketplace.
- Marshall the components of the marketing mix.

© Jonathan Groucutt 2006
Foundations of Marketing

This makes the link between the functional area and strategy. It is important that you come to understand and appreciate the different relationships between the functional strategic elements of business.

Slide 2.4   Strategy

What is Strategy?

Mintzberg *et al.* (2003) describe strategy as:

'the pattern or plan that integrates and organization's major goals, policies and action sequences into a cohesive whole. A well-formulated strategy helps to marshal and allocate an organization's resources into a unique and viable posture based on its relative internal competencies and shortcomings, anticipated changes in the environment, and contingent moves by intelligent opponents.'

© Jonathan Groucutt 2006
Foundations of Marketing

Definitions are useful in creating a general understanding. You have to be aware that, in business studies, an idea or concept can have several definitions. Some are merely a contemporary update of an early definition – for example, the meaning of marketing. However, there are revised definitions that challenge traditional wisdom. In such cases, you will be expected to know the varying definitions and why they vary. This could be your first encounter with comparing and contrasting views and ideas, an approach that will be immensely valuable when you come to your dissertation.

Slide 2.5   Strategy requirements

A Strategy Requires

- Appropriate level and type of resources.
- These resources need to be deployed efficiently and effectively to support the organization's corporate objectives and goals.
- There needs to be flexibility to be both proactive and reactive to changing environmental and competitive conditions.

© Jonathan Groucutt 2006
Foundations of Marketing

As you will encounter throughout your degree programme, business tends to be process driven. Therefore, it is important to understand what is actually required for an action or perspective to take place.

Slide 2.6   Strategy levels

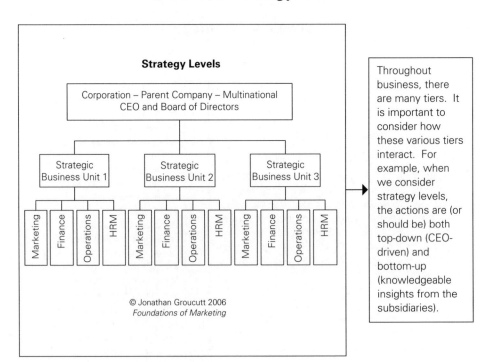

Strategy Levels

Corporation – Parent Company – Multinational CEO and Board of Directors

Strategic Business Unit 1

Strategic Business Unit 2

Strategic Business Unit 3

Marketing | Finance | Operations | HRM

Marketing | Finance | Operations | HRM

Marketing | Finance | Operations | HRM

© Jonathan Groucutt 2006
Foundations of Marketing

Throughout business, there are many tiers. It is important to consider how these various tiers interact. For example, when we consider strategy levels, the actions are (or should be) both top-down (CEO-driven) and bottom-up (knowledgeable insights from the subsidiaries).

Slide 2.7   Marketing audit

The Marketing Audit

Kotler *et al.* (1989) describes this as:

'an independent examination of the entire marketing effort of a company, or some specific marketing activity, covering objectives, programme, implementation and organization for the purpose of determining what is to be done, appraising what is being done, and recommending what should be done in the future.'

© Jonathan Groucutt 2006
Foundations of Marketing

Slide 2.8   Referencing

References

Kotler, P., Gregor, W. & Rogers, W. (1989) The MA comes of age.*Sloan Management Review.* 30 (2) (Winter) pp: 49–62.

Mintzberg, H., Lampel, J., Quinn, J.B. & Ghoshal, S. (2003) *The Strategy Process: Concepts, context and cases.* (4th ed.). Harlow: Prentice Hall.

Porter, M.E. (1980) *Competitive Strategy: Techniques for analyzing industries and competitors.* New York: Free Press.

Porter, M.E. (1985) *Competitive Advantage.* New York: Free Press.

Porter, M.E. & Millar, V.E. (1985) How information gives you competitive advantage in Porter, M.E. (1998) *On Competition.* Boston, Mass: Harvard Business School Press.

© Jonathan Groucutt 2006
Foundations of Marketing

Typically, at the end of the lecture session there will be a reference list of the texts – journal articles to which the tutor has referred. This provides you with additional sources of information that you should explore. This will help reinforce your knowledge and understanding.

Slide 2.9 Next session

Next Session

- The Branding of Products and Services.
- This has become an integral component of marketing, business and everyday life.

© Jonathan Groucutt 2006
Foundations of Marketing

This indicates the context of the next session and provides guidance for you to prepare for that session. Reading the topic area in advance and linking it to the contemporary world can provide you with a greater understanding of the fundamental issues. It also prevents having to 'catch up' every week after the lecture session.

 Connections: See types of assessment in this chapter and Chapter 12

Example 2.1 shows a practical exercise undertaken by first-year business undergraduates. The objective here is for the students to examine products that they are particularly familiar with in light of three other criteria –price, promotion and place (location). This allows students to investigate products with which they are familiar prior to exploring more esoteric goods and services.

Connections: This relates to the points made in Chapter 1 about goods and services that form part of your life, thus helping you to explore the essential features of a business

Example 2.1   A practical exercise undertaken by first-year business undergraduates

PRODUCT (Refer to your Favourites)	PRICE (What was the price of the product? What type of pricing do you think it is?)	PROMOTION (How is the product promoted?)	PLACE (Where did you buy this product? Where else is it available?)
CDs			
Clothing brands			

Types of assessment

Throughout your degree programme, you will encounter various types of assessment. The aims of an assessment are generally to:

- Provide a variety of different methods that test or challenge different levels of knowledge, understanding and skills.
- Test your level of knowledge, critical reasoning and various skill sets (for example, your ability to develop a persuasive argument).

In this section, we briefly explore some of the key assessments that are often used within a business programme (see Table 2.3). Several of these are discussed in greater depth in later chapters. Some of these assessment techniques might already be familiar to you while others might be new.

Assessment component	Assessment objectives
Numerical tests	Numbers form a basic part of business (for example: accounting and financial analysis). Therefore it is vital that you are able to handle numbers/calculations of various complexities.
Sourcing information	Increasingly students have access to online databases. These potentially provide a wealth of information at the touch of a computer keypad. Some universities and colleges use tests early in the first term/semester to check your ability to search and gather specific information from the online databases. For you to be successful in a business degree you must be able to use the various online databases efficiently and effectively.
Assignments	These normally ask you to critically evaluate one or more issues in a real or fictitious company. From your analysis you are asked to draw conclusions. Assignments can be group and individual. In terms of group work it is important that everyone makes an equal contribution to the outcome. Assignments may be written in report or essay format. Usually you will have several weeks to research and prepare your response. The important issue (as reflected elsewhere in this book) is to start straight away on the assignment – do not leave it to a few days before submission date. It will be too late!
Case study analysis	This is another form of assignment. Here you will use a case study on a particular organization and/or industry to critically examine specific issues pertaining to the organization/industry. Case Studies can comprise anything from one page to 20 pages. They may be used both as an assignment and as a discussion document within a seminar.
Poster presentations	These are usually a group activity where you are assigned a specific task. For example, you might be asked to find ways of visually demonstrating a company's supply chain (from factory to retail outlet) and what models can be used to examine supply chains. So within the physical limitations of a poster your team needs to: (1) Be inventive. How are you going to demonstrate supply chains (and the relevant models) in a visually exciting way? (2) Demonstrate that you understand the models and how they operate. You need

Table 2.3 Key assessments

Assessment component	Assessment objectives
	to achieve this without the benefit of several pages of typed pages of explanation, as you might find in an assignment. Thus it can be a real challenge of the imagination to produce a successful poster. However, while there is a real learning motive behind poster presentations they are also great fun too!
Examinations	These are usually held at the end of a term/semester and are designed to evaluate your knowledge and critical reasoning skills within a set time frame (normally two to three hours). These can take various forms (1) Essay-based where you examine a possible choice of free-ranging questions. (2) Essay-based where you are required to answer questions that focus upon a case study (this may be pre-seen prior to the examination). (3) Multiple-choice where you choose what you believe is the answer from a selection of possible answers. The answers are usually marked on special forms that are subsequently computer read to provide an accurate and fast printout. Some multiple-choice examinations are undertaken at a computer increasing the speed of marking and feedback.

Table 2.3   Continued

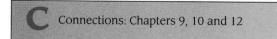

C   Connections: Chapters 9, 10 and 12

● When do you take time to study?

Please do not leave the studying of topics until just before an examination. Learn as you go along, both within a particular module and across your programme. Making this activity a continuous process helps to ensure that you are not under time pressure in the final days before an examination. This will also help you to follow the lectures more easily. So, you need to include study time in your weekly timetable.

I recommend that you spend more hours studying outside the lecture room as you do within it. This time should be spent in two ways:

1   Ensuring that you have learnt what has been explained in the lecture theatre;
2   Reading around the subject. You are reading for a degree, thus it is important that you read around the subject, broadening your horizons as you go.

You will find any subject much easier to learn and understand if you can see something of the context within which it operates.

You will have been given a programme timetable. Use it to schedule ongoing study time. Even though it is tempting, do not let any other activities encroach on your study time. If you keep to this plan, people will respect your wishes to study at certain times, and you can build a social programme around when you are available. By being disciplined, you will be surprised by how much free time you really do have (and also by how much you are learning along the way).

 Connections: Chapter 4, section on designing a successful study timetable

● Know the regulations

You will find that many colleges and universities are excellent examples of a bureaucracy (as advocated by sociologist, lawyer and economist Max Weber (1864–1920)). Weber's work will be identified in any lectures/workshops that you have on management. Colleges and universities are usually renowned for being awash with regulations, paperwork and teams of administrators who oversee various functions. While regulations (for example, entry requirements, conduct, assessment and progression) are important, initially they can be overwhelming. It will be impossible for you to remember all the regulations pertaining to your modules and degree programme. However, be aware of the basic requirements and keep a paper copy of all regulations in a folder. This will, at least, help you when in doubt. Also, know from whom you can seek advice when required. In many institutions there are field advisors, year tutors and/or programme/course directors who can assist you.

● Learning resources

It is vital that you understand how the library operates and are fully aware of the resources that it contains – both physical and electronic. You must read around the subject – *not* everything (as previously stated) is contained within lecture and seminar notes.

Online academic journals

Academic journals are extremely useful for obtaining a greater understanding and appreciation of a subject. They are a valuable resource for researching background material for your assignments and dissertation.

Typically, journal articles are peer reviewed (the same process is used for textbooks) prior to acceptance for publication. Usually, two or more academics are asked to review the paper, making comments where they feel that it adds new knowledge and where it can be improved. In many ways, it is a very similar process to your tutors appraising your assignments. The article might either be accepted without changes or revised prior to publication.

C Connections: Chapter 9, section on peer review

The following is a very brief selection of what is now available online. Access will also depend upon the licence agreement between your college/university and suppliers. What you have to bear in mind is that such licenses are extremely expensive and beyond what you would be able afford if it were just down to you. Therefore, it is in your best interest to use such resources while they are available to you at no cost.

The following are well-known online academic journal databases:

- Business Source Complete offers full text articles from over 5,000 journals and quality business magazines (over 1,000 academic journals). This equates to literally thousands of journal articles that you can search electronically. For example, it contains the *Harvard Business Review* dating back to 1921, which is an excellent resource in its own right.
- Emerald provides full text articles from over 100 business and management journals.
- Ingenta makes available full text articles from various academic journals.
- Journal of General Management is a journal of international management.

Of course, you can be overburdened with too much information. My suggestions when searching for online information are:

1   Give yourself time. Throughout this book, I suggest that you start work on assignments and examination preparation as soon as possible. Never leave it to the last moment, as you will severely increase your risk of failure! Searching for relevant information takes time – it is not something that you can do in just 30 minutes. As stated earlier, your objective is to think like a business manager. In order to make the right decision, a business manager needs accurate and relevant information. Thus, in order for you to write a knowledgeable assignment, you need to access the right information. Give yourself two to three days just to search for the information – this is even before you start your evaluation of the most relevant information;

2   All online databases have usually very good search facilities. What you need to do, in the initial stages of your search, is focus upon key words. In some subject areas, these might be quite narrow. However, in others you might want to use a range of key words to see what appears. For example, if you were examining redundancy policies within a Human Resource Management assignment, you might want to consider the following key words and phrases:
    - Redundancy
    - Downsizing
    - Restructuring and re-structuring. (You will have to consider whether or not the search engine will delineate between hyphenated and non-hyphenated words.)

- Business closures
- Divestment
- Closure of businesses
- Termination of businesses
- Exit strategy.

3   Make a note of the articles that you believe that are most relevant. With some journal databases, you can tick the articles that you believe are relevant for later downloading and printing;

4   Once you have downloaded and printed the relevant articles, you need to assemble them in an order of importance. Once you have completed that task, you can begin extracting the relevant background data for your assignment. What you will have to bear in mind is that this will also take time. The length of time will depend upon your understanding of the business issues and the level of your English language skills.

Internet search engines and sites

Familiarize yourself with the various Internet search engines. Through these you can enter the dedicated websites of major international companies. These websites often contain a diverse array of information from corporate history, product/brand range and developments, financial structure and performance. The Internet can provide several sources of information:

1   Details of companies from their own corporate websites. Remember that this is their view of the world, not necessarily how others perceive them;

2   Company and industry watchers, such as the financial house Standard & Poor;

3   Broadcasters, such as the BBC and CNN. They have dedicated areas of their websites to business issues and relevant programmes such as the BBC's *The Money Programme;*

4   Newspapers and news agencies, such as *The Financial Times* at ft.com (Please note that ft.com has various levels of entry, some are free while for others a subscription rate is charged);

5   Organizations such as the World Trade Organization, World Economic Forum and other internationally respected bodies;

6   Reputable publishers and think tanks (a specialist government or commercial research organization; for example, Demos in the UK) raise challenging questions and issues for further discussion.

Health warning!

Whilst the Internet can provide a wealth of resource material, it also contains dubious material. Just because a website states that it discusses either the principles of marketing or strategy does not mean that the information is reliable or, indeed, accurate. The above six areas should help you to steer clear of dubious material.

Quality newspapers and business magazines

It is important that you become familiar with quality international newspapers/magazines such as *African Business, Business Week, The Financial Times, The Economist, Fortune International and The Middle East.* They contain useful practical examples of how companies operate. In addition, there are features on management and business subjects such as marketing and human resource management.

Trade or industry publications

Various business or industry sectors have their own range of publications. These vary enormously in terms of their scope, quality and level of detail. For example, the areas covered include automotive, aerospace, cosmetics, engineering, mining, transportation and utilities.

Trade and industry publications can be useful in providing you with:

- Background to the industry and/or a particular company.
- Current changes that are affecting that industry – for example, changes in legislation how and they might affect companies operating within that industrial sector.
- A contemporary perspective on the strength of competition and the opportunities for new companies to enter the marketplace. Such information could be useful if, for instance, you were conducting a Porter's Five Forces analysis on the sector.

While trade and industry publications do have a value, it is advisable that you do not rely on them for all your assignment sources. You will need to balance these with appropriate academic journal articles.

Television news, current affairs and business documentaries

As with newspapers and business magazines television news broadcasts will discuss contemporary company and industry sector issues. From time to time, there will be special current affairs and business documentaries, such as *The Money Programme* on the BBC and *World Business* on CNN. Financial news updates are available 24/7 on networks such as Bloomberg TV (www.bloomberg.com) and CNN (www.cnn.com). There are also business TV channels such the satellite- and cable-delivered The Business Channel www.the-businesschannel.com

The BBC worldwide website can also be a valuable source of information and analysis. Visit www.bbc.co.uk for details. In addition, several news agencies, including the BBC, issue daily podcasts and programme videos online.

Radio programmes

The BBC World Service has numerous business programmes such as *Business Brief, Business Daily, Global Business, World Business Report and World Business Review.* You can also hear BBC radio programmes after they have been broadcast through the BBC's

Radio on Demand service. Visit www.bbc.co.uk for details of these programmes, schedules and your opportunity to listen to them.

Business, market research and company reports

It is important that you become familiar with the market, business and company reports available through online library databases. These include Mintel, Euromonitor, Thomson Gale, Thomson One and Business Insight.

Business DVDs

Also available, in some regions, are various business-oriented DVDs, some of which are previously broadcast television documentaries.

● The knowledge triangle

In this chapter, we have considered several important first steps to your success. Therefore, it is perhaps appropriate, at this stage, to reinforce in Figure 2.1 what I call 'the knowledge triangle'. In order for you to be successful, you have to engage in lectures, seminars and exploration of the subject area (that is, reading). If you fail to engage seriously in any of these, you risk the collapse of the triangle. All three areas are important to your overall success.

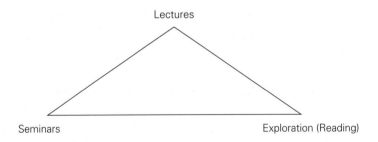

Figure 2.1   The knowledge triangle

● Leisure and relaxation – balancing work and social time

You might think that this is oddly placed within a book on study skills – far from it. University life is not just about studying day and night – in fact, it is not in your best interest to do so. You have to create a balance between studying and having a life separate from the purely academic environment. Now, let's be clear – that does not mean handing assignments in late (see later sections of this book). It is about planning or organizing your life so that you have both study and leisure time.

It is important that you relax as well as study. The programme will be hard work. However, in order to maximize your opportunities, it is vital that you have fun as well. If you enjoy leisure activities (passive or active), do not sacrifice them entirely in order to study and revise.

Yes, you probably will reduce the number of leisure hours as the assignment deadlines and examinations approach. However, do ensure that you plan for time to enjoy yourself. You need to ensure that you are keeping your social and people skills alive. They are part of our lives and also the business environment.

Remember – it is important that you seek quality time with both friends and family (Illustration 2.1). This way you can seek to have a balanced life both now and in the future.

Illustration 2.1   Friends enjoying quality time together in the peaceful setting of a botanical garden in Washington State, USA.
© Jonathan Groucutt 2000

Reflection zone

Here are a few key summary points for you to reflect upon:

- Be clear as to why you want to study a business degree and what you will gain from the experience.
- Understand that studying at university might be a very different world compared with your previous experiences. Consider the approaches that you might need to take to adapt your learning styles.
- Reflect upon how your programme of study is devised and consider how the various modules interlink.

- Consider your language capabilities – if you have difficulties, seek advice and guidance.
- Consider how you can maximize benefits from the lectures and seminars. For example, how you can support the overviews gained in lectures through additional reading.
- Be aware of the various types of learning resources that are now available to you. Consider how you can use them effectively and efficiently.
- Realize the importance of balancing work and social time.

3 Getting to Know Your Tutors and the Administrative Staff

'Experto credite.'

[Trust one who has gone through it].

Aeneid, Book 11, 1.283,
Virgil (Publius Vergilius Maro), 70–19 BCE, Roman poet

Contents

- ▶ Introduction
- ▶ Managing expectations
- ▶ Different types of faculty
- ▶ The administrative team
- ▶ Understanding the role of your tutors
- ▶ Communicating with your tutors
- ▶ Tapping into their wealth of knowledge
- ▶ Reflection zone

Introduction

The purpose of this chapter is to prepare you for working with your tutors and the administrative staff, and understanding their individual roles. Many students arrive at university and really do not know how to interact with either the teaching staff or the administrative staff. This is often understandable. Hopefully this chapter will place the relationship between tutor, administrator and you in some form of realistic context. Indeed, as we interweave business studies with a business mindset, perhaps you should also consider your tutors as business managers. Equally, as in business, the administrative team is there to provide knowledge and support.

I should state from the outset that cultural differences will affect working relationships and I will refer to these within this chapter.

Managing expectations

As stated through out this book, you will be charged – or, indeed, empowered – with managing expectations. These levels of expectations might be far in advance of those you have been previously accustomed. For example, you might have studied in an environment of rote, where you copied down everything that was said to you. Moreover, you might well have treated that material as 'gospel' – never to be challenged. Within a university context, this is far from reality (or, at least, should be). University, as indicated in previous chapters and sections, is about you reading and thinking about issues and ideas. This is, after all, the only way for new ways of thinking and new concepts to ever see the light of day.

In order for you to succeed at a business school, you need to know what is expected of you. This might be the level and depth of reading you undertake and the degree of your participation in lectures and seminars. Your tutors will be seeking a level of engagement that you might not previously have been accustomed to – for example, in presentations. You might look upon this as a frightening experience (whether you have experience of this or not). However, do not perceive this as something to fear. Instead see it as an opportunity to hone your business skills (presentations will be an important part of these) and, where there is assessment, to build your assessment base.

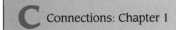

C   Connections: Chapter 1

● Different types of faculty

It is perhaps worth providing a short note on the different people and their roles within a business school.

Head or Dean of School

They are, in essence, the Managing Director of what would be termed a Strategic Business Unit (SBU) of an organization, in this case a university. Equally, though, it could be an SBU of an organization such as the multinational company Nestlé. The turnover of business schools can range from US$ one or two million to several hundred million at the higher end of the spectrum.

Heads of academic departments

They are usually charged with running specific departments within the business school; for example, Business and Strategy, Marketing and Strategy, Organizational Behaviour and Human Resources Management, Accounting and Finance. Titles do vary across the global university sector. Equally, the role of heads of department also vary – in some institutions they are 100% engaged in running the department exactly as if they were business managers within a commercial environment. In other institutions, their role as head of department is a more a part-time function, with the remainder of their time engaged in teaching and/or research.

Lecturers

Titles and level of grades vary from institution to institution and from country to country. So, you can have lecturers (Assistant Professors), senior lecturers (Associate Professors) and principal lecturers (Associate/Full Professors). To a greater or lesser degree, these tutors will be engaged in a range of teaching, research and administrative roles.

Associate lecturers (also known as adjunct faculty and visiting lecturers)

These are in essence freelance academic staff. They might either teach at other colleges/ universities and/or work in business. Often, business consultants and senior managers embark upon part-time lecturing for a variety of reasons. For example, they might seek to give something back to education after their own business success and/or enjoy working with younger people. Most often, they will have a wealth of business experience and the ability to articulate the relationship between the theory and practice. Sometimes, when students enter a seminar room and discover that the tutor is an Associate and not a permanent member of staff, they think they are getting a second rate deal. This could not be further from the truth. They have a wealth of experience from which you can greatly benefit. Buy into this concept and you will have three or four years of free business consultancy. This is an experience worth a fortune in the commercial world.

PhD/DBA students

These are students studying for either doctorates in philosophy or business administration. They might be involved as guest speakers to discuss a particular topic and/or as a seminar leader. As with associate lecturers, they might also have a wealth of business experience and academic knowledge to share.

● The administrative team

The range of administration varies enormously from one business school to another, often depending upon its size and range of programmes. Just as within a major company, the administrators are vital in making sure that the organization runs smoothly.

You will interact with them at various times and in different contexts over the duration of your programme. These are some of the possible interactions:

- **Accommodation:** This is usually pre-arranged. However, there might be issues, from time to time, that you might need to discuss. For example, noisy first-year students in your accommodation block when you are trying to revise for your final year exams.
- **Computer help desk:** This might be face-to-face or over the telephone. Increasingly, universities use intranets to convey information to both staff and students.
- **Examinations:** The examinations office will inform you, either in writing or electronically, of your examination dates and exam rooms. There will be specific procedures to follow.
- **Submission of coursework:** Depending upon the number of students on a module, the place of submission might be an administration office.

These and other administrators are there to help you. However, you must understand that you are not the only student on campus and that you have to *work with them* to obtain the best possible outcomes. This is exactly what happens within a real business situation.

● Understanding the role of your tutors

As stated in Chapter 2, your tutor will most likely have several functions within the organization. These can be very time consuming activities. Your teaching team is most likely to be engaged in many of the following activities:

- Research – conducting both primary and secondary research, writing up their findings and submitting for publication by certain dates within the year.
- Preparing materials for lectures and seminars (they might be leading/teaching on several modules at various levels during a semester/term). The planning and execution of such activities are very time consuming.
- Supervising dissertations at both undergraduate and postgraduate levels.

- Supervising doctoral research students.
- Consultancy on behalf of the university. This can take them away from the university for several days per semester/term.
- Developing links with other universities and organizations (including companies).
- Attending faculty and university committees. (Bear in mind that universities operate, to a greater or lesser extent, on committee structures. These will range from department to regular quality assurance committees). As stated earlier, universities – whether public or private institutions – can be very bureaucratic in their operation. Often, this is for the very good reason of maintaining and developing quality standards.
- Developing new modules and degree programmes. The development of a postgraduate programme might take six to ten months before it actually reaches validation (or approval) stage. Only if it is successfully validated can students be recruited onto the programme.
- They might even be running a department (this includes managing staff, timetabling and many of the above listed items).

The point of this list is to demonstrate that tutors have many roles and responsibilities within a university. They may not only be engaged in delivering the one module you are studying as part of your overall degree.

Communicating with your tutors

As stated earlier, place yourself within a business context and consider how you would be expected to communicate within that environment. Learning how to do it within your college or university environment will help prepare you for business, thus providing a smoother transition.

Email

While email may have many benefits – for example, 24/7 communication opportunities – it has many disadvantages:

- There is sometimes an assumption that everyone is on 24-hour call. Within a university, we are not usually dealing with life-and-death situations, as in either medical or military circumstances. Do not, therefore, expect your tutors to be on 24-hour call simply because you decide to send an email (appropriately or not) at 3am on a Sunday morning. Many universities operate a five-working-days approach. That is, the aim is to answer your email within five working days. As stated earlier, your tutor might be engaged in many activities. Business studies programmes tend to gain a large influx of students, some modules might be as large as 500 students (under European law this would be designated as a medium-sized enterprise, with a full management and administrative team). The 'immediate' response is perhaps a touch beyond reality, if you really think about it. Always try and place yourself in your tutor's shoes, and just to imagine how it might feel.

- While email might have liberated communication for all ages of the global community, SPAM has created what can only be described an Internet traffic jam. While universities use SPAM filters, they have to be careful not to exclude relevant emails (be they yours, from a learned society or from the Dean – and yes, it does happen). Your tutors might receive in excess of 100 SPAM emails per day, each one needs to be checked (not opened) just to make sure that a student's email has not been inadvertently placed in the SPAM folder instead – yes, this does happen too! Therefore, to reduce the risk of being classed as junk mail, it is suggested that you place the name and number of your module in the message box. This should alert both the system and your tutor to the fact that this is a genuine email. Equally, you need to add your name either within the main body of text or at the end of the email (as you would do in a letter).
- Overall the use of mobile texting abbreviations, such as 'u' for 'you' is inappropriate in an email. As stated within the Preface, you should consider yourself not so much as being in a purely academic environment, but rather as in an environment that prepares you for the real business world. In that context, could you see yourself using texting forms as a basis of your email to, say, your line manager? Leave the 'u' as 'you' for your friends. It is an inappropriate format for the staff at a university and you just might be overwhelmed by the negative response.

Telephone

- Some tutors will prefer emails to telephone conversations as (a) it enables them to keep a record of what has been discussed; and (b) if they have a large teaching load (and many do) they often will not be in their office to take the calls.
- If you do decide to call your tutor, check at the time of the call that it is convenient to talk. Even though the tutor might have answered the ringing phone, it might not be the best time to have a lengthy conversation. Moreover, do not expect the tutor to recognize your voice instantaneously. As stated earlier, business schools tend to have large student populations and your tutor might have hundreds of students in their modules during a semester/term. You cannot expect them to know everyone!
- Be clear as to what you want to discuss. Ideally, note down some bullet points beforehand that cover the key issues. Arrange them in a logical order. This will help you to communicate your issues/questions to the tutor effectively and efficiently.

Office hours

- In most institutions, tutors operate designated office hours for each term or semester. These are normally surgery hours, where students can just drop in. However, it is suggested that you send an email in advance stating that you wish to meet up during the scheduled office hours. It is also useful to state, briefly, the key purpose of the meeting. This will, where possible, permit the tutor to assemble the key facts necessary to make your meeting worthwhile and valuable. Some institutions and tutors clearly state the purpose of office hours (for example, not for dissertation students, as these would have a separate meeting time/place). Therefore, make sure that you have made yourself familiar with these parameters in advance of any email or visit.

● Tapping into their wealth of knowledge

It might be helpful, at this stage, to provide background that places the role of your tutors into some form of context.

Your tutors will probably have two or more degrees and belong to one or more business-orientated or learned institutions. Many of these memberships are by invitation only.

They (though not all) have most likely worked at middle- to senior-management levels within an organization, including not-for-profit, voluntary and government. Moreover, if they are either visiting or adjunct faculty, they are likely to be currently engaged in business operations, usually as a consultant. This means that they can bring direct experience into the seminar or workshop. This can be of immense value to you in understanding the realities of business operations.

There are, of course, the issues of 'age' and 'wisdom'. As a twenty-something, you might consider your tutors old. However, they might not be as decrepit as you think! As the quote from the Roman poet Virgil that opened this chapter aptly suggests, they might have 'been, done it, and collected the T-shirt along the way'. In other words, they might have the real business (and personal) experiences that perhaps only reside within your imagination.

Once again, tap into that knowledge and vital experience. True, not everyone who teaches business studies, in its various guises, has done it for real, so to speak. However, those who have will usually be quick to draw on their own experiences either to support or counter conceptual views.

Never be frightened to engage – it might be extremely rewarding and the key to the rest of your life.

Reflection zone

Here are a few key summary points for you to reflect upon:

- Understand the structure of your business school and from whom you can seek advice and guidance. Administrative staff members are equally as important as the academic staff. Moreover, they might have a better understanding of the regulations and where assistance can be sought than the academic staff.
- Appreciate and understand the various roles and commitments of both academic and administrative staff.
- Consider how best to communicate with your tutors. What are their preferences and at what times are they available to see you?
- Consider how you can benefit from both the intellectual and business knowledge of your tutors. They have a wealth of knowledge that will help you gain much insight into the world of business, industry and commerce.

4 Preparing for Study

'Be ever questioning.'

Hyman George Rickover, 1900–1986,
Admiral, US Navy

Contents

- ▶ Introduction
- ▶ Your personal exploration
- ▶ Making the connections
- ▶ Thinking critically
- ▶ Your physical environment
- ▶ When do you study?
- ▶ Staying focused
- ▶ Group/team discussions
- ▶ The high-risk approach to studying
- ▶ What is the purpose of a module guide or workbook?
- ▶ Lecture and workshop skills
- ▶ Your approach to research
- ▶ Using textbooks and other resources
- ▶ Key points for designing a successful study timetable
- ▶ Reflection zone
- ▶ Further reading

Introduction

In this chapter, we will explore how to prepare to study for a business degree. While some of the ideas and concepts are applicable to any programme, I will focus on the issues directly related to a business degree.

Your personal exploration

Many subjects at university level, by their very nature, can only be studied within the confines of a physical laboratory. As stated earlier, this is not the case where either business or management are concerned. While you are studying business, you must appreciate that it will envelope a significant proportion of your life – just as it probably will in your life beyond university. Business, perhaps more than any other subject, encapsulates how we, and others, live – whether by choice or imposition. Business, more than many other subject areas, has a breadth of responsibility for both current and future generations. Therefore, the study of business is very much a serious matter affecting not only you, but also untold generations to come.

To understand business, you will need to explore beyond the confines of the lecture and seminar room. It is most likely that you will be asked, as part of your programme, to explore the wider world – perhaps through surveys and observational data gathering (more on this later). However, you can help build your own knowledge base by exploring the wider world that surrounds each and every one of us every day of our lives. Throughout this book there are references to the world beyond the university campus – after all, that is where the real world of business lies and of which you will be part of once you graduate.

To be truly successful in your studies, you have to be inspired. That inspiration might come from those around you (family, friends, colleagues and tutors). However, your inspiration to study business and management subjects might actually arise from the business world itself. Therefore, you need to connect with the business world, which can happen in several ways, for example:

- When you go shopping, consider the range of products and services that are on offer. Reflect upon how the products reached the stores, what they comprise, how they are positioned on the shelves and the price charged. Viewing business as it affects you will help provide you with a greater understanding of the subject.

- Consider also theory and practice. As part of your general management/human resource management studies you will come across the work of Frederick Taylor (1856–1915). Although his work practices – commonly known as Taylorism – date back to the turn of the twentieth century, they are still observable today. For instance, the person at the supermarket checkout, it could be argued, operates within a Tayloristic environment. You might want to consider whether or not the whole checkout process could be organized differently. Indeed, could it be fully automated (certain European supermarkets have installed automated systems)? However, you would to also need to consider the consequences of such a step change. How would employees react? Is it what consumers really want? Would it work? What are the cost implications? Would it actually make the checkout process more efficient? As you can see, from just one 'simple' issue comes a multiplicity of questions – all related to business and management.
- Watch the business news on TV, read the business press and generally engage in, and be alert to, the changing nature of business.
- Watching movies and TV dramas. Now, you might think this slightly odd. However, you might be surprised what can be learnt from watching quality dramas. Indeed, when the award-winning US legal drama series *LA Law* (1986–92) was broadcast, many law professors at American universities made it required viewing for their students. The class sessions following the latest episode were used to debate the legal issues cited in that particular episode.

    We can also appreciate business dilemmas from quality movies such as award-winning *Big Night* (1996). This is the story of two Italian émigré brothers, Primo (played by actor Tony Shalhoub) and Secondo (played by actor Stanley Tucci), in 1950s America. They open an authentic Italian restaurant, *The Paradise*, in the resort of Key Port, New Jersey. Primo is a master chef who seeks perfection – yet, the restaurant is failing to attract customers who appreciate such gourmet food. Across from *The Paradise* is another restaurant that has a booming business. It is also run by an émigré – Pascal (Ian Holm) – but he has a very different philosophy to the brothers. He provides his customers with the very American 'fat juicy steak'. He espouses to Secondo, 'Give people what they want, then, later, you can give them what you want': in other words, it is all about understanding what the customers wants now and then working to change attitudes. Consider how attitudes to the types of food we now consume have changed in many countries over the past ten years or so. For instance, increasingly in the UK there has been a move back to the use of organically produced rather than mass factory-farmed produce.

    Big Night is a movie that can be viewed on so many different levels, from sibling rivalry to trust and the difficulties of running your own business.
- Reading novels. Vivid portrayals of business life are painted in a variety of novels, both classic and contemporary. For example, Anthony Trollope's *The*

Way We Live Now; Theodore Dreiser's *The Financier*, *The Titan* and *The Stoic*; F. Scott Fitzgerald's *The Last Tycoon*, David Lodge's *Nice Work*, Tom Wolfe's *The Bonfire of the Vanities* and Émile Zola's *Money*.

● Where possible talk with people engaged in business. They do not have to be the Chief Executive Officers (CEOs) of multinationals – however if the opportunity arises, listen to what they have to say). The owner of a local store can equally as well provide you with an appreciation of the factors that impact upon his or her business. Let's not forget that business ranges from the micro (employing one or two people) to the multinational (employing thousands).

● Making the connections

As stated in the Preface to this book, the crucial issue in business studies is making the connections. Often, when students enter university they see a module as an independent unit of study, simply because it has a mark attached to its assessment. That is a danger-ous way of looking at modules. I call this 'Silo Thinking', where a student views a mod-ule as a self-contained unit that has no bearing on any other module studied over their degree programme. Nothing could be further from reality. Every module within a busi-ness studies programme is, by its very nature, interrelated. To fail to realize this is to place your whole degree programme in jeopardy. You must view a business degree from an holistic perspective. In other words, it is like a giant jigsaw puzzle and you are required to fit the different pieces together to construct a realistic view of the world – both now and in the future (perhaps the more difficult aspect of business studies – more on this later).

This leads us onto silo thinking (as depicted in Figure 4.1). We often view life or sub-jects as a series of silos (see Figures 4.1 and 4.2). On their own, they have a clear mean-ing. However, greater meaning is provided when they are linked or connected together. Throughout your studies, think about how these different issues can be connected. This approach leads into thinking critically, as discussed below.

The difficulty continues, in that we often create sub-silos of knowledge and informa-tion. What we really need to do is to find a way of linking this knowledge. In reality, we

Figure 4.1   Silos of knowledge

Figure 4.2   A vertical slice of the main silo

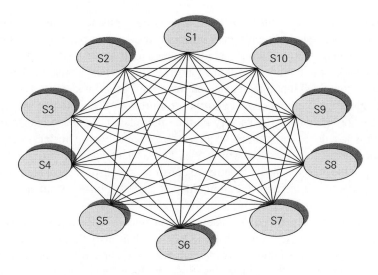

Figure 4.3   The interlinking of the silos to create a relational architecture

should consider all the elements of business to be interlinked – perhaps in the form of an architecture, as depicted in Figure 4.3. Here, there is a clear relationship between the various elements. S1 could be finance, S2 marketing, S3 operations and so on.

The understanding of these 'environments' is important in the overall appreciation of how business operates within our contemporary and often dynamic world. A critical issue to bear in mind is that these environments are not static; they are in a constant state of fluidity. This is an issue that is often overlooked by both writers and students alike. By the time you have read the mini cases within this chapter ('An International Airline' and 'Republic of Zimbabwe – PESTLE factors') the events they depict might have changed manyfold, and probably dramatically. Thus, the mini cases are for illustration and for you to consider how they have changed since this book was published.

The fluidity of these environments illustrates one of the dilemmas facing organizations (both nationally and globally) today. Organizations must both understand and be able to monitor or scan these environments in an attempt to be both proactive and reactive to changing conditions. If an organization fails to 'read' and understand the dynamics within these environments successfully, it might soon face, on the one hand, a reduced market share or, on the other, total extinction.

Business activities are influenced and controlled by a mixture of external and internal factors. These are often referred to as the 'macro' and 'micro' environments. The micro (or internal) environment refers to the elements usually within the company's immediate environment – for example, its workforce and the local community.

What is the macro environment?

This is often described by various mnemonics – for instance:

PEST (Politics, Economics, Society and Technology). This is sometimes also presented as STEP.

LE-PEST-C (the LE represents Legal and Environmental, while the C stands for Competitors – thus bringing competitors out of the micro environment (or internal environment) into the macro environment).

SPECTACLES (Developed by Cartwright (2002). This covers Social, Political, Economic, Cultural, Technological, Aesthetic, Customers, Legal, Environmental and Sectoral (Cartwright, 2002).

PESTEL/PESTLE

PESTLE Factors

For several reasons, PESTLE is the format adopted for this book:

1   It clearly defines the major external factors that impact upon the organization both nationally and internationally;
2   It covers a much wider relevant perspective than a PEST analysis;
3   Easy to remember – always useful;
4   The Oxford English Dictionary meaning of the word 'pestle' is 'a club shaped instrument for pounding substances in a mortar (bowl)'. This, to some extent, can be used to often describe the affect on business organizations of the PESTLE factors. They can actually 'grind down' a business. Think, for instance, beyond the political factors. If the economic environment is unfavourable, then a company – even one with a good product – can still face bankruptcy.

Examples 4.1 and 4.2 give two very brief examples of such connectivity and application. First, the airline industry and, second, considering developing a business in the Republic of Zimbabwe.

> ### Example 4.1   Mini case: an example of connectivity – an international airline

Consider any international airline – for example, American Airways, British Airways, China Eastern, Singapore Airlines or Qantas. Every element of their individual businesses must be connected in order for them to operate a profitable business that benefits all their stakeholders. Otherwise, their businesses would fail, with consequences for their customers, employees and shareholders.

Macro

Political

This not only refers to the politics within an airline's own country. Today, we are politically connected – not necessarily in terms of political beliefs, more in terms of political actions. For example, countries may choose to 'de-regulate the skies', allowing more carriers to form. This happened in both America and Europe, and precipitated the growth of low-cost airlines. At another level, political tensions between nations can result in sanctions, embargoes and, even, military actions. Such events or actions will impact/influence airlines.

Economic

In a similar vein to politics, economics can have an influence both in the home market and internationally. National economies have become ever more interlinked. A recession in one market can have repercussions in another, as exemplified during the latter part of the 20th century by economic downturns in America and Europe. High levels of inflation within home nations will impact upon an airline's ability to purchase necessary supplies for aircraft maintenance. Equally, in the combined situation of stratum to hyperinflation and high unemployment the level of disposable income will be reduced. Individuals who previously took overseas vacations will have limited spending power, with a need to focus on the basics. (You can also link this to Maslow's (1954) 'Hierarchy of Needs' model.) In such cases, domestic airlines may well suffer. Of course, in periods of high national economic growth with increased levels of disposable incomes there may be greater propensity to participate in international travel.

Societal

With an increasing view of the world as a 'global village' (McLuhan and Fiore, 1969), both individuals and groups have sought to experience other cultures and places. Initially, this may be achieved through television (the early sales of programmes internationally) and, since the 1980s, global satellite transmissions with access to literally hundreds of channels (link to the influence of technology). Moreover, the ready availability of internationally branded products and services has influenced people's perception of the world and how they seek to live their lives. Migration, especially within economic blocs (such as the European Union), has increased societal diversity and knowledge. Today, it is common for many students to study outside their own country – some of them will have flown physically long distances to attend university or college.

Technological

This can be viewed on two levels:

1 Aircraft manufacturers develop new ranges of aircraft covering the short and long haul markets. These tend to be: (a) more fuel efficient, thus reducing particulate pollution

and costs; (b) quieter, thus reducing noise pollution levels; and (c) often larger, and thus able to carry more passengers. An example is the Airbus A380, which can carry 600 passengers;

2 In-flight systems are available that can enhance the passenger experience.

Companies outside the airline business have often driven the changing technological landscape. Examples include the development of faster, smaller computers and the creation of new materials and manufacturing methods.

Legal

Various factors can be included:

1 The legal permission required to fly across a country's airspace;
2 The legal requirement of certain regulators (for example, CAA, FAA) that the aircraft meet certain airworthiness safety requirements;
3 Requirements for night flights into and out of certain airports. Some airports are in essence closed to all but delayed flights and emergencies late at night/early hours;
4 Restrictions on licences to operate out of certain airports – this may prevent an airline developing certain potentially high value routes;
5 Restrictions on building additional facilities at airports, including more runways that may benefit the airlines but be seen to disadvantage those living near the airport.

Environmental

This is the impact of environmental factors on the airline business. One example is severe and extreme weather conditions. In December 2006, at the height of the vacation rush the world's busiest international airport servicing over 90 airlines (Heathrow Airport near London, England) was virtually closed due to dense fog.

Although modern aircraft can fly in such conditions, it is the ground movement of aircraft that increases risk of an incident. All major airports have ground radar that shows to controllers in the airport tower the position and movement of aircraft on the tarmac and runways. However, ground radar is only one element in ground movement safety. Controllers high in their towers frequently watch movements through binoculars while talking to pilots and other controllers. With visibility reduced to a few hundred metres, airport officials deemed the risk level of a ground incident too high and reduced the number of flights, both into and out of the airport, to around 40% of capacity (BAA, 2006). Such restrictions impacted upon domestic, short-haul (Europe bound) and long-haul travel, with airlines forced to cancel flights. Heathrow is British Airways' hub or base and, as a result, the company was financially impacted as flights had to be cancelled (on 22 December they cancelled some 170 short-haul and domestic flights out of a total of around 400 (BA, 2006a and b).

Micro

Here, we are considering stakeholders, which typically include airline and related supplier employees; the local community (those affected by airline noise, pollution, traffic congestion and so on); the customers (economy, business and first-class passengers – each with their own needs and desires); competitors (for example, how they will react to price changes and/or the introduction of new additions to already competitive routes).

You will be asked to consider the various external environmental factors that influence or impact upon an individual business or industry. In Example 4.2, we consider the state of the Republic of Zimbabwe (as of May 2007). The information is set out in tabular form. However, you could just as easily use a mind map. It is important to understand how the macro factors affect a country for these will have an impact upon (a) indigenous companies/industries and their ability to operate; and (b) those regional and international businesses that either trade within a country or seek to do so in the future. This might also include whether or not they engage in Foreign Direct Investment (FDI) – actually building factories in that country.

As you will see from the very brief overview in Example 4.2, the Republic of Zimbabwe is an interesting example as it depicts a country on the verge of collapse. Of course, that does not mean the country will remain in this state for years to come. Indeed, if you consider the history of countries you will find that many of today's richest countries were once poor – Sweden is a good example of such a case. Even so, Zimbabwe clearly has a very long haul before it has the standard of living enjoyed by the citizens of Sweden.

Example 4.2	Mini case: Republic of Zimbabwe PESTLE factors
Factors	**Description**
Political	Although a multiparty state, President Robert Mugabe's ZANU-PF party has held power since 1980. It is a politically repressive regime and the international community has isolated it over human rights abuses, including its land clearance policies. The political policies have driven the country to increasing levels of instability and violence. Several governments have imposed sanctions and have advised their citizens not to travel to Zimbabwe or to conduct business with the regime.
Economic	The implementation of several political policies has been highly detrimental to Zimbabwe's economy. Primarily an agrian economy, the forced seizure of commercial farms led to a dramatic fall in productive output. Agriculture was traditionally a source of exports and foreign exchange. Now, the country is a net importer of food.
	The nationalization of foreign-owned businesses through expropriation resulted, in essence, in de-industrialization. According to the World Bank real Gross Domestic Product (GDP) – a measure of prosperity – declined by 4.5% in 2006, which was the eighth consecutive year of negative growth since 1997 (World Bank, 2007). Year-on-year inflation rates have fluctuated (yet, overall, have continued to grow) since 1990, when it had already reached stratum inflation levels of 15% (RBZ 2007). In 2005, it was 237.9% year-on-year with 2004, yet it increased to a staggering 1,116.5% in 2006 (World Bank, 2007).
	Unemployment was estimated at 80% while, in July 2007, the Zimbabwean Central Statistical Office recorded year-on-year inflation running at 7634.8% within month-on-month inflation at 31.6% (CSO, 2007), making it the highest in the world.

▼

Factors	Description
	This has an immediate impact upon both businesses and customers, as prices for goods and services change (often several times) on a daily basis. This makes even staple foods such as bread, milk and eggs out of the reach of most people (consider the connection to Maslow's Hierarchy of Needs). Moreover, the country's exchange rate is overvalued, fuelling further economic decline.
	The government's actions to combat inflation and the declining economic stability (as of October 2007) have been:
	1 To instruct the Reserve Bank of Zimbabwe to print more money and at higher denominations (although, at the time of writing, there were plans to introduce a new currency to stem black market activity in currency transactions). The printing of more currency and at larger denominations only serves to devalue the currency and increase inflationary pressures as the currency becomes basically worthless;
	2 To place restrictions on prices and wages. Reductions in the price of commodities by up to 50% have been required by law. The difficulty here is the issue of the goods still being priced beyond the means of most of the population, especially the poor and unemployed (BBC, 2007a and b).
Societal	Society is greatly affected by the combination of political and economic stability. There is a 90% literacy rate – possibly the highest in Africa. However, the population cannot afford books and magazines due to hyperinflation. There has been substantial emigration of professionals to neighbouring countries to create a better life for themselves and their families. This exodus of the knowledge and skills base will further handicap the country's already failing economy.
Technological	There are significant technological changes taking place globally. These range from computer software/hardware to the development of new materials and processes (for example, the construction of cars, buildings and so on). However, the combination of the political and economic situation prevents the country from exploiting these technologies for the good of the nation.
Legal	This can be considered from two perspectives. First, how the government uses the law to impose its will – for example, through land reforms. Second, the legal frameworks that support the development and regulation of business. According to the World Bank, it normally takes 10 steps and an average of over 96 days to launch a business. Companies that need to comply with permits and licences have to complete 21 steps and this normally takes 481 days (World Bank, 2006).
Environmental	Zimbabwe is a country of outstanding natural beauty, which includes Victoria Falls. Thus, it is ideal for tourism – yet, the combination of politics and economics has led this into decline. Moreover, severe droughts (combined with the land reforms) have led to food shortages.

This is considering purely a one-nation state at the time of writing (late 2006–late 2007).

There are, however, several important considerations:

- The macro factors do not operate in isolation There are interrelations that can be extremely complex.
- The world is dynamic and thus any such analysis must be ongoing – situations can, literally, change overnight. You must, therefore, consider what the impact would/could be of such complex changes.

● Thinking critically

This is an area that will be repeatedly referred to throughout this book, the reason being that it is core to studying a business degree. Throughout your course of study, you will be asked to analyze and evaluate concepts and ideas – therefore, you will need to think critically about everything. As Cottrell (2005) states: 'critical thinking is a cognitive activity . . . Learning to think in critically analytical and evaluative ways means using mental processes such as attention, categorization, selection and judgement.'

As Cottrell (2005) further states: 'critical thinking is a complex process of deliberation which involves a wide range of skills and attitudes'. The following is a range of skills and attitudes developed from Cottrell's work. The important thing to remember is that a critical approach to thinking about issues and ideas does not only apply to reading textbooks and journal articles (more on this later). On a business programme, you will also need to make critical evaluation of the views of others within group work situations. You might have already had some experience of this, or it might be completely new to you and something that you find daunting. However, as you will see, it is a crucial part of the real business world.

C   Connections: Chapters 9 and 10

- Identifying other people's positions, arguments and conclusions:
  You will find that there are numerous models and concepts discussed in business studies. You will need to understand the views not only of the originators of these models, but also those who disagree with them. As will be discussed in later chapters, you will often be called upon to compare and contrast views on particular ideas, such as the value of strategic alliances and acquisitions.
- Evaluating the evidence for alternative points of view:
  You have to go beyond the view that Author X simply dislikes a particular concept developed by Author Z. You need to be able to consider the merits (or values) of the different perspectives that authors might promote.
- Weighing up opposing arguments and evidence fairly:
  You will need to consider the various arguments (or views) for and against a theory or indeed the choices a company might need to make. Moreover, you will

need to consider these views objectively. You might totally disagree with a particular argument; that is a perfectly valid approach. However, you must clearly show that you have been objective in your appraisal of that point of view.

- Being able to read between the lines and identifying false or unfair assumptions: This can be a very difficult exercise and something that often comes much easier with experience. This is like a friend saying one thing to you, yet their body language or posture suggests something totally different. You are trying to decipher the difference between the two and thus attempting to decide, as a result, what to do. The same is true in the study of business and is most likely (though not exclusively) related to the external or macro environmental forces. A good example is how governments often relate to businesses, whether they are indigenous or foreign. The government might, for example, overtly state that it welcomes foreign direct investment (FDI), yet it imposes restrictive laws that reduce the effectiveness of such direct investment. So, what is the government really saying?

- Recognizing techniques used to make certain positions more appealing than others, such as false logic and persuasive devices:
Logic is generally the search for a method that separates valid reasoning (the ability to comprehend, reflect, abstract, analyze and draw conclusions) from invalid reasoning. Thus, false logic can be defined as a method that attempts to provide a valid reasoning when none exists. For instance, you will access resources for assignments and dissertations that might be written by academics from various universities. Many students will take what is said at face value because they have been brought up to believe that academics are to be revered and never questioned. So, for instance, if an academic wrote a paper in such a way with, what appears to be, compelling evidence that the colour blue is actually the colour black, would you believe it? Well, many would. Think of this way, the whole of advertising history is based upon the premise that 'Brand X is good for you', that 'Brand Y washes clothes better than any other brand', that '9 out of 10 cat lovers prefer Brand Z than any others', and so on. In some cases, this might be true. However, in many cases the promotion, albeit effective, is based on a false logic. So, when you review an academic paper, consider the validity of it. Ask yourself the question 'Does it make real sense?'

- Reflecting on issues in a structured way, bringing logic and insight to bear:
Be systematic in your approach – just as a forensic scientist would be at a crime scene hunting for clues and piecing together the jigsaw puzzle.

- Drawing conclusions about whether arguments are valid and justified based upon good evidence and sensible assumptions:
Throughout your course work, you will normally be required to provide good evidential support to your findings and draw conclusions. Perhaps the important issue here is to consider whether or not your conclusions have any validity in the real world. For example, let us say you are asked to consider the various strategic options available to McDonald's over the next five years. You might suggest that they should include a wide range of healthy organically-grown choices due to

increasing concerns over obesity, the risks from saturated fats and so on. Moreover, you might suggest that they can expand their range by acquiring various companies focused on health food. Taking the various micro and macro factors into consideration, you promote this as a means for McDonald's to sustain an advantage within the competitive fast food marketplace. There is a clear rationale for this suggestion and it would make a good conclusion. However, if you suggested that the fast-food company McDonald's should stop being a food business and start building space rockets, it is unlikely that your conclusion would be as valid.

- Presenting a point of view in a structured, clear well-reasoned way that convinces others:
  As indicated earlier in this section, many students, even when requested, resist from providing their own point of view. In some cases, this is simply fear of getting it wrong – going for the 'safe, trusted' textbook views. In other cases it might be cultural, in that it is deemed wrong to promote your own views when there are views stated by academics in textbooks and journal articles. In some cultures, it is deemed disrespectful if a student challenges the views of their learned superiors. While that might be honourable, the only way ideas are developed and enhanced is by challenging them. As long as it is undertaken with respect for the other person's views, then no disrespect should be incurred. Progress is about challenging what we consider to be the current norm.

What are the benefits of thinking critically?

Once again, Cottrell (2005) provides a valuable insight. She considers the benefits as follows:

- Improves your level of attention and observation.
  In other words, this helps you to look at the world within a much wider context. Reflect back to Chapter 1 and the discussion on the value of observations.
- Creates more focused reading.
  This is particularly important when it comes to a major project such as your dissertation.
- Improves your ability to identify the key points in a text or other message (for example, a seminar).
  This means that you will be less likely to be distracted by less important material.
- Improves your ability to respond to the appropriate points of the message.
- Helps you develop the skills and the knowledge to communicate your own points/perspectives more easily and confidently.
- Helps you develop the necessary analytical skills and the knowledge of when to apply them and in which circumstances.

● Your physical environment

Your physical environment is extremely important in contributing to the effectiveness and efficiency of your studying.

Here are a few hints:

- Choose an environment that is comfortable for you. Some people prefer to read in total silence, others prefer quiet music playing in the background. You must choose the environment that best suits your learning style.
- When you are studying, ensure that you are somewhere with plenty of fresh air and natural as well as artificial light. This makes reading and note taking much easier. It also helps to prevent you from falling asleep! Also ensure that the room temperature is comfortable.
- Make sure that you have all the resources you need to hand – pens, paper, textbooks and lecture notes. Plan the areas you will study before you commence. By ensuring that you have the prerequisites, this will prevent you from having to stop and hunt for resources. Planning will help make your studying easier.
- Use a comfortable chair and set it at the right height for your desk.
- For students studying on a part-time basis, you might want to consider studying at work. Again, this depends on whether the environment is conducive to studying. Additionally, you should check with your employer, if only out of courtesy, to see whether they have any objection.

When do you study?

You will have been given a programme timetable. Use it to schedule ongoing study time. Even though it is tempting, do not let any other activities encroach on your study time. If you keep to this plan, people will respect your wishes to study at certain times, and you can build a social programme around when you are available. By being disciplined, you will be surprised at how much free time you really do have (and also by how much you are learning along the way).

Staying focused

Concentrating during your study sessions is fundamental to your personal success. It is natural that, when you study, you might start daydreaming – thinking of other things. These daydreams might be about music, people, places or events. They might be positive or negative emotional thoughts. Generally, there is nothing wrong with these thoughts. They are part of being a person. However, they can be a distraction when you are trying to study.

Whatever these thoughts, it is vital that you remain focused on the task at hand. You need to stop daydreaming and focus on your studies. So, when these thoughts enter your mind, mentally drag yourself back to your studying. Tell yourself that you must stay focused.

Group/team discussions

You might find it very useful to discuss issues with your friends. This might be face-to-face in small groups (these can be held in the canteen or empty lecture rooms) or via email.

Small groups provide an environment for debate and constructive argument. You can compare ideas/thoughts/theories and practical applications.

NOTE There must be a word of caution here. Whilst it is highly beneficial to discuss class/course topics, there needs to be care when undertaking assignments. Some assignments might be group assessed, whilst others are clearly individually assessed. Please read assignment questions carefully to determine whether they are group or individually assessed. If two or more assignments bear striking similarities, plagiarism or collusion might be alleged. This will impact upon the marks allocated to the assignment. Please read the Regulations Handbook and the section on plagiarism in this book.

The high-risk approach to studying

This is where the student decides to leave everything to the very last moment. This is in the vain hope that cramming information will allow them to perform well in the examination. Of course, there are always the one or two situations where the student has succeeded with such an approach and has found 'glory'. However, it is a very high-risk strategy and one that is best avoided.

What is the purpose of a module guide or workbook?

These are generally guides detailing the module that you are studying. The form and content of these will vary depending upon your college or university's requirements. Typically, they will contain the following:

Rationale for the module
This can be divided into three constituent parts:

- The justification for the module in terms of your overall business learning.
- How this module fits with the other modules, both within the same academic year and across the life of your degree programme.
- How this module will benefit you once you have left college/university and entered the working environment.

Learning outcomes
Modules tend to have overarching learning outcomes. These are the things that you should be able to do/understand once you have successfully completed the module and its assessment.

Within the learning outcomes there might also be transferable skills. These normally include (both individually and collectively):

- Active problem solving (this might extend beyond solving a problem within a piece of assessment to solving a disagreement within your team).

- Communication can link to how you communicate both written and orally within the assessment regime (including assignments and presentations) with your peers and your tutors.
- Self-management (time management and the ability to be focused on the work, submission by key deadlines).
- Team working has become an important part of many business degree modules. The early introduction to team working will help you to understand how vital it is within the contemporary working environment.

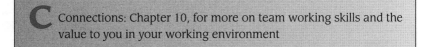

Connections: Chapter 10, for more on team working skills and the value to you in your working environment

- The use of information technology (for research and other purposes) helps you to hone your computer skills. This is not only important in helping you to explore valuable and relevant information on, for example, the Internet. Such practice might well help you to word-process information faster and more accurately. Within any business environment, anywhere in the world today, you will be expected to be able to use a range of computer packages. Indeed, you will generally be expected to do much of your own typing, no matter what your level of seniority. So, this is also a good way of honing your keyboard skills (that is, until voice recognition software becomes universal).

Hours of study required

There will be a set number of contact hours where you will be in lectures/seminars and/or workshops. However, these are really only 'scene setters' to provide a taste or overview of the key issues. You will be expected to dedicated significant time to reading around or exploring the subject, preparing in advance for the seminars/workshops and working towards your completion of your assessments (be they examination, presentations, assignments or a combination).

Reading

As stated in the Preface to this book, the need to explore the material on the module subject area cannot be understated. Reading is a vital component to helping you achieve success.

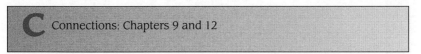

Connections: Chapters 9 and 12

Structure of the module

It is important to have an idea of how the module is actually constructed, what issues are discussed and what are the key readings. Figure 4.4 provides an example of a semester plan for a postgraduate module on business strategy. This illustrates week-by-week activity that will allow the student to prepare readings (and ancillary note production) in advance.

Semester week	Lecture topic	Reading	Workshop activities
Week 1	An outline of strategic management concepts to be introduced on the course and how they link together. Introduction: What is strategy? Levels of Strategy Analyzing the external environment via the PESTLE framework.	Hill and Jones, chs 1 and 2; Appendix – analyzing a case study and writing a case study analysis; Johnson *et al.*, chs 1 and 2	Coursework briefing. Newspaper article as a basis for discussion of topics covered.
Week 2	Identifying the competitiveness of an industry using the Porter's 5 forces analysis and leading to the identification of key drivers of change.	Hill and Jones, chs 1 and 2; Johnson *et al.*, ch. 2	Newspaper article as a basis for discussion of topics covered. Group mini presentations.
Week 3	Appreciating the Industry Life Cycle and associated critical success factors. Use of Strategic Group Analysis as a means of identifying competitors in an industry and the grounds on which they compete.	Hill and Jones, chs 1 and 2; Johnson *et al.*, chs 2 and 5	Presentation and discussion briefing.

Key chapters that, as a basic, you should read. However, it is useful to link to contemporary business issues that may be found in quality newspapers and magazines.

Outlines of the workshop activities to be undertaken. In some cases, you may be asked to provide material(s) in advance or on the day to demonstrate that you have undertaken some background reading on the subject.

In some modules you will be asked to undertake group presentations. These may not be allocated any marks. However, they will help in terms of both presentations and your team-working skills.

The week-by-week outlines of the key topics to be covered and debated. Such a list helps you to read ahead.

	Presentation and discussion session		
Week 4			
Week 5	Introduction to internal analysis. Distinctive competencies, competitive advantage and profitability.	Hill and Jones, ch. 3; Johnson et al., ch. 3	Video on the retailer, Zara and discussion.
Week 6	Creating and sustaining a competitive advantage: efficiency, quality, innovation and customer responsiveness.	Hill and Jones, ch. 4; Johnson et al., chs 2 and 5.	Video case study and discussion.
Week 7	Bringing internal and external analysis together – SWOT.	Hill and Jones, ch. 5; Johnson et al., chs 2 and 3.	Developing a SWOT analysis
Week 8	Presentation and discussion session and module evaluation		

Video is just one teaching and learning tool that could be used. If you have access to a TV it is always useful to watch the business news and any business-related documentary. Good insights to case study material may well be presented that is valuable to your studies.

Modules should bring together an often disparate series of ideas or concepts to aid your understanding. In this particular module, students should be able to produce a high-calibre SWOT analysis on a particular company and the industry within which it operates.

Figure 4.4 A semester plan synopsis

However, you must also remember that business is both dynamic and fluid. To some extent, a business module and degree programme should demonstrate the same dynamics and fluidity in line with external factors. The more dynamic tutor might decide to alter the plan, especially if something major happens within the business world – for example, the collapse of a global business. This is generally deemed acceptable, as long as it is within the module's learning outcomes. In my view, such dynamics are to be encouraged, as they provide you with a more realistic view of the business world.

● Lecture and workshop skills

In this section, we consider some of the basic skills that you will need to develop to be successful in your degree programme. Some of these skills you might have already mastered as part of your previous studies. Some, on the other hand, might be new. If you have used them before, you might seek ways of enhancing them further. It is important to remember that university or tertiary education is at a different level – and, perhaps, intensity – than you have previously experienced. By seeking to hone your skills from the start, you will better place yourself in a winning position.

Active listening

Active listening is a skill we all need to acquire. Effective listening is obtained through practice and training, over a period of time. Listening is not only about hearing words; it is about actively processing the information (interpreting and evaluating) you hear.

Active listening highlights a key feature in the listening process. The listener must be actively engaged in this process. Do not sit in a lecture room and pretend that you are listening – all you are really doing is hearing. Think about what the tutor is saying. You need to approach listening with an open mind – not blank, or accepting everything being said. Listen and appraise what is being said in a non-judgemental manner, actively seeking to make the experience a positive one.

Note taking

This skill will enable you to make the most of your lectures and seminars.

Note taking is not *verbatim* (that is, word for word) recording. Do not expect (or even attempt) to take down every word that the tutor says. It is tempting to try; however, that is not what a lecture is about. Moreover, by the end of the hour-long session you will have a sore wrist, illegible notes and literally hate the subject.

In a lecture, generally, you are seeking to obtain three things:

- Facts
- Concepts
- References.

Facts and references are easy to note down, as they are usually presented in the form of a handout, on the OHP, the Microsoft PowerPoint® presentation or on the wipe board. They can be written down as they appear.

The most difficult part of a lecture to note down is the concepts, the ideas and the tutor's perspectives. These items often take a considerable time to explain and, thus, you might be tempted to write down everything. However, if you do this, there is a very high probability that you will not understand what the tutor is saying. We also need to be honest and say that there are few tutors who are skilled in delivering a truly clear and concise presentation. The level of effectiveness of delivery can, therefore, impede understanding.

Concentrating on writing does not allow you to spend the time concentrating on listening. As such, you should prepare for all your lectures beforehand. Read up on the subject being taught. You can use this preparatory time to understand the key issues, and then you can link them to more complex issues.

If necessary, take brief notes in the form of basic ideas and then link to other concepts. You can follow up after the lecture with detailed descriptions and annotations. It always pays to go over your notes after the lecture in conjunction with the core textbooks to check your understanding and fill in any gaps in your understanding. Much of a lecture is amplification of the concepts. It is intended to make the essential character of the concepts more understandable.

Always allow space within your notes for your own use. It might be helpful, for example, to write the lecture notes in blue or black ink, and then use red or green pens to write down your own thoughts on the subject.

There are two main forms of note taking – linear notes and patterned notes.

Linear notes These are the ones that you are most likely to see. Linear notes use subject headings, sections and subsections with bullet points and underlining to emphasize important points.

Patterned notes These are like mind maps. They provide a two-dimensional presentation of the subject area. They allow you to utilize your visual and graphic memory of a lecture as well as your memory of words. This will benefit your revision.

In addition, patterned notes are easily expandable, allowing you to add new material without having to break the logical sequence of your notes. For example, consider the following question: 'What are the key models that are associated with strategy?' This is a very simple question – however, it allows us to display, using this method, the key ingredients to the question. As you will see from Figure 4.5, we are able to provide a very visual diagram that identifies some of the key concepts in strategy. This is visually more striking than a list on a page. You could use different coloured pens to annotate such a diagram to make further links and to raise questions.

Audio-tape recording of lectures

Some students like to tape their lectures, so that they can prepare notes afterwards, in addition to those taken in class. Should you wish to tape your lectures, please seek permission from your tutor. Most will probably agree. Some, however, do not like it. It is important to remember that all the material that you are taping is the copyright of the

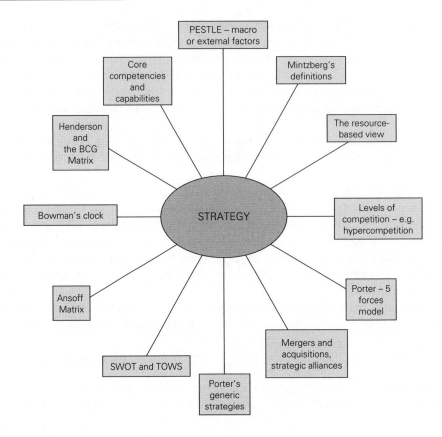

Figure 4.5 An example of a basic mind map

tutor concerned. Therefore, any unauthorized reproduction, in any form, for sale is *strictly illegal*.

Of course, what you have to consider is the length of time it might take to transcribe the tape. First, you have to eliminate the material that you do not feel is relevant, then you need to create a relatively accurate transcription of what is left. However, this is just an early stage. In order to make this really work for you, I would suggest that you further annotate your notes from your reading.

Audio recordings have benefits. However, you must be prepared to dedicate time and effort for it to be used effectively.

● Your approach to research

As suggested in this chapter and others, you will need to read around the subject area. Furthermore, you will have to consider the *value* of the books and journal articles that you will read. It is worth noting at this stage the importance of four key concepts – validity, reliability, triangulation and generalizability. These concepts are important in two ways:

- You need to have some understanding of the background to the idea, concept or theory:

  Academics and researchers write comment pieces as well as work based upon empirical research. Not everyone will agree with either the commentary pieces or the outcomes of the empirical research. The diversity of views and ideas is important for the development of knowledge itself. Furthermore, some ideas and concepts might have universal practicality, some might have either less or none. You need to think about the quality and value of the sources that you use. Some colleges and universities will guide you towards certain types of resources – journals and quality business magazines. Equally, there will be guidance (see later section) on where you have to be careful in your sourcing of information. There are some very good websites – however, there are also many of poor quality.

C Connections: Chapter 2, section on learning resources

- The depth and breadth of your evidential support:

  When you are writing either an assignment or dissertation, your tutor is looking for your perspective – not just a repetition of the theory. What do you think about this theory and why? If you have a particular view of a theory, then you need to be able to support that view. Your evidence will usually come from commentary and research in textbooks, journal articles and business magazines.

  Think of it this way. You are a lawyer defending a person who has pleaded not guilty to a crime.

  > Lawyer: 'Judge and Jury, let me tell you that my client is innocent of all the charges. This is the case for the defence.'

  This is certainly a view, and the lawyer's client might well be innocent of the crime. However, no evidence has been produced to demonstrate, at least, that the lawyer's client *could* be innocent. Just stating that they are innocent is insufficient.

  In the context of your work, you need to provide evidence to support the views proposed in your assignments and dissertation. You need to be the lawyer providing the evidence.

Validity

Here, you need to judge whether or not the information provided is based upon tried and trusted research methods. Is the information that you are going use acceptable?

Reliability

This can have two meanings:

- How reliable is your source of information? As stated earlier some sources on the Internet might be more reliable (or trustworthy) than others. Always think: 'Is this source of information reliable? Can I trust it?'
- How reliable is the outcome of a survey? In other words, if we repeated the survey would we obtain similar results whether now or in the future? In your reading, you will discover that there can be both similarities and significant differences when surveys are repeated (or tested further), especially over time. Therefore, when using survey-based data (especially if the survey was conducted several years ago) consider its reliability today. The views of twenty-year-olds in the 1970s might not be the same as those of today. Perhaps the survey needs to be repeated to gain a better insight in to today's twenty-year-olds.

Triangulation

In virtually every piece of work, there will be some degree of bias. This bias might be intentional or unintentional. In order to reduce the impact of bias and to help in the validation process, we should examine more than one source of data or research. Surveying or evaluating several sources on the same topic (for example, a particular model), will place you in a better position to understand its strengths, weaknesses and level of applicability.

Generalizability

This is the extent to which a concept, idea or an outcome from a piece of research (for example, a survey) can be generally applied in a wider context. For example, a survey of Russian men might show that they consider chocolate a confectionary that women consume, not men. Could this view be generally applied to all men in Russia, to all men in Europe and so on? So, when examining surveys and other forms of data consider whether or not it can be generally applicable in a wider context.

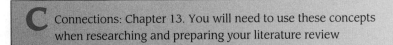

C Connections: Chapter 13. You will need to use these concepts when researching and preparing your literature review

● Using textbooks and other resources

As stated elsewhere in this book, you will need to use a combination of resources effectively and efficiently to be successful in your degree programme. Depending upon the module you are studying, there will be a list of core texts, indicative and supplementary reading. The core texts are usually carefully selected by the relevant subject specialists to provide you with the background to your studies.

Your tutors devote time to the selection of texts that:

- Meet the academic standards required for the particular module.
- Provide a mixture of theory and practical application. On business courses it is important to be able to apply theory (where appropriate) to real world cases.
- Provide a critical appraisal of the subject.
- Provide relevant additional exercises for you to undertake.
- Signpost clearly the various topic areas under discussion.
- Are contemporary to your programme of study.
- Provide guidance to further reading.
- Are realistically priced to meet your study requirements, not only for one module but also for several modules across the programme.

It is important that you own at least one of the core texts per module. This provides you with the background to the subject area.

When you look at a textbook for the first time, it is important that you consider the following steps. They will help you (a) understand the author's approach; (b) appreciate the structure of the book (including the layout); and (c) reflect upon the content of the relevant sections and chapters.

- Read the contents pages/section headings. You will find that some texts (especially American) are more detailed in this area than others. From the textbook, note the relevant sections/chapters relating to your lectures/assignments.
- Now compare with the index. This is important to gain a complete picture of the information available within the text. For example, in the contents page there might be a chapter headed 'Ethics'. However, by checking the index you might discover several other entries for 'ethics' in other sections/chapters. These might be *relevant* to your research.

Making notes from textbooks

In making notes from textbooks, it is not about writing down what has been written *verbatim*. While you might want to use specific and referenced quotes from the work, these should generally be used to introduce an idea or concept and to help to support your perspectives. A tutor wants to see, in your written work, evidence that you actually understand the issues and ideas. A simple listing of quotes from various identified sources does not provide *real* evidence of understanding. It could merely prove that you are good at finding various viewpoints and referencing. Think of this from a business perspective. Finding out about different competitor organizations is one thing. However, what you do with that information in relation to your organization has greater practical value. As previously stated, think about how your search for understanding 'fits' with the business world.

Before producing any notes, read the section once/twice to gain an idea and understanding of the author's thoughts and the main points. Most important is the ability to read material critically, searching out the main arguments/issues.

This process helps you to:

- Gain an appreciation of the author's approach to the subject.
- Clarify the issues in your mind.
- Signpost for you points that you might find difficult to understand (these can be re-read for further clarity).

Read the section again and take notes. This will assist your retention and understanding of the information (see Figure 4.6).

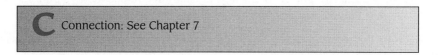

Connection: See Chapter 7

To help you collate information from various sources, I suggest that you divide a sheet of paper (which you can later hole-punch, if not already so provided) with a margin on the left-hand side. Some spiral pads, for example, already come with both punched holes and a wide pre-drawn margin. It is for you to choose which one is best for you.

When you have completed reading the relevant chapter and made notes, you should undertake a selection of brief exercises. This could take one of two approaches:

1   Using quality newspapers and/or the business press, seek out real examples of the issues being discussed within the textbook. Examples could include any of the following:

- An organization is paralyzed by strike action. You might want to explore the issues behind the strike and how they relate to textbook discussions on such issues as industrial relations, internal communications, external communications, conflict resolution in business, the reaction of competitors and the potential impact upon the company's current business strategies.
- A major company might be considering an acquisition of another; for example, the Indian conglomerate Tata's acquisition of the Anglo-Dutch steel marker Corus in January 2007. You might want to consider such questions as whether or not the acquisition followed the stereotypical view of acquisitions, as often outlined within the texts. Moreover, you might want to consider how such an acquisition affects the global steel market? Would such an acquisition be able to regenerate the steel production market in the UK? What could be the impact upon the workforce as a result of the acquisition?

   As you can see there are virtually endless possibilities in terms of self-generating questions. What these do is help you gain an increasingly informed understanding of the issues.

2   Today, the vast majority of textbooks pose end of chapter questions for you to consider. Additionally, your tutor might have presented you with knowledge

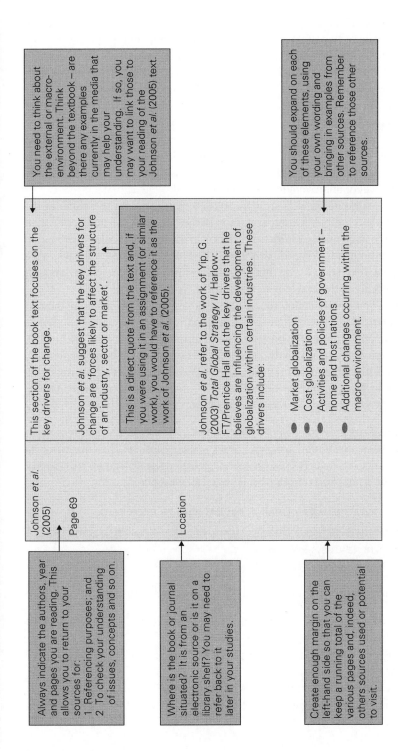

You need to think about the external or macro-environment. Think beyond the textbook – are there any examples currently in the media that may help your understanding. If so, you may want to link those to your reading of the Johnson et al. (2005) text.

You should expand on each of these elements, using your own wording and bringing in examples from other sources. Remember to reference those other sources.

This section of the book text focuses on the key drivers for change.

Johnson et al. suggest that the key drivers for change are 'forces likely to affect the structure of an industry, sector or market'.

This is a direct quote from the text and, if you were using it in an assignment (or similar work), you would have to reference it as the work of Johnson et al. (2005).

Johnson et al. refer to the work of Yip, G. (2003) Total Global Strategy II, Harlow: FT/Prentice Hall and the key drivers that he believes are influencing the development of globalization within certain industries. These drivers include:

Johnson et al. (2005)

Page 69

- Market globalization
- Cost globalization
- Activities and policies of government – home and host nations
- Additional changes occurring within the macro-environment.

Always indicate the authors, year and pages you are reading. This allows you to return to your sources for:
1 Referencing purposes; and
2 To check your understanding of issues, concepts and so on.

Location

Where is the book or journal situated? Is it from an electronic source or is it on a library shelf? You may need to refer back to it later in your studies.

Create enough margin on the left-hand side so that you can keep a running total of the various pages and, indeed, others sources used or potential to visit.

Figure 4.6   A format for making notes from a textbook

checks (brief sets of questions to check your knowledge and understanding of the module at that particular point in time).

- Select one or two of these questions and write brief notes in answer to the questions. Set yourself a time limit of, say, 20 to 30 minutes per question.
- Once you have completed your answer, re-read both the relevant chapter section and your notes to check your level of understanding.
- Make any necessary amendments to your answers. You might want to use a different colour (marker pen) to highlight your changes.
- If you have had significant difficulties in answering a question, then place it to one side and revisit it again (as a question) in a few days' time. Once you have completed a second attempt, check it with your first attempt to see what level of improvement has been achieved.
- When taking notes, it is strongly advised that you state the name of the author and the publication at the top of the page in your notebook. Then note the page number from the textbook in the left-hand column or margin of your notepad, alongside your notes. This allows easy referral back to the original text should you need to clarify any particular point, and for referencing at the end of your assignment (see Figure 4.6).
- Unless you are intending to use a specific quotation, do not copy the text *verbatim* (that is, word-for-word). Instead, consider what the author is stating and rephrase or paraphrase it. Paraphrasing is a very useful skill, particularly if you are analyzing a long section of text. When paraphrasing is used, no quotation marks are used. However, you must still attribute the ideas to the appropriate author. Here is an example from an edition of Philip Kotler's book *Marketing Management*.

> Kotler (1998) argues that targeting is often controversial, and causes concern when marketers take advantage of vulnerable groups. However, he does state that not all attempts to target special groups meets with criticisms. The real issue is not who is targeted but how and for what purpose.

NOTE: When reference is made to an author, the text must be referenced.

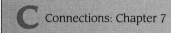

C Connections: Chapter 7

Paraphrasing will increase your understanding of the subject matter.

- Read the section in the book again, this time alongside your notes. Check that you have an understanding of all the salient points.
- Once you have completed your notes from the various texts, take a break and clear your mind.
- Then re-read and consider the various issues raised in the texts and your notes.
- Jot down your thoughts (with supporting information) and see how they link in with those of the authors.

● Key points for designing a successful study timetable

Prepare a timetable of topic areas that you intend to study. This will allow you to cover all the key areas. Put variety into your timetabling. It is advisable not to spend a whole day on one topic area (for example, Introduction to Accounting). Create variety by spending time on, say, a management topic followed by a marketing problem. Variety in your planning also helps to keep you refreshed and aids retention.

When preparing a study timetable consider the following:

- Look at your programme/course timetable then consider how you will space the necessary hours over the week. Remember that it is also important for your overall wellbeing to allocate time for your leisure activities.
- Decide upon the most appropriate time for you. In the example timetable provided, I have time starting at 7.00 AM and finishing at 10.00 PM. This is only a guide. Some people work better early mornings, perhaps before attending the morning lectures; others are more effective working early to late evening. You must decide what will be most effective and rewarding for you.
- Allocate your study sessions over the subject areas. Include extra time to topics/subjects that you find particularly difficult. Taking such action now might prevent difficulties at, for example, examination time.
- Decide on the length of your study sessions.

NOTE: Do take breaks. Take the opportunity to relax. You cannot work continuously otherwise your performance will drop considerably. As a general rule, study for a maximum of 50 minutes then take a break of 10–15 minutes. During the break, walk around, exercise the body, perhaps have a drink. The important thing is to take the break – this helps to refresh you and improves your concentration when you return to the study activity.

Study sessions

Divide the individual study session into sections:

- Consider the topic under review. Link it to the learning objectives/outcomes of the module (these are normally to be found in your module guide).
- Read the relevant sections in the textbooks and make appropriate notes that summarize the key ideas/concepts.
- Review your notes. Then reflect on how they link back to the learning objectives/ outcomes.
- You must be clear in your mind that you have understood the key issues. If you have not, you should re-read the relevant sections/notes.
- As previously stated it is important not to consider topics in isolation – but, rather, collectively. Consider how your various modules interlink. For instance, a company might have a great product that they wish to launch into the marketplace. However, if the level of management competency is poor the company is unlikely to get the best out of the product. Indeed, both the company

and the product could fail. Equally, if there are insufficient financial resources available the launch might be ineffective, with potential negative consequences for both the product and the company.

Creating a study timetable

This might look formidable, even awesome – but it is not, in reality. The objective here is to get you to think about what are your best study times. Figure 4.7 is based upon a real undergraduate programme over the course, for example, of a 12-week semester. Sheets for you to use are contained on the book's website for you to download.

Why do a timetable?

Business degrees are normally intense. Just think of all the group work, individual assignment, reading around the subject area and examination preparation that you will undertake over the length of the programme. For some programmes – for example, a one-year MSc in management – the time allocation to study (in the widest sense) will be very intensive indeed. Moreover, it will be particularly taxing if your first degree was not in business and you are starting from the beginning.

Always expect the unexpected

> 'To expect the unexpected shows thoroughly modern intellect.'
> *An Ideal Husband* (1895), Oscar Wilde, 1854–1900, Irish novelist, playwright and poet.

'Expecting the unexpected' has two significant meanings when planning your study schedule for a business degree.

- We often assume, quite wrongly, that everything is going to go to plan, that nothing is going to interrupt our schedule. An integral part of this assumption is that technology never fails. How wrong can we be! In planning our schedules, we must assume that there will be interruptions, online logins will fail and computers will crash. If we try to build some flexibility into our schedules, then this very action takes account of 'things working against us'. Of course, we cannot plan for every eventuality. However, it might alleviate some of the worries attached to a rapidly approaching deadline with very little evidence of any work accomplished. It also is a sharp reminder never to leave any assignment or revision to the last minute, for that is when something is bound to go wrong!
- The second meaning relates to the business environment itself. If you are regularly scanning the business environment, as part of your normal exploration of the subject, you will become more aware of developing issues. This might allow you to anticipate changes within the business environment, much like entrepreneurs who foresee an opportunity within the marketplace. If you are seeking out the 'unexpected', then you might be able to incorporate these thoughts (if relevant, of course) into your various assessments and class contributions.

Times	Monday	Tuesday	Wednesday	Thursday	Friday	Saturday	Sunday
7.00			Reading				
8.00	Research/reading			Reading			
9.00	Research/reading	Lecture	Lecture	Lecture	Lecture		Coursework
1.00	Research/reading	Seminar	Seminar	Seminar	Seminar		Coursework
11.00		Review the lecture & seminar		Review of recent seminars	Meeting colleagues to discuss team work projects		Coursework
12.00	Lunch	Lunch	Lunch	Lunch	Lunch	Lunch	Lunch
13.00	Reading	Reading			Reading	Lunch	Lunch
14.00	Lecture	Lecture	Sport	Part-time job	Review of lectures & seminars		Reading
15.00	Seminar	Seminar	Sport	Part-time job	Research & reading		Reading
16.00	Seminar	Seminar	Sport	Part-time job	Research & reading		
17.00							
18.00							
19.00	Review the day's lecture & seminar	Review the day's lecture & seminar	Meeting colleagues to discuss team work projects	Meeting friends	Meeting friends		
20.00							
21.00 – 24.00	Watch/listen to the news	Watch/listen to the news	Watch/listen to the news	Watch/listen to the news	Watch/listen to the news	Watch/listen to the news	Watch/listen to the news

Figure 4.7 An example of a study timetable

Reflection zone

Here are a few key summary points for you to reflect upon:

- Note the importance of personal exploration in broadening your understanding of the wider world and, in particular, the business environment.
- Appreciate the importance of making connections between the various modules that comprise your degree programme.
- Consider how you can enhance your critical thinking skills and apply them to your study.
- Seek to create the right physical environment that best suits your approach to effective studying.
- Appreciate how to use the contents of your module guide effectively to enhance your study activities.
- Seek techniques that will enhance your lecture and workshop skills, for example, in creating effective notes.
- Understand the relevance of validity, reliability, generalizability and triangulation to all the assessments that you will undertake.
- Consider how best to use textbooks and journals articles to supplement your lecture and seminar notes.
- Appreciate the need to create a study timetable that also incorporates leisure time.

Further reading

Buzan, T. (2002) *How to Mind Map: The Ultimate Thinking Tool That Will Change Your Life* London: HarperCollins.

De Bono, E. (1990) *Lateral Thinking: A Textbook of Creativity* Harmondsworth: Penguin Books.

De Bono, E. (1996) *Teach Yourself to Think* Harmondsworth: Penguin Books.

De Bono, E. (2000) *Six Thinking Hats* Harmondsworth: Penguin Books.

De Bono, E. (2004) *De Bono's Thinking Course* London: BBC Active Books.

5 So, Who Marks Your Work?

'People ask for criticism, but they only want praise.'

Of Human Bondage (1915)
W. Somerset Maugham, 1874–1965, English novelist

Contents

▶ Introduction
▶ What do markers seek from your work?
▶ Processes
▶ Reflection zone

● Introduction

It is useful for you to have an understanding of how your assessments (assignments, examinations and dissertations/projects) are usually marked. As this might vary from institution to institution and country to country, I am promoting my view of an ideal scenario. The rationale for including this chapter is to communicate some of the complexity that goes into marking your work. Let's be clear here, it is not a 'black art' and it is vital that there is transparency. It is more than often sheer hard work on the part of the assessors to mark the submissions to a high standard by a set deadline. Moreover, having a greater understanding of the processes involved might well help you understand what markers seek in your response to the assessments.

● What do markers seek from your work?

This is a question that students often ask of both themselves and tutors. Information contained within your student handbook should provide you with a general schematic of the areas you should be covering within your assessment. Typically, an examiner will be asking themselves the following questions of your work:

- Has the student displayed a depth and breadth of knowledge and understanding? In other words, has the student shown that they have read around the subject and used these various sources to demonstrate that they understand the complexity of the issues in some detail?
- Has the student been able to apply the theory to practical situations where appropriate and required? Moreover, has the student challenged such applicability?
  There is often a belief that because Professor X comes up with a theory then that is it – perfection reigns! Perhaps all theories have a value – however, are they applicable in all situations? That is something that needs to be questioned. By reading a variety of literature, you will begin to realize that many of the past and current business/management theories have, to a lesser or greater extent, been challenged.

- Has the student focused this knowledge and understanding into the question being asked?

  Unfortunately, especially in examinations, students often 'dump' everything they know about, for example, strategy onto the answer book. While they might clearly demonstrate that they have read widely, they have not focused on what has been asked of them. Sadly, this can result in a fail grade, not just for that answer but also for the module. Therefore, it is imperative that you focus on the specific requirements of the answer and apply your knowledge accordingly.

- Can the student provide a reasoned (and rational) argument for a particular perspective?

  For example, clearly not everyone agrees with the development of specific business models (see the earlier point in this section). Therefore, you need to know (and be able to state) the different perspectives held.

- What's the student's own perspective? Is there supporting evidence for that perspective?

  This evidence will usually come from the textbooks, journal and business articles that you have read. This is particularly important in dissertations, where you will be expected develop your own point or view (or voice).

● Processes

As stated at the beginning of this chapter, I have sought an ideal approach to the marking process. Not all institutions might take this route, and thus I suggest that you check on the particular processes used within your college/university.

- **First marker** Depending upon the student numbers on the module this can be either your module or seminar leader. They are tasked with marking the work in line with the marking criteria, which are usually set out either in a module/student guide and/or separately when you receive the assessment details (for example, the assignment).

- **Second marker – moderator** Again, depending upon the student numbers of the module, this is usually the module leader. Depending also upon the size of the student cohort, the moderators might review all the marks or a sample set. If it is a sample set, it is usually divided into the following groupings: the fails, borderline passes/categories and top grades. The moderator usually has the power to amend marks. In some institutions, if the moderator wants to change marks this is usually discussed with the first marker and an agreed mark is presented.

- **The marking of dissertations** It is worthwhile stating here that there is a slight variation on the above process where dissertations are concerned. A dissertation is, usually, marked by a first marker (the student's supervisor) and then a second marker. Once they have written their draft reports, both markers discuss the merits of the work. At this stage, neither marker has seen the other marker's suggested mark or market range (for example 60–65). By comparing and contrasting their individual findings on the dissertation, the two markers will, usually, come to an agreed view of the final mark. Very rarely do the two markers come to *exactly* the same mark – although it can happen. Usually, though, they should be within a few marks of each other. If they are not, then it is a matter of discussion as each debates the merits or otherwise of the work. If no agreement is reached (for example, one marker believes it is a 'fail' and the other believes it is a 'pass'), then it must go to a third marker. The third marker can be either an internal member of staff or the external examiner. Whichever is the case, they should not be told either the views or the proposed marks of the former two markers as they need to draw their own independent conclusion.

- **External examiner** This is usually a senior academic from another institution who is appointed by the college or university. They will be specialist within the particular subject area; for example, Human Resource Management, Accounting or Economics. They will read a sample of the assessments and comment upon standards and the quality of work produced. Usually, they do not have the power to change marks. However, they may suggest if the marking has been too harsh or, indeed, too lenient. It is then up to the examination committee to decide whether or not the marks should be accepted or referred for re-marking to an appropriate standard. In the UK, for example, although the external examiner does not have the power to change marks, they have to complete an annual report for the university for which they are an examiner. In that report, they are asked to comment upon standards and it is here that they can articulate their perspectives upon both the positive and negative aspects of the programme, department and school. This report is public information and must be available via the university's website. Therefore, it is an important source of information for perspective students and parents who are seeking information on academic standards.
- **Chair of the examination committee** A senior member of college/university staff who checks (usually with an administrator) that the information on the various mark sheets is correct.
- **Examination board** These boards might also be known by the title 'Subject Examination Committee'. These usually comprise the chair, module leaders, seminar leaders, external examiners and senior administrators. The objective of the committee is to determine that fairness has prevailed across the marking and that no individual student or group of students has been disadvantaged. For example, if the pass mark is 40 for a module, a student who receives a mark of 39 could be considered as being disadvantaged: Is the mark of 39 a 'fail' or a 'borderline pass'? It could be too close to call. Therefore, the examination committee might take the view that it should be moved to a pass grade of 40. However, this will also be accompanied with a note to module leaders to be clear at both marking and moderation as to whether the work is of a standard that merits either a pass or fail grade and not left at an 'almost'. In such circumstances, a mark of 39 is clearly not fair on the student. If the work does not warrant a pass, then it should be clearly marked as a fail. If it is just a pass, then it

should be clearly marked as just a pass. In addition to demonstrating academic rigour, there must be fairness.

- **Appeals process** Colleges and universities usually operate an appeals process for students who might feel disadvantaged by the grades that they have received. However, it is important to realize that such appeals are normally reserved for specific situations. You cannot appeal against a grade simply because you do not like it – that is clearly an irrational act! You might believe that you have submitted an assignment that deserves, say, 75%, but which has only been awarded 62%. The tutor feedback should provide you with the clues as to why you received the 62%, as opposed your anticipated 75%. Moreover, you will also need to compare your perception of levels of attainment with those of your tutors, who will have the experience of assessing university-level work. It is important that you think of this as you move from a pre-university environment to a university. As stated earlier in this book, a higher level of both commitment and output will be asked of you and it is important that you understand this from the outset to avoid the risk of disappointment.
- **Grounds for appeal** Usually, grounds for appeal encompass the following (however, you must check your own college/university regulations).
  - There were mitigating circumstances of which the examination board, for good reason, were not aware at the time that they made their decision. (This might be your own ill health or that of a close member of your family.)
  - An error had been made (for example, you were provided with the wrong examination date, the wrong examination room, the wrong paper or some of your work was lost).
  - An administrative irregularity has occurred or university regulations were not followed.

An appeal should really only be for exceptional circumstances and is clearly not intended for someone who just does not like their grade. If your grade is not what you had hoped it to be, obtain the feedback on where you went wrong, then use that feedback to enhance your work for the future. This will be taking a positive step forward.

Reflection zone

Here are a few key summary points for you to reflect upon:

- Seek to understand what tutors want to see from your work in terms of breadth and depth of knowledge, application and the communication of your own perspectives.
- The value in providing evidence to support your perspectives.
- Understand the often complex processes that are involved in assessing your work from markers through to examination boards.

6 Cheating: Copying, Collusion and Plagiarism

*'I hate like death the situation of the plagiarist;
the glass I drink from is not large, but at least it is my own.'*

La Coupe et les Lèvres (1832),
Alfred de Musset, 1810–1857, French poet and playwright

Contents

► Introduction
► Forms of cheating
► Why do some students cheat?
► Detection
► Consequences
► The potential wider impact of cheating
► Seeking guidance
► Reflection zone

● Introduction

Musset's quote is very apposite. He takes the view that although he might not be a great artist, at least he is an honest one. The same view is clearly applicable to you, the student. Yes, you want to be successful – but at any cost? As you will see in this chapter the risks might actually be greater than you imagine.

You might be wondering why there is a chapter on cheating in a study skills book. The answer is simple:

●   To advise you what generally constitutes cheating and dishonest behaviour so that you can seek to avoid it.
●   To warn you against taking that route by demonstrating the possible consequences of your actions. The impact upon your future can be severe.

The fact that you have registered to spend a few years of your time and energy undertaking a degree programme shows some commitment. Otherwise, if you just wanted a few letters after your name (that have absolutely no value whatsoever) you would simply knowingly purchase a degree from the Internet – 'US$500 for a BA degree in 5 to 15 days based upon your "life experiences"'. Quite clearly, a legitimate degree cannot be obtained in such a ridiculously short time scale. The purchasing of such degrees is an absolute waste of money. However, as you will see in this chapter, students are prepared to pay extortionate sums of money to cheat their way through their degree programme. Therefore, anything is possible.

The fact that you have not taken that route at least shows that you are prepared to invest some time and effort into obtaining a degree. The issues of cheating, however, are not as simple as many of us would like to think. While this chapter is geared to giving you emphatic advice against any form of cheating, we must also seek to understand the reasons why some people (knowingly and unknowingly) take this route. If you see yourself in any situation that is discussed within this chapter, now is the time to challenge yourself. By challenging yourself, you might prevent yourself taking the wrong route and losing your degree.

● Forms of cheating

In this section, we review the different forms of cheating that some students undertake. This is in no way condoning such actions but merely illustrating the various forms. The objective here is to highlight the issues in order for you to safeguard yourself – in other words, to prevent you from falling, wittingly or otherwise, into taking such actions.

Copying from another student's work

This is where a complete assignment, project or dissertation has been copied *verbatim* from another student. The student might have colluded (see below) or, indeed, unknowingly had their work copied. One example is where a student copied out a dissertation housed in a university library. Copying out 10,000 words or so requires no skill whatsoever. Of course, a supervisor during regular dissertation meetings with a student can usually detect if the student knows their subject or not. If an outstanding piece of work is produced and it does not match the student's performance profile, then there is cause for suspicion. This suspicion might well lead to an investigation.

Collusion

This is where students collaborate together on their individual assignments rather than undertaking the work separately. In essence, one work is produced and submitted by two or more students. If the students believe that suspicion will not fall upon them, then this is a gross naïvety on their part. As stated in Chapter 5, there are usually several marking stages and detection could occur at any one of these stages.

Purchasing assignments

We cannot ignore the fact that Internet-based companies have been formed to provide students with assignments and dissertations. The companies concerned use disclaimers similar to 'the tailored assignment is for guidance only and the student must develop it further'. Yet, if anyone had paid, for example, UK£50.00 for one assignment, would they seek to 'develop it further', considering that it is merely 'a research aid'? This is clearly not the goal of the student who seeks to circumvent the pursuit of knowledge and academic standards. The costs of these assignments can vary from UK£50 to UK£4,000 depending upon subject and time imperative.

What you have to remember is that, under the gloss, these are for-profit organizations – there is definitely no philanthropy here. They will not rescue you if the university charges you, under its regulations, with cheating. The supplier of the assessment will simply say that 'it was a business transaction and what the student decides to do with it is at their own risk'. So do not expect any help.

Students who purchase such assessments lose in several ways:

- **Financially** These online services are expensive. So, who pays?
- **Morally** They seek to gain an unfair advantage over colleagues who have honestly undertaken the research and written up the assessment.

- **Detection** Clearly, there is the risk of being detected and having to face the necessary consequences (See later section on consequences).
- **Risk of being caught out by employers** They might be discovered to be an individual who knows absolutely nothing about their subject, thereby risking dismal without a reference. What are their potential job opportunities then?

Getting your friends to write the work for you

Students sometimes ask their friends to write either the assignment or dissertation for them. There might be some payment in exchange; although it is unlikely to be at the level stated above. However, there are a few assumptions to be considered:

- Your friend understands the subject well and thus can clearly address the issues in the question. What if they are a willing provider but do not understand the key issues surrounding the question? They might still provide a piece of work that fails. So, it might be no different to the work that you would have produced. In fact, you might have produced a piece of work that actually would have passed!
- Your friend does not understand the subject and decides to plagiarize other sources – for example, textbooks and journal articles. As you do not understand what has been written, you do not know whether your friend has plagiarized or not. The markers become suspicious and the result is that, for example, you have to retake the whole module again (see issues on plagiarism later in this chapter). Therefore, you have achieved nothing apart from a note on your academic record that you plagiarized your assignment or dissertation.
- If your friend is at the same institution, they too might well find themselves in front of a panel to explain their own actions. Again, the penalties will vary from institution to institution but could result in expulsion.

Plagiarism

Plagiarism is to take the work of another person and use it as if it were your own in an attempt to mislead the examiner.

Examples of plagiarism:

- Citing other people's models or theories as your own.
- Where short sections of text have been copied *verbatim* without acknowledgement. This happens where a student copies sections from another source (books, journals, the Internet and lecture notes) and fails to place the section in quotation marks and acknowledge the sources.
- Where long sections are copied. This happens where a student copies whole sections or chapters and portrays the work as their own. Again, there is no reference to the original source of the material at any stage within the submission. Not only is this plagiarism, but also it clearly demonstrates a lack of subject understanding. If the student understood the subject area, they would be able to assimilate information from various sources.

Let's consider an example. A student has to produce an assignment on the mystique of the computer. The student writes:

> Stanley Kubrick's film 2001: A Space Odyssey (1968) introduces us to HAL 9000, a highly intelligent voice responsive computer. HAL, prophesying Artificial Intelligence, displays certain human qualities – not only hyperintelligence but emotion and self awareness (Jonscher 1999). However, HAL displays a much more sinister threat to the two crew of the spacecraft. In the end, it becomes a battle between a human and a machine, resulting in HAL being shut down. Perhaps, in the end, we feel a strange mixture of relief and sorrow; relief in that a machine has not taken control of human activity, yet sorrow because it has displayed a 'human' quality. Most especially, when HAL recounts how 'his' creator taught him language through the nursery rhyme 'Mary had a little lamb.'

If the student had written the above *verbatim* (without any acknowledgement and quotation marks), then they would have committed plagiarism. The above is a direct quote from Groucutt and Griseri (2004).

What should the student do?

1   The best solution is paraphrasing the text in your own words and making reference to the source of information. If you look at the sample text, you will see that the authors referred to Jonscher (1999).
2   The second best solution is to place the whole section in quotation marks and refer to the source at the end of the paragraph. While that is legitimate, it is best used only on small quotations. Moreover, you do not want to be seen quoting large chunks of material one after the other throughout your work. All you are really doing is such cases is cutting and pasting other people's ideas. You are not really comparing and contrasting ideas, evaluating them and coming up with your own point of view.

Overall, you need to demonstrate that you have used material wisely, cited the sources diligently and shown that you understand the issues. It is an integral part of the learning process to discuss and analyze the ideas of other people. It shows the examiner that you are reading around the subject, taking account of different perspectives. However, you must take care to acknowledge all thoughts, ideas, writings, images, concepts and concepts that are the work of others.

Why it is not a good idea to plagiarize

Do not try to outsmart the tutor/examiner. A student might copy from a text in the belief that the tutor might not know the text. Tutors might spot key words or phrases that will alert them to possible plagiarism, whether they are familiar with the text or not. This will set off an investigation that could spell the end of your academic career.

Copying from the text might not even answer the question; it might only answer a very small part of the question. So, you are lulling yourself into a false sense of security if you feel that copying from one or two authors (no matter how notable they might be) will actually provide you with a relevant answer to your assignment (see example cited later in this chapter). Such an approach is naïve in the extreme. Never underestimate your tutors!

Examination malpractice

Some students will knowingly endeavour to circumvent the examinations system. It is important to note that any irregular behaviour – prior to or during examinations – can be classed as cheating.

This includes:

- Obtaining, by any means, the question paper in advance of an examination.
- Impersonating another student. In this case, both students would face disciplinary action.
- Unauthorized use of notes – usually smuggled into the examination room.
- Copying another student's/candidate's work.
- The use of programmable calculators or other electronic equipment when this has been prohibited.

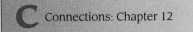

C Connections: Chapter 12

● Why do some students cheat?

While it is not acceptable to cheat under any circumstances, it is nonetheless worth considering why some students take this action. By considering such actions, we can try and, perhaps, counteract this behaviour.

Fear of failure

This is something that affects all of us, often at many stages in our lives. However, the vast majority of people seek to overcome their fears honestly and do the best they can in undertaking the given task. Failure might still occur. However, as entrepreneur Henry Ford (1863–1947) stated 'Failure is the only opportunity to begin again intelligently' (Garrett, 1952). Henry Ford was not successful with his early automotive ventures. However, he learnt from his failures and was able to use this knowledge (what went wrong and why) to create the Ford Motor Company. This became the dawn of mass production and, in creating this approach, forged one of the largest companies in the world. In other words, Henry Ford learnt from what went wrong and what went right – he learnt from his experiences and used that to his best advantage.

For many students, such fears are culturally driven and based upon losing respect.

C Connections: Chapter 12

This fear can drive some students to act dishonestly in order to gain a degree. However, it is far better to be honest in your endeavours and fail the assessment/module than to be caught cheating. The disgrace of an investigation, and possible expulsion from university, is far greater than submitting a poorly argued assignment.

Ego

A brash ego is often based upon the view that they have escaped detection before and thus will continue to cheat. A student might be of the opinion that this is the way to succeed in the 'cut and thrust' of an aggressive dynamic business world. In reality, it is not and those who choose this route are usually discovered. A recent example of such discovery was the prosecution of the executives attached to the gigantic failure of the energy company ENRON.

● Detection

A student might believe that, with cunning, they can escape detection. However, the means of detecting unethical behaviour are many and varied.

1   As with all good, effective detection work, experience can play a major part. For example, I remember reading a very good essay then seeing one line in the final paragraph that made me uneasy. It just did not fit – clearly there was something wrong. I raised this with the module leader and the student was called in for a meeting. It transpired that the student 'hadn't had the time' to work on the assignment because they had gone on a skiing vacation and thus had 'downloaded everything from the net'. They had to retake the module.

2   Increasingly, students are asked to present an electronic copy of their work. A random sample of work is chosen (or work that is suspected of potential plagiarism) for scanning through specialist software that detects work from journal and book sources. The sophistication of such software will increase over time, thus catching many who plagiarize other people's work in the name of their own.

3   Students who undertake a doctoral thesis (PhD or DBA) have to undertake a *viva voce*. This is an oral examination (or defence) of their work. It is one thing being able to write the words – but can you defend your understanding of what you have written? Increasingly, where either plagiarism or other forms of cheating are suspected students can be called to an interview and asked questions based upon the assignment. If they know the work and the subject area, the student should be able to 'defend' their abilities. If not, from where did the work purported to be that of the student emanate?

● Consequences

This section is subdivided into 'Academic' and 'Business', as there is value in considering the impact of cheating within both environments.

Academic

The investigation and interview When a tutor reports a student for cheating, there is usually an investigation, which will mean that any marks/grades will be withheld from that student. The investigation seeks to determine whether or not there is a case to answer, in other words can a clear link – for example, to Internet sites – be established? If this is the case, the student is normally asked to attend a meeting. In many institutions, they are entitled to have another student accompanying them. A tutor (often called an 'academic conduct officer') will, either alone or with other tutors, ask the student questions based upon their work. Although such meetings should be quietly and efficiently conducted, it will remain a nerve-racking experience for the student concerned. If the student is proved to be guilty of misconduct, then the institution can apply various penalties.

Penalties These vary according to the level of offence and from institution to institution. However, as a guide these are the potential consequences of cheating:

- Retaking the assessment
  The student is required to retake the assessment having had their originally submitted assessment deemed to be a fail. On the retake, the maximum grade achievable might only be a basic pass grade.

- Retaking the module
  This would be in addition to the other modules the student would have to take during the semester/term. The student would have to consider what additional pressures this would place upon him or her.

- Retaking the whole year again
  Let's say the academic year comprises eight modules and the student has been caught cheating in two. Let's also say that the student did not cheat in the other modules – however, only the student knows that and cannot prove it. Nonetheless, the university suspects that this student might be a serial cheat and thus decides to disqualify all the student's grades for that year. Therefore, the student has to start the whole year over again. This not only provides an embarrassment for the student but also adds another year of study and fees. How would your financial provider – be it your parents or the State – feel about paying out another year of fees under such circumstances?

- Expulsion
  A university might take the view that, in order to maintain its international quality reputation, anyone caught serial cheating will be dismissed from the university. Consider the humiliation for the expelled student. They have to face both family and friends, and might have difficulty in obtaining another college place or, indeed, a viable job.

Your own business experiences

Companies seek individuals who are reliable, and have integrity and honesty. While this is important at all organizational levels, the more complex the role, the more sensitive the information, the more critical these qualities become. A person who has cheated at university to obtain their degree might now consider this a normal practice. Indeed, it might in their eyes be the only way they can succeed – for the sheer truth is that they used other people's work and thus do not fully understand the business and management concepts. In a company they will be put to the real test.

Scenario 6.1   Cheating: the aftermath

The following scenario is based upon a real case of an MBA student who cheated in an assignment. The assignment question required the students to consider aspects of buyer behaviour. Student A started his assignment by stating that he would respond to the question by using a case study. Usually this would be a good approach, allowing the student to bring together the differing aspects of buyer behaviour to address the core issues of the question.

By paragraph two suspicions were raised when the words 'Larry is an MBA graduate who wants to buy a computer'. These words were familiar . . . but from where? Within the hour, the assignment was being compared to the text in Philip Kotler's book *Marketing Management*. Apart from the deliberate or careless spelling mistakes in Student A's assignment, only one word had been changed. In Philip Kotler's example of buyer behaviour, he had used the name 'Linda' whereas Student A had changed it to 'Larry'.

Clearly, this student was not very intelligent for not only did he copy it word-for-word from a textbook, 'his' answer did not sufficiently address the question. He would have most likely failed the assessment anyway, even if his plagiarism had gone undetected. Perhaps he would have had a greater opportunity to pass if he had undertaken the research and written up his findings in his own words?

On being informed that he would have to retake the whole module again, Student A said he could not because he had an internship in Switzerland.

Student A would probably have been asked to research and write reports for this company. They would expect a high standard – after all, he was soon to complete his studies with an MBA. If the student were unable/incapable to research and write a 3,000-word assignment, would they be able to produce a management report to Swiss business standards? Or would Student A resort to cheating, plagiarizing other managers' and companies' work? This was pointed out to him and he was asked what he thought the consequences could be when detected? Student A had no response.

The consequences could have been:

- Instant dismissal and being escorted security from the building.
- As Student A was not a Swiss national, he would have had a limited work visa. However, as he was now out of a job he would have had to leave the country.
- The company would have informed the university of its actions. The university, believing that its reputation had been affected, might have also taken action against the student.
- Whether the student would have been dismissed from the university or not, he might not be able to call upon the university for a reference.

Needless to say, in this case Student A's internship was cancelled.

Let's now examine Scenario 6.1. The purpose of this scenario is to demonstrate the following:

- Once having taken the cheating route, Student A might have been forced to continue cheating in order to cover up for his lack of knowledge.
- Companies, in order to protect their reputations, will usually take action (within the legal frameworks of the home/host country). As stated in Scenario 6.1, this can mean instant dismissal.
- A student who has successfully circumvented the university system might be arrogant enough to believe that they can circumvent any system. Such an attitude could lead to a variety of actions, including serious white-collar crimes. In such cases, it is not only dismissal from the organization but also often significant fines and prison sentences. Governments are increasingly aware that for businesses, industries and economies to be successful, there must be a principled foundation. Without such foundations, companies can collapse – to the detriment of both the local and national economies. In 2006, prison sentences were handed down to former executives of the collapsed US energy business ENRON and the founder of the South Korean *chaebol* Daewoo. These were significant prosecutions and a reminder of the need for integrity and honesty in business.

The potential wider impact of cheating

It is worth considering the wider potential impact of cheating by some business students:

- As there is, sadly, an increase in Internet 'essay sites', colleges and universities will possibly move towards having the larger proportion of their assessment by examination. This can disadvantage honest students whose performance is rated higher in continuous assessment than in examinations. Many people prefer continuous assessment than examinations, as this brings out the best in their work. For example, the opportunity to drill down into the data and provide real critical analysis on the subject under investigation.
- Company managers might increasingly view business degrees as worthless as, in their view, assignments can simply be purchased online. Large companies, in particular, might decide to take non-graduates, on the basis that they can be trained by means of the companies' own tailored courses.

Seeking guidance

While there are students who will knowingly cheat, there are many others who unwittingly find themselves accused of, for example, plagiarism. If you are in any doubt as to how to approach your work, seek help and advice. This comes in various forms:

- At induction, you might have received general guidance on how to approach your assessments – in other words, what to do and what not to do.

- College and university libraries usually have guides to good referencing and how to avoid plagiarism.
- Your workbook or guide for each module might contain relevant information.

Connections: Chapter 4

- Discuss any concerns, either with your module leader or personal tutor before you submit your work.

Reflection zone

Here are a few key summary points for you to reflect upon:

- Understand the various forms of cheating, such as plagiarism, and how to avoid them.
- Understand the consequences of being caught cheating.
- Consider why some students might choose to cheat and the detrimental effect such actions have on academic standards and employability.

7 A Brief Guide to Referencing

'You will find it a very good practice always to verify your references, sir!'

In John William Burgon, *Lives of Twelve Good Men*
(1888) vol. 1: 73,
Martin Joseph Routh, 1755–1854, English classicist

Contents

- ▶ Introduction
- ▶ Referencing styles
- ▶ Potential difficulties
- ▶ The difference between a reference list and a bibliography
- ▶ A few general thoughts
- ▶ Reflection zone

● Introduction

Throughout this book you are asked to consider the following:

- The necessity to explore (both in terms of depth and breadth) the subject area using a range of sources. These sources will have included academic textbooks, business books, journal articles, business publications, quality newspapers, radio and TV programmes and Internet sources.
- The validation, reliability, triangulation and generalizability of these sources.

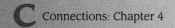

C Connections: Chapter 4

- The justification for your own perspectives, using evidence drawn from this range of sources.

In every assignment, as well as in your final dissertation, you will have to demonstrate the above. Your evidential support in both your assignment and dissertation will come by means of your use of referenced sources. It is important that you acknowledge the source of any theory or information used in your assignments and dissertation, whether you are using a quote or describing someone else's observations in your own words.

You should ensure that:

- Words or phrases taken *verbatim* from published works are placed in quotation marks and the source acknowledged.
- Quotations take the form of brief relevant extracts. (Only exceptionally exceeding 100 words in length.)

Where lengthier use of a published work is appropriate, you may summarize or paraphrase an author's words. However, the source of the summary or paraphrase must, again, be fully acknowledged by textual reference.

As an example, here is a direct quote from Groucutt, J. (2006) *Foundation of Marketing* (Basingstoke: Palgrave Macmillan).

> In their original article Booms and Bitner (1981) intended their original additional 3Ps to be limited to service marketing. However, there are academics and writers, for example, Levitt, who suggest that 'there are only industries whose service components are greater or lesser than those of other industries. Everybody is in service' (Levitt, 1972). Raqif and Ahmed (1995) contended that a marketing mix was needed that cut across the boundaries of goods, services and industrial marketing – a generic marketing mix. Increasingly the Booms and Bitner marketing mix framework has been adopted to meet that need (Groucutt, 2006).

This quote illustrates the importance of:

- Seeking evidential support for your perspectives and points of view
- Referencing those perspectives and opinions within the main body of your text.

● Referencing styles

There are two forms of referencing: the Vancouver and the Harvard (also known as the parenthetical and author-date) systems. Your college or university will usually take a view on the one that you should use during your studies. The purpose here is to explain briefly the two referencing styles ands how they operate. However, it is important to bear in mind that these are not perfect systems. Look at a range of textbooks that uses the Harvard system, for example, and you will see minor variations. Publishers often adopt a variation to suit their own purposes. The most important things to remember are:

- Have you acknowledged the views of others? This includes referencing all tables, graphs, and photographs as appropriate.
- Have you made an attempt to construct a list of those acknowledged sources?

If you do not follow some form of reliable system then you risk being accused of plagiarism.

C Connections: Chapter 6

Vancouver system

This is also known as the author-number style of referencing. The style was developed by the US National Library of Medicine and adopted by a committee (later to become the International Committee of Medical Journal Editors) at a 1978 meeting in Vancouver. This has since become a standard reference style for many scientific publications. However, it has also become a standard format for many business textbook and journal publishers. Two reasons are often cited for using the Vancouver system.

1   That the text flows better and, thus, there is enhanced readability;
2   It is less obtrusive than having names and dates appearing within the main body of text.

Let us present the quotation on p. 94 using the Vancouver style:

> In their original article Booms and Bitner (1) intended their original additional 3Ps to be limited to service marketing. However, there are academics and writers, for example, Levitt, who suggest that 'there are only industries whose service components are greater or lesser than those of other industries. Everybody is in service' (2). Raqif and Ahmed (3) contended that a marketing mix was needed that cut across the boundaries of goods, services and industrial marketing – a generic marketing mix. Increasingly the Booms and Bitner marketing mix framework has been adopted to meet that need (4).

References in the Vancouver style are cited in numerical order. There is less punctuation than with the Harvard style (see later section) and journal titles are abbreviated.

The references would be stated in the reference list as follows:

(1)   Booms, B.H. Bitner, M.J. Marketing strategies and organization structures for service firms in J.H. Donnely and W.R. George (eds) Marketing of Services, Chicago: AMA. 1981.
(2)   Levitt, T. Production line approach to service. HBR 1972 (Sept–Oct) 41–52.
(3)   Rafiq, M., Ahmed, P.K. Using the 7Ps as a generic marketing mix: an exploratory survey of UK and European marketing academics. Mk Intel and Plan. 1995 13 (9) 4–16.
(4)   Groucutt, J. Foundations of Marketing. Basingstoke: Palgrave Macmillan, 2006.

Observation

Consider the structure of the reference, particularly:

1   The numerical order;
2   The punctuation;
3   The date at the end;
4   The fact that you need to consider the potential difficulties of using a numbering system.

You might find yourself in the situation of repeating a reference to a particular author. This can be directly following one quote or later on within your text. Let's use the above example, with a few modifications.

> In their original article Booms and Bitner (1) intended their original additional 3Ps to be limited to service marketing. However, there are academics and writers, for example, Levitt, who suggest that 'there are only industries whose service components are greater

or lesser than those of other industries. Everybody is in service' (2). Raqif and Ahmed (3) contended that a marketing mix was needed that cut across the boundaries of goods, services and industrial marketing – a generic marketing mix. Increasingly the Booms and Bitner marketing mix framework has been adopted to meet that needed (4). Groucutt believes that the 7Ps is 'all well and good' but that there is room for expansion (5).

The reference list will read:

(1)   Booms, B.H. Bitner, M.J. Marketing strategies and organization structures for service firms in J.H. Donnely and W.R. George (eds) Marketing of Services, Chicago: AMA. 1981.

(2)   Levitt, T. Production line approach to service. HBR 1972 (Sept–Oct) 41–52.

(3)   Rafiq, M., Ahmed, P.K. Using the 7Ps as a generic marketing mix: an exploratory survey of UK and European marketing academics. Mk Intel and Plan. 1995 13 (9) 4–16.

(4)   Groucutt, J. Foundations of Marketing. Basingstoke: Palgrave Macmillan, 2006.

then

(5)   *Ibid.*, p: 159

If you later refer to the same text (say, as source 19) then you would use:

(19)   Groucutt, *op cit*. p: 328.

If you had more than one author, you could use *et al.* on repeats. It is abbreviated Latin for *et allii* – which means 'and others'.

For example, the first citing would be:

(7)   Mintzberg, H. Ahlstrand, B. Lampel, J. Strategy Safari. London: FT/Prentice Hall 1998.

then, if cited sequentially:

(8)   Minzberg *et al.*, *ibid.*, 1998.

If the work has been cited earlier (at number 7, in this example) then later (number 14, in this example) then you would use:

(14)   Minzberg *et al.*, *op. cit.*, 1998.

Observation

Ibid. is abbreviated Latin for *Ibidem*, which means 'in the same book or passage'.

Op. cit. is abbreviated Latin for *opere citato*, which means 'in the work quoted above'.

Et al. is abbreviated Latin for 'and others' and is used where there are more than two authors. This saves writing out all the names again.

Any text that is in Latin must be presented in italics.

Referencing websites

(9)   BBC. BAA to face competition inquiry. London: BBC 2007. www.news.bbc.co.uk/
go/pr/fr/-/1/hi/business/6509311.stm (accessed 30 March 2007).

Harvard system

This is also known as the author-date and parenthetical system. The Harvard system was derived from the library cataloguing system at the Zoological Laboratory at Harvard University. It was first used in an academic paper in 1881 by Edward Mark, who was Professor of Anatomy and Director of the Zoological Laboratory (Mark, 1881). Over time, many textbooks and journals have adopted the Harvard system in one variation or another (see later note on variants).

If we refer to the example taken earlier, then we can illustrate how you would reference this in the Harvard format:

> In their original article Booms and Bitner (1981) intended their original additional 3Ps to be limited to service marketing. However, there are academics and writers, for example, Levitt, who suggest that 'there are only industries whose service components are greater or lesser than those of other industries. Everybody is in service' (Levitt, 1972). Raqif and Ahmed (1995) contended that a marketing mix was needed that cut across the boundaries of goods, services and industrial marketing – a generic marketing mix. Increasingly the Booms and Bitner marketing mix framework has been adopted to meet that need (Groucutt, 2006, p: 159).

The reference list will read:

Booms, B.H. and Bitner, M.J. (1981) 'Marketing strategies and organization structures for service firms', in Donnely, J.H. and George, W.R. (eds), *Marketing of Services* Chicago: AMA.

Groucutt, J. (2006) *Foundations of Marketing* Basingstoke: Palgrave Macmillan.

Levitt, T. (1972) 'Production line approach to service', *Harvard Business Review*, September/October, pp: 41–520.

Rafiq, M. and Ahmed, P.K. (1995) 'Using the 7Ps as a generic marketing mix: An exploratory survey of UK and European marketing academics', *Marketing Intelligence and Planning*, Vol 13, No 9, pp: 4–160.

Observation

Consider the structure of the referencing particularly:

1   The alphabetical order based on surname;
2   The punctuation;
3   The date following the author(s) name;
4   Journal titles are stated in full;
5   The titles of textbooks and journals are either underlined or set in italics.

Variants

As indicated earlier, there tend to be variants on the original referencing systems. Indeed, your college or university might have a variant to the styles indicated above. Generally, these are minor variants – for example, no brackets around the date or the first name written in full rather than just an initial.

The key is that the more you practice the required style, the better you will become at applying it.

● Potential difficulties

From time to time, you will come across sources that do not fit neatly into the above boxes. The following are possible examples that you might encounter.

Where there is no author

Occasionally, you will encounter documents or articles that have no specified author. Here are a few possible examples – a company (for example, Nestlé and its Annual Report and Accounts), the BBC (global radio and TV broadcaster and Internet news provider), *The Economist* (quality business newspaper), Mintel (provider of marketing reports, specifically on UK markets). In each case, you will use the name of the provider of the information – for example:

Mintel (2003) *Vending – UK report*, Mintel International group, February.

Where the author has two or more sources in the same year

This is applicable if you are using the Harvard system. Where you have the same author and the same year, you separate the documents by using 'a', 'b', 'c' and so on. The use of letters would appear within the main body of text as well – for example, (NCIX, 2004a).

Here is the reference listing:

National Counterintelligence Executive USA (NACIX) (2004a) *The Economic Espionage Act of 1996: A Brief Guide.* Washington, DC: NCIX.
National Counterintelligence Executive USA (NCIX) (2004b) *Annual Report to Congress on Foreign Economic Collection and Industrial Espionage* Washington, DC: NCIX.

Citing personal communication

Often, especially when working on dissertations, we might have access to individuals who provide us with opinion and information. As with any other source, they must be acknowledged, both in the main body of text and the reference list. If you are quoting directly, then their words must be in quotation marks.

Muir, J. (2005) *Personal Communication*, Muir Engineering Pty Ltd, Tasmania: 5 September.

The use of Latin within cited references

For this example, let us cite the original paper that started the promotion of the Harvard system.

Mark, E.L. (1881) Maturation, fecundation and segmentation of *Limax campestris, Bulletin of the Museum of Comparative Zoology*, Vol. 6, Part 2, no. 12, pp: 173–625.

> **Observation**
>
> In this citation, although the title of the article is presented in standard characters *Limax campestris* is presented in italics because it is a Latin name.

The difference between a reference list and a bibliography

This is often a confusing area for students.

Reference list

This contains only the material that you have cited within the main body of your assignment/dissertation. The two must clearly match up.

Bibliography

This contains two types of material:

1   All the material you have cited within the main body of your assignment/dissertation;
2   Material that you have read as background but have not cited within the assignment/dissertation. This background material, for example, could be a company's history, the evolution of a particular school of thought and so on.

A few general thoughts

The vast majority of colleges and universities will have their own documents (often online) that will guide you through the referencing maze. If you have any doubts at all – ASK!

While we all strive for perfect referencing, it is seldom achievable. Even the best writers and academics are prone to make minor errors. The emphasis is on the 'minor'. It is most unlikely that your tutors will penalize you for having the comma in the wrong place (although they might indicate it). The real issues are whether or not you have made a realistic attempt to reference properly and have been, overall, honest in your approach.

Reflection zone

Here are a few key summary points for you to reflect upon:

● Appreciate the overall value of citation.
● Appreciate the difference between the Harvard and Vancouver styles of referencing.
● Consider how you can enhance your referencing skills.

8 When Things Go Wrong – You Are Not Alone

'One must be a god to be able to tell success from failures without making a mistake.'

Anton Pavlovitch Chekhov, 1860–1904,
Russian author and playwright

Contents

▶ Introduction
▶ Focusing on underlying issues
▶ Reflection zone

● Introduction

This chapter considers some of the 'things that can go wrong' in terms of studying for a business degree. The focus here is on the academic rather than the personal issues that might affect you, although such events can clearly have an impact upon how you feel as an individual.

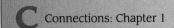

Connections: Chapter 1

Reference to Chekhov is apposite in that, while not engaged in running a business as such, he knew about failure and success. In 1868, he enrolled at a classical gymnasium (or high school). His eight-year course took him ten years because he failed in two classes and was kept down twice. However, he later trained as a doctor (by all accounts, not a very good one) at Moscow University. Clearly, though, his passion was writing, becoming a prestigious writer of short stories.

Apparently all of Chekhov's early full-length plays were deemed failures. The *Chayka* (The Seagull) had a disastrous first night performance in St Petersburg. However, when revived in 1889 it was a great triumph. This marked the turning point for Chekhov in terms of his plays, as the later productions of his masterpieces *Dyadya Vanya* (Uncle Vanya) in 1900, *Tri Sestry* (The Three Sisters) in 1901 and *Vishnyovy Sad* (The Cherry Orchard) 1904 would bare witness. Today, Chekhov is considered one of the master storytellers and playwrights of the twentieth century. His work will continually be read and performed on the stage for many generations.

In some countries, the words 'fail' and 'failure' have much stigma attached to them. These words are compared to 'losing face', 'letting people down' and 'being a disgrace to the family'. These are harsh views, for failure is often the means through which we truly learn and improve our performance. In some countries – namely, North America – the words 'fail' and 'failure' are associated instead with 'trying', 'experimenting', 'risk taking' and 'endeavour'. The belief is that unless you make business mistakes and (importantly) learn from them, you do not truly appreciate how to build a real business. The entrepreneur, physicist and inventor Thomas Edison (1847–1931) apparently once stated: 'I have never failed. I've just found 10,000 ways that won't work.' (Note: The date of publication of the original quote is unknown.)

As well as considering measures to help your progression, this chapter also requires you to ask yourself some perhaps difficult, yet important, soul-searching questions. However, they are questions designed to help you to consider your future options.

Focusing on underlying issues

A fundamental point to remember is that everyone fails at something in his or her life. Even the most successful business people have had failures. As stated in Chapter 6, the entrepreneur Henry Ford (1863–1947), considered the father of car mass production, had setbacks and disappointments. Yet, he came back with a vengeance in 1903 with what was to become the Ford Motor Company.

In your business studies, you will examine human resources management issues and the problems associated with entrepreneurship. Through your reading and discussions, you will come to understand that even the most successful entrepreneurs have often failed more than once. However, they have persevered with a combination of creativity, determination and self-belief in order to succeed.

Indeed, ask any entrepreneur about failure and disappointment and they will usually provide volumes of examples.

The real question is: What do you do with failure and disappointment?

Consider why you failed the assessment, the module(s) or indeed the programme.

The assessment

In Chapters 9, 11 and 13, the importance of feedback is discussed. It is this feedback that will explain what went wrong and what you need to do to rectify the situation. As stated throughout this book, the areas where students often fail are:

(a) Lack of an understanding of the models, theories and concepts;
(b) Lack of an ability to apply models, theories and concepts;
(c) Inability to promote his or her own ideas supported by relevant and quality evidence;
(d) Inability to firmly ground him/herself in the rational and the real world.

By turning this failure around you have demonstrated that you can take onboard the issues and rectify the situation. This is exactly what you would need to do in business. Not everything will go according to your marketing plan, corporate plan and so on. Therefore you have to be able to react to the changing situation and adapt in order to be once again successful.

Modules and the programme

If you have failed several modules, then you will have to consider how you can rectify this through retaking modules and improving your assessment performance. Clearly, this can be a challenge, especially as it might add another year to your programme of study. However, many students do benefit from such an extra year and their performance does improve.

However, if there is significant failure across a broad range of modules you need to consider the causes and the possible remedies. If it is simply due to not studying and 'over-partying', then it can be rectified through retaking the modules and engaging in the studying process. However, if you have studied hard and have significant failures then you perhaps need to consider the following:

- Is this the right degree for you? You might have started off and enrolled in the belief that it was right for your needs. However, it is only when we get involved in a situation that we sometimes really become aware of both the positives and negatives of that situation. This is very similar to accepting a job offer. You might have, for example, undertaken research on the company, spoken to employees and walked around the company's plant. However, it is not until you start working there that you become fully appreciative of the corporate culture and expectations. The same applies to a business degree programme. This might be the wrong business degree programme for you – or, indeed, the subject of business is the wrong subject for you: therefore, you might consider changing your area of study.

- Is it the right institution for you? A university is a combination of tangibles and intangibles – facilities, people, programmes, schools (or faculties), various approaches to teaching and learning, academic and vocational ideals, departments and a corporate culture. As with the job example stated earlier, first impressions might not be your lasting impressions. Sometimes the chemistry is not right and you realize that you are studying at the wrong institution for you. This does not mean that there is anything inherently wrong with the institution – indeed, it might be one if the best in the world – however, it is not right for you. Therefore, you might need to consider a move to one where you, as a person, feel more comfortable.

- Is it the right time to study for a degree? In many countries, there is an assumed progression of unbroken study from primary through to tertiary education. This suits many individuals – however, not all. Sometimes individuals embark upon a degree programme too soon in their lives and, as a result, fail. However, if they spend one or two years working in business they might be better equipped (in terms of knowledge and skills) to undertake a business degree. The practical experience can provide an extra insight that supports the academic perspectives.

Reflection zone

Here are a few key summary points for you to reflect upon:

- Seek to obtain feedback from the module leader on your assessment strengths and weaknesses. Use this feedback (a) to plan your re-assessment; and (b) help you to improve your overall level of performance.
- Prepare a revision timetable.
- If you have failed several pieces of assessment and/or modules, then book an appointment with your personal tutor or the programme director. Prior to the meeting, consider the questions indicated earlier in this chapter. They are difficult questions but they are, however, worth considering and discussing. You need to consider what is right for you, and now might not be the right time for you to undertake a degree programme.

'Our greatest glory is not in never falling but rising every time we fall'.
K'ung Fu-Tzu (Confucious), 551–479 BCE, Chinese philosopher

9 Assignments

'The devil is in the detail and everything we do in the military is a "detail".'

Hyman George Rickover, 1900–1986,
Admiral US Navy

Contents

► Introduction
► Why assignments are used as a method of assessment
► Assignments and the business perspective
► Group and individual assignments
► Assignment formats
► Examining a case study
► Peer review
► Presentation of assignments
► A word on getting started and writer's block
► The purpose and value of feedback
► Using feedback effectively
► Making deadlines work for you
► Reflection zone
► Further reading

Introduction

Admiral Rickover was responsible for developing the US Navy's nuclear ship capabilities, a major task in its own right and one that was apparently fraught with many difficulties. His quote is an extremely important one because the 'devil *is* often in the detail'.

Whether you are writing an assignment or making a business presentation, you have to consider the detail that often forms the backbone of your work. You might be great at viewing the bigger picture, that is all well and good – but the detail is how you are going to enact what you propose. This is often where business students fall over. They suggest this or that as a strategy but fail to understand the tactical issues.

By appreciating the detail, you should place yourself in a better position to:

- Understand the approach that you need to take in order to obtain the necessary research material to complete your assignment.
- Appreciate how detail underpins models/concepts. For instance, in your first term/semester, you might have demonstrated your basic understanding of a model by simply replicating the framework. However, as you progress through your programme you will be expected to apply the model. The more you are able to apply the model, the more you are able to understand how it operates. Moreover, such an approach will help your critical evaluation skills, allowing you consider both the positive and negative aspects of the model.
- As you become familiar with critical thinking tools you will be able to drill down into the research material that you have gathered. This will allow you to examine the material in order to test its validity and relevance to your assignment. Moreover, in time you will be able to seek out a variety of information that might well support a particular point of view (this is often called triangulation).

 Connections: Chapter 4

- The degree of applicability is important. It is often assumed that because a business theory or model exists it must be applicable in all cases. This is simply not true. The degree of applicability of models will depend upon various circumstances and conditions. Therefore, by seeking out the detail you will have a better understanding of the degree of applicability.
- Business needs 'blue sky' thinkers, those individuals who have the ideas and concepts, create the models. These people are important to the development of organizations and industries. However, in order for the 'blue sky' concepts to have any chance of becoming a reality, there has to be an appreciation of both micro and macro issues – that is, the detail that both underpins and influences the concept.

By seeking to understand the detail from the outset places you in a position to:

- Approach your assignments with confidence.
- Improve your performance as you gain more insight.
- Prepare yourself for future employment.
- Develop your written presentation skills.

In this chapter, we explore how best to approach assignments and how, through tutor feedback, continually to seek to improve your work over the progression of your degree programme.

Why assignments are used as a method of assessment

Assignments are used as a method of assessing a student's ability to research and analyze a particular problem or issue. When a student successfully accomplishes this task, it will show the examiner that the student has an understanding of that particular topic/subject area.

Additionally, it can help students who are strong at research and analysis but who might be less able at examinations. This might be due to examination nerves or pressure.

Assignments and the business perspective

View every assignment not purely as a piece of coursework but as a document for a board of directors. This approach helps you in several ways:

1   It makes you focused, especially in terms of meeting deadlines;
2   It helps you to develop a professional mindset – a professional, business-like approach to your work;
3   It helps you to focus on communicating information in a clear, concise manner.

● Group and individual assignments

There are various types of assignment that can be used to explore both your understanding of the subject area and your analytical approach to the subject. It is important to be mindful that a tutor might use more than one type in assessing capabilities over the course of a module. For example, a tutor might use a combination of group and individual assignments.

The various types are briefly outlined below.

Group assignment

This is where a pre-selected or self-selecting group (usually between two and five students) embark upon a set assignment. For example, the task could be to construct a critical review of the current situational position of a particular company within its competitive environment. Typically, each member of the group will then seek to identify and research key issues, which are fed back to the whole group. From this information, the group, through each individual, will produce the material that will be melded into the final submission.

Often associated with group assignments is a group presentation. This is an important component as it usually accrues marks.

For the group to operate efficiently and effectively it is advisable that:

- The group members are able to contact each other outside class/university time. This will normally mean the swapping of phone numbers and email addresses. Of course, ethical codes of behaviour must be observed once there has been an exchange of contact details.
- The group meets on a regular basis to share information and discuss issues.
- There is an agreement between all members of the group to participate actively in the assignment. There is always the risk that there is a student within the group who will avoid any work. This student might take the view that the rest of the group will continue to perform to a high standard (thus covering for the non-cooperative student) to gain the grades. This might particularly be the case if some of the group members are in line for possible distinctions/first class honours degrees. In an attempt to overcome this unfair weighting of effort, you might choose to implement a group agreement. The agreement binds all members of the group to fulfil their fair share of work. Within this agreement, you might have penalties for those who do not actively participate. These penalties can be in the form of reduction of marks for the particular non-participant. The remainder of the marks should be allocated fairly across the other members of the group. However, before you embark upon such agreements you should seek permission from the module leader. It will be their responsibility to see that there is fairness for all members of the group.

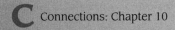
C Connections: Chapter 10

Individual assignment

(1) A 100% individual assessment is where the assessment is based purely on individual work. This might be one or two pieces of written or presentational work.

(2) A percentage individual assessment is where the assessment is a percentage of the total assessment output. For example, there might be 50% associated with group work and 50% associated with individual work. Using the earlier example, the group might be assigned to examine the organization's current situational position. The individual assessment might then ask you to make recommendations that the company could adopt over the next two to five years in order to gain and sustain a competitive advantage.

Formative and summative assignments

Formative assignment

This is normally a short piece of work that is often a compulsory element of the module but which doesn't accrue any marks. They are usually only one or two pages in length and focus on a particular issue that will be related to your summative assignment.

For example, in your summative assignment you are asked to examine the impact/influence of both the micro (the internal factors) and macro (the external factors) of a particular organization. Your formative assignment might require you to set out briefly the macro factors that will impact/influence the organization. Now, this cannot be simply a bullet point list of the macro factors – Political, Economic, Societal, Technological, Legal and Environmental (PESTLE) – it has to be more specific. For instance, under 'Economic' you might focus on inflation, exchange rates, interest rates, the level of disposable income, balance of payments, and so on.

Advantages of a formative assignment
As formative assignments are usually set within the first few weeks of a module, they can be particularly valuable.

1 It gets you started on your research so that you are not leaving it to the last minute;
2 It is allows tutors to gauge your initial abilities in several areas:
   - Your overall understanding of the formative assignment question.
   - Your ability to write succinctly – in other words, to the point.
   - Your ability to cite evidence – thus, demonstrating your ability to start researching the question and referencing your sources.
   - Your overall writing skills.

 Connections: Chapter 2, section on language capabilities

3   Tutors can use the formative assignment to provide you with feedback that you can use to enhance your summative assignment. (The value of feedback is discussed later in this chapter and elsewhere in this book.)

Summative assignment

As the name suggests, this is the summation of your work – hence, the assignment that you would summit either as full or part of the module's assessment.

● Assignment formats

As indicated in Chapter 2, assignments come in various forms. The following is a sample of what you might be presented with, both as individual and group assessment.

Essays

You might well be familiar with this standard form of assessment. Basically, they comprise:

An introduction – scene setting, for example, the background to the organization or model being investigated.

The main body of text – this is where you would present your analysis of the problem (the question).

A conclusion – as with any other concluding section of a document, you would draw together aspects of your analysis. Your conclusions would include your own perspectives. However, it is always advisable to provide evidential support for your views.

Posters

One means of depicting business and management issues is through a poster presentation. Initially, you might think 'Surely this is something for a primary or elementary school?' However, posters can help you to depict particular issues visually. For example, they can be used to show the factors that influence the effective distribution of goods or the regional macro factors that affect the setting up of a new business.

Posters:

- Are often used in your first year of study.
- Can be used to introduce you to group work activities.
- Provide a vehicle that enables you to visualize business and management activities. Visualization is a useful technique that allows you to understand the inner workings of businesses and related organizations. We gain and retain more information visually than we do aurally.
- Can also be great fun! Who said that studying business had to be dull and boring?

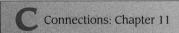

C Connections: Chapter 11

Report format

When you enter the commercial world you will probably to be asked to write reports on a variety of issues and subjects. Therefore the aim of using report writing in your business degree is to help you become familiar with the process.

Here are a few guidelines to writing a business report:

- What is the purpose of the report? Unless you have a clear understanding of the purpose of the report, then it is unlikely that you will achieve the stated objective. To help clarify the purpose, ask yourself the following question: 'As a result of reading this report the reader will ...'. So, for example, if you were asked to examine the rising cost of oil and its relationship to the airline industry you could say:

  As a result of reading this report the reader will understand the impact of rising oil prices on the profitability of an airline. From this the reader will be able to consider various strategies to reduce the negative impact. This might include cutting other costs and raising fares.

You can use this 'purpose' as a means of guiding you through the research and writing process. It will help you to stay focused.

- Consider who will be reading this report: The instructions to your assignment might designate who is the target audience for your report – for example, the CEO of the airline company. In some cases, you might not be informed of the potential reader. You might therefore decide to state the target reader clearly at the beginning of your report. Again, understanding from the outset the identity of the person reading your report helps you to focus. It also helps you to consider the following sub-questions:

  How much background knowledge does the reader already know about subject area? If you are addressing your report to an airline's CEO, you will not want to spend a great deal of time detailing the company's history for them. The reader will already know.

  What is the level of their technical knowledge? Again, the assignment brief might indicate the level of technical knowledge of the proposed reader. For example, the proposed reader might be the logistics manager of a major chilled food supplier. In this situation, for instance, you are likely to focus on the link between theory and practice through application. The logistics manager will be seeking solutions and not a repeating of basic theory in isolation.

The structure of reports

Reports tend to follow a particular structure:

Executive summary – This is an overview or snapshot of the document's contents. This will include the outcomes of your analysis, any recommendations and your conclusions.

The key is writing this so that it is no more than an A4 page in length. Your overall aim is to write it so that anyone reading it will be able to grasp the fundamental issues of the report.

Introduction: This should provide some background to the report. The report might, for instance, be examining the human resources policies of a particular organization. In this situation, you would need to provide some background to that organization and its policies, even before you seek to evaluate them.

Key issues – Analysis: This is where you examine the key issues of the question. Here, you would consider the relationship between theory and practice. For example, consider the following question:

> A Middle Eastern telecommunications company has won a contract to supply all the telecommunication needs of a major German company. The telecommunications company will second managers to the German company and be based at their headquarters in Munich. Prepare a report outlining the potential managerial issues, focusing on human resource management. In your report, suggest solutions to any potential difficulties.

Here you might consider the relationship between different nationalities (for example, Hofstede's power-distance relationships), reporting lines and the difficulties that expatriates face when working overseas (such as missing their families and friends). You might rely on a combination of theory and practice to explain the issues as well as possible solutions.

Recommendations: Here, you would state the actions the organization should undertake. However, you must say why you are making these recommendations: give the evidence that supports your view. Let's consider the above question. In this situation, managers will be away from home on a secondment that might last, for instance, a year. The manager might become homesick, depressed and not perform to normal high standards. You might suggest regular visits home and/or arranging for family visits. Yes, this will cost the company money; however, the company might also reap the rewards from the performance of a dedicated manager. Moreover, it demonstrates to others that the company seeks to care for its staff. You could cite a body of evidence both from academic journals and business publications that supports this view.

Conclusion: This is where you draw together the different strands that you have examined within the report, both the positive and negative issues. Your conclusion might be that if the Middle Eastern telecommunications company, working with its German partner, enacts your recommendations, then the relationship (and, thus, the contract) will have a greater chance of success.

Examining a case study

A case study is an examination of either a real or fictitious organization. Case studies can be used in several ways to help you understand how businesses operate, for example:

- As a seminar activity and assignment question

You might receive a full case study on a fictitious hotel covering its market, the competition, finances, human resources and management. During each teaching session, you might be presented with specific problems that you have to solve within working groups. Thereby, on a session-by-session basis, you are accumulating additional material on the company and making decisions. At the end of the teaching element of the module, you might be presented with an assignment question. This will normally encapsulate the issues that you have examined on the session-by-session basis.

Possible scenario: Over the sessions you see that the hotel is under-performing in virtually all areas. The end session assignment question could focus on whether or not the hotel should be closed. You could be asked to make recommendations, justified with evidence. You might decide to keep the hotel operational but with substantial changes. Over the course of the sessions, you have realized that, overall, the management of the hotel is highly inefficient, perhaps with one exception. You would need to consider the implications (legal, financial and operational) of changing the management structure. However, if you can provide the supporting evidence (your justification), then you might be able to turnaround a failing business.

- Case study assignment

At your first lecture/seminar, you could be given a case study together with a series of questions. The objective is to use the case study document(s) as a platform for research in order to address the proposed questions. Example 9.1 illustrates this.

Example 9.1 How to work with a case study	
Example	**Commentary**
Case study:	Here, the case is being used to provide background information. Starbucks is a company operating within a highly competitive environment. No matter how recent the case, much will have happened since its publication. Thus, there needs to be some updating. Moreover, such an approach encourages students to explore the issues. It is important that the information used is both relevant and contemporaneous, especially in light of the nature of the task.
Starbucks' international operations	
Note:	
● The case study provides you with a platform upon which to develop your knowledge and understanding of the issues. It is your responsibility to explore additional material on the case study company and the issues stated in the assessment.	
● You will receive guidance on sources to help you examine case studies.	
Task:	An assignment based on a case study can either be in the form of an essay or, as in this example, a report (see earlier text on reports).
You are to provide a management report that addresses the following key issues:	
● Critically evaluate the entry strategies that have been adopted by Starbucks	With both these questions the student could adopt the role of a management

Example	Commentary
for developing their international presence. What lessons do you think can be learnt by Starbucks and other companies from Starbucks' experiences? (50%)	consultant advising the business. This is often a good mindset to adopt, as it will help you to focus on the core issues. Equally, you will know that (as a consultant) you will have to justify your recommendations with quality evidence.

- How do you think Starbucks should develop their international markets in the future and why? (50%)

Example	Commentary
Your work must be set out in report format of not more than 10 pages of A4. Use 12-point Arial and double-space your work. The 10 pages, however, exclude cover sheets, reference list and Appendices (however you are only permitted *three* pages of appendices).	You will find that some assignments have word limits while others have page limits. Additionally, in this example the tutor has imposed a page limit on the number of appendices that can be used. There is a clear rationale for this requirement. It encourages you to be focused and critically evaluate what you are going to include/exclude. When there are no page limits on appendices, students often create an appendix that is double the size of the actual answer to the question. So, they end up including all the diagrams (remote from the actual discussions of the diagram), copies of articles, annual reports and various other documents. Such an approach is usually a mixture of enthusiasm and not knowing what to leave in or take out.
Any tables/diagrams used must be linked to the main body of text.	
Your work must be fully referenced in the Harvard format.	All information that is obtained from other sources must be referenced.

C Connections: Chapter 7

Example	Commentary
Submission date: 5 March at 4 pm, Office 9.	The length of time given for the analysis of a case will vary, depending on institutions and individual tutors. As previously stated, it is better to start considering the case immediately you receive it.

The following outlines some of the issues that you need to bear in mind when analyzing a case study.

A case study usually presents an historic record with supporting data on an organization. Case studies are often descriptive in structure – a statement of facts. Your objective is to interpret that data and, often, set it within a contemporary context.

Reflecting upon the question(s) posed, you need to prioritize the issues and/or problems influencing/impacting upon the organization. You might want to conduct a SWOT analysis to help you prioritize. Consider the organization's particular strengths and weaknesses (the internal issues). Then examine the opportunities and threats posed by the external environment. Examine the patterns and issues that emerge. What do they tell you about the organization and the world it operates within?

There are generally no right or wrong answers. The quality of your answer is more often than not defined by:

- How systematic you were in your approach. Have you been logical in your approach to the issues/problems encountered by the company? You will also need to demonstrate a systematic approach in your submitted report, showing that there is logic to your presentation.
- The identification of the key issues – your prioritizing.
- The quality of the resources used to 'investigate' the case organization – for example, journal and business articles.

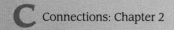

C Connections: Chapter 2

- The level of knowledge, comprehension, application, analysis, synthesis and evaluation you have demonstrated.
- Your recommendations – do you present several options? What is your supporting evidence for these recommendations? Are your recommendations feasible? Sometime students make recommendations that are either implausible or unsubstantiated. For instance, 'increasing revenue generation by 50% over 12 months on a UK£2 million turnover business that is struggling within a shrinking domestic market'. True, the company might need to increase its revenue generation. However, 50% might be physically unrealistic and the company might need to consider additional options. For example, the company might need to reduce its costs (with resultant consequences, such as redundancies), seek new non-domestic markets and improve operational efficiency.

As with any assignment, you must check your spelling and grammar. Where possible be succinct and precise. Use sub-headings to delineate the issues, ideas and recommendations.

Peer review

A colleague might be asked to review your assignment prior to submission. This will normally take place as part of perhaps a seminar activity. The peer review session is designed so that you can have an active discussion with a colleague on the merits/demerits of your assignment.

These can be both very active and rewarding debates. They should not be thought of as a chore – but, instead, as a means of developing your work further.

The objectives of peer review are:

- To provide, through an impartial reader (normally a fellow student), objective feedback on the quality of the work.
- To highlight areas that, in the judgement of the reader, are strong and those that are weak and thus in need of further development.
- To make sure that the assignment question has been answered fully.
- To help promote individual self-development and awareness.

How peer review operates

The following is an example of a process that could be used:

- Your assignment is swapped with that of a colleague.
- Read your colleague's draft assignment carefully. Remember, the objective is to provide *constructive feedback*.
- Once you have read the draft, complete the peer review questionnaire. It is important that you are fair and honest in your feedback.
- Once you have completed the peer review questionnaire, discuss it with your colleague.
- Once you have fully discussed the peer review, request your seminar leader to sign it to show that the peer review was conducted within the seminar. Once this has been done, hand this document back to your colleague. Your colleague might have to attach it to their final assignment when submitted. (This will depend on the requirements as set out in your module guide – which is, in turn, dependant on the regulations within your own university/college.)

Example 9.2 illustrates a peer review questionnaire.

Example 9.2 Peer review questionnaire

In order to appreciate the value of this peer review, the original assignment question or brief is stated below. The following is an abridged version of a real first-year undergraduate assignment.

You are a product manager. You have been asked by your board of directors to produce a report on the viability of launching of a new product into the UK market. Specifically, they want to know:

- The market potential for this new product including segmentation.
- How to position the product within the market.
- Macro-environmental factors that might impact (both positively and negatively) on such a product.
- The extent (and power) of the competition within the marketplace.
- Your recommendations – should they go ahead with this product or not and WHY?

You have to choose only **one** of the following product areas:

- Shampoo
- Chocolate
- Coffee
- Clothes (this could, for instance, be a new style of jeans or sports shoe)
- A magazine

For example, you might want to choose to launch a new magazine. You will need to consider what type of magazine. This might be for a particular women's interest group or for those readers interested in a particular hobby. The choice is yours. However, you will need to be specific.

What you must include in your assignment

You are expected to:

- Be contemporary in your analysis. You must be able to show that you have analyzed current issues facing your particular market.
- Use current journal articles (you **must** refer to at least two journal articles in your report – this is a compulsory requirement).
- You **must** refer to at least one Mintel* or Euromonitor* report (this is a compulsory requirement). However, please note that the information you use from these reports must be integrated (and referenced) into your report.
- Assignments not conforming to these requirements will receive a zero mark.

To help you, here is a selection of Mintel reports that are available through the university's online library service.

Mintel (2003) *Shampoos and Conditioners – UK*, May, Mintel International Group.

Mintel (2003) *Men's Shirts – UK*, November, Mintel International Group.

Mintel (2004) *Coffee – UK*, January, Mintel International Group.

Mintel (2004) *Home Interest Magazines*, June, Mintel International Group.

Mintel (2004) *Chocolate Confectionary – UK*, November, Mintel International Group.

Actual peer review questions

1 Has your colleague considered the key elements?

Namely:

	YES/NO	
● The market potential for this product including segmentation	[]	[]
● The positioning of the product within the market	[]	[]
● Macro-environmental factors that might impact upon the product	[]	[]
● The extent and power of the competition	[]	[]
● Their recommendations. Are these substantiated?	[]	[]
2 Has your colleague clearly used the Harvard Referencing System?	[]	[]
3 Has your colleague made any mistakes in using the Harvard Referencing System? For example, is there is a lack of author citation within the main body of text? If so, please state.	[]	[]
4 Has your colleague used a variety of sources of information to answer the question(s)?	[]	[]
5 Could your colleague improve the use of information sources? If YES, in what way could they achieve this?	[]	[]
6 Has your colleague checked their spelling and grammar? (Please point out any serious spelling and grammatical errors on their draft copy.)	[]	[]

7 Readability – tick one of the following boxes:
 Is the assignment:
    Difficult to read and therefore to understand?
    Therefore needs significant changes   []
    Quite readable? Needs some further development   []
    Very readable? Needs minor changes.   []
    Excellent? Highly readable and easy to understand   []

You can make further comments on readability here, if you wish:

Note: * Mintel and Euromonitor are independent market research companies that produce a wide variety of reports. Many universities will have access to these or other types of market research reports for you to use.

● Presentation of assignments

You are often required to present your assignments in a particular format. This will often depend on your type of course, your department and programme guidelines. It is vital that you follow these to the letter. However, the following might also provide you with some guidance.

If, for example, no guidance is provided to you, the following might be a suitable route to take:

- Word processed in 12 point Arial font and double-spaced. This font size is clear to read. The double-spacing allows tutors sufficient space to make comment.
- Margins should be in the reasonably generous – for example, top and bottom margins of 2.5 cm, left-hand and right-hand margins of 3.2 cm. This is for two reasons:
  - Good margins help the visual presentation. Text that goes to the very edge of the page often looks too dense and unreadable. Reasonable margins can help the readability of the work.
  - There is space available for the examiner to make comments next to the actual assignment text. This might be the praising of a particularly good point or the raising of a question on your interpretation of data. Whichever it might be, this is potentially useful feedback for you. (See later comments on the effective use of feedback.)
- Make sure that there is at least one line space between paragraphs. Again, this makes the presentation look good and aids readability.
- Use sub-headings to break up the text. Large sections of text can often be difficult to read, as one paragraph appears to merge into another. Use sub-headings to break up the text and help to create structure to your work. Subheadings will help you group important facts and ideas together.
- Graphs and other diagrams should be generated in MS PowerPoint® or similar packages. Such programs provide a professional look to the diagrams, as well as clarity.
- All pages should be numbered. This is particularly important. If pages are mislaid they can be quickly re-grouped and it enables tutors to refer easily to a particular page by using the front assessment sheet. Moreover, it is a frustrating exercise for the tutor to have to read through the script first in order the number the pages.
- The assignment should have a front cover stating:
  - Module name
  - Title of the assignment
  - Your name
  - Module number
  - Your Student Number (this assists in proper identification and recording of marks)

○ Submission date
○ Word count (if applicable – as stated earlier, some assignments have page rather than word limits).

● It is advised not to place the assignment in plastic wallets or ring binders. They should be stapled in the top-left hand corner only. Again, this might vary between institutions. Typically, a sample of marked assignments will be sent to the external examiner for the module. To expedite this action, the sample is usually photocopied and either the copies or the originals sent to the external examiner. The photocopying is both a precaution and a means of allowing the student to see feedback on their assignment.

C Connections: Chapter 5

● Seek to write well-constructed paragraphs. Please avoid simply listing bullet points, as this will not demonstrate how you thought about the issues.
● Try to avoid long sentences. Generally speaking, sentences over 20–25 words can become very convoluted and thus difficult to read. Sentences of 60 or more words are usually difficult to interpret. Try, where possible, to keep sentences short and snappy.
● Read the question carefully – consider what is required from you. Are you clear in your mind as to what you need to do?
● Do not be afraid to be critical of a report or journal article. If, for example, you feel that the report does not reflect the real market situation, then say so. However, you must provide evidence to say why you have come to that conclusion. Good tutors will want you to develop analytical and critical skills.

C Connections: Chapter 4, section on critical thinking

● Whilst at university you will normally be requested to write in an academic style. That means well-structured grammar, referencing and in the third person (that is, no 'I', 'we', 'you', 'me' or 'our'). Look at a good textbook or journal article to get a flavour of the style. Remember that your assignment is not the only one that your tutor reads. They might have 50 or more to mark over a short period. Place yourself in their shoes. Think about how you would want the text presented to you for reading and marking. Therefore, think about your writing style.
● The phrase *'et cetera'* is often abbreviated to 'etc.' – for example, 'Human resources management includes recruitment, selection, orientation etc.' The use of 'etc.' often makes the assumption that the reader knows what you are thinking. This might not always be the case and so it is best avoided.

- Avoid making very generalized statements. Sometimes statements are too generalized and are not substantiated – for example, 'A lot of people in the UK have mobile phones.' What is meant here by the words 'a lot'? To some people, 10% would be 'a lot'. Can it be more accurately quantified? In this particular example, it could be quantified and substantiated by stating (and referencing) published survey results – for example, from the UK National Statistical Office.
- For academic purposes all secondary research material must be carefully referenced.

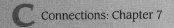

Connections: Chapter 7

- It is highly recommended that you keep both a hard copy and a digital copy of your assignment. It is a reality that, from time to time, assignments are lost. Therefore, you should be able to provide a back-up copy if, as and when required. Additionally, in an attempt to reduce plagiarism many institutions also require you to be able to provide a digital copy (either disc or memory stick) so that the assignment can be checked against plagiarism detection software.

Collating your work with the assignment grids

Whether or not assignment grids (see Figure 9.1 for an example) are used will be very much down to your institution and/or your module leader. Assignment grids are usually for the tutors. However, they can be very useful for you when preparing your assignments. From the grids, you can gauge some level of what is required to achieve a high grade. What you need to do is match your standard of work with the indicators on the assignment grid. True, it is not as easy as it might sound. However, it will provide you with indicators from which to develop your work.

The grid in Figure 9.1 might not be universal and should only be used as a guide.

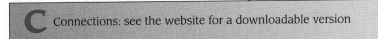

Connections: see the website for a downloadable version

● A word on getting started and writer's block

The French mathematician, physicist and theologian Blaise Pascal (1623–62) was responsible for inventing, amongst other things, the calculating machine, the barometer and the syringe. In his posthumous work *Pensées* (Thoughts), he wrote 'The last thing one knows in constructing a work is what to put first.'

I have taken the liberty of considering this as a mixture of where to begin and how to keep going. You might think that only novelists and writers of non-fiction suffer from writer's block, either at the beginning of the work or during its development. Yes, they do and, while it can be frustrating, they usually have more time to meet their deadline than you.

Criteria	70%+	60–69%	50–59%	40–49%	<40%
Content and range – understanding and comprehension	Demonstrates a comprehensive and detailed knowledge of the topic area. Shows depth and breadth in their approach to the assignment.	Displays reasonable knowledge of the topic area. The student is aware of a variety of ideas and frameworks.	Displays factual and/or conceptual knowledge base. Appropriate terminology is used. However, some issues, concepts, models are not fully explored.	Evidence of limited knowledge of the topic area. Some appropriate terminology is used. Very descriptive.	Lacks evidence of knowledge relevant to the topic area. Does not demonstrate a sufficient understanding of the terminology.
Research (including validating materials)	Demonstrates ability to research the topic area. Has used a wide range of specifically high-quality resources beyond the basic sources stated in the module guide.	Demonstrates the ability to research topic area. Has used a variety of good quality resources.	Some evidence of reading around the topic area beyond the standard texts. However, variable quality of texts used.	Very limited research – only indicative/directed reading used. Little or no critical evaluation of the literature used.	Very little or no evidence of research conducted to address the question. Material used irrelevant or largely irrelevant to the task set.
Critical analysis and evaluation	Material is interpreted, critically evaluated, categorized and prioritized to an exceptionally high standard. Interrelationships are clearly developed and illustrated. Implications are fully explored. Excellent linkage to models, theories, concepts.	Material is interpreted, critically evaluated, categorized and prioritized. Appropriate frameworks are used for the analysis. A range of implications for the company is explored. Good linkage to the various models and theories.	A limited range of material is interpreted and critically evaluated. The level of critical evaluation might be limited. Some attempt at categorization and prioritization. However, this might be very descriptive.	A very limited attempt to evaluate the material. Very basic and very descriptive in format.	No evaluation of material. Statements are very descriptive. Lacks any form of critical analysis or evaluation.

Synthesis of ideas and information	Demonstrates an ability to bring together (in a highly coherent and intelligent form) various strands of information, concepts and ideas. Very perceptive approach.	Demonstrates an ability to collect together various strands of information in a reasonably coherent format.	Demonstrates an ability to collect information together within a predictable and standardized format.	There is a partial collection and collation of information. It is categorized in an acceptable (supplied) structured format.	There is no organization of the material – either information or ideas.
Recommendations and conclusions	Well-substantiated recommendations. Critical issues raised and discussed (e.g.: the possible contradictions in the material). Excellently constructed conclusion that draws together the major key elements or issues.	Good substantiated recommendations logically presented. Well-constructed conclusion that draws together many of the issues that have been critically evaluated.	Recommendations are limited in scope. However, there is some substantiation and this is generally accurate. A reasoned, if limited, conclusion.	Recommendations very limited in scope. Some substantiation and only partially accurate. Very basic conclusions are drawn. May not link back to the previous analysis.	Either no recommendation(s) or no substantiation of those recommendation(s) provided. Recommendations and conclusion may not link to the assignment question(s). Significant inaccuracies that demonstrate a lack of understanding of the topic and subject areas.
Presentation (including visual and written elements)	Excellent presentation. Logically organized. Very well written and structured. Meets all the requirements for report format. Excellent referencing.	Logically organized. Well written. Meets most of the requirements for report format. Well referenced.	Good organization. Logical structure. Generally well written but with some grammatical/spelling mistakes. Meets several elements of report format. Good referencing.	A basic attempt at organization and structure. Generally poor grammar and spelling for this level. Meets some of the requirements of report format. Quality of referencing variable.	Lacks overall structure. Generally disorganized. Very poor grammar. Very poor spelling. Overall inconsistent. Does not meet requirements of report format. Very poor or non-existent referencing.

Figure 9.1 An example of an assignment grid based upon grids used by the Business School, Oxford Brookes University

Often, students who have had very little experience of writing longer essays believe that they have to start at page one and write the complete work from start to finish. Again, this is an issue that occurs when it comes to writing a dissertation (see Chapter 13). This view could not be further from the truth. Very few people have the ability to sit down at a computer or typewriter, or with a pen and paper, and write from start to finish. The American composer Bernard Herrmann did, as did Georges Simenon, the Belgian-born writer of detective novels. However, we would perhaps reserve the word 'genius' for such people. The rest of us are, sadly, not as gifted. Either through experimentation or with guidance, we have to find our own route to 'putting pen to paper'.

You might have difficulty in getting started (and it happens to all of us). Equally, you might have a moment where you cannot make sense of things and continue with your writing. If so, here is an approach you might want to emulate.

In the inspirational movie *Finding Forrester* (2000) written by Mike Rich, Sean Connery plays eccentric and reclusive Pulitzer Prize winning author William Forrester. He befriends an Afro-Caribbean teenager from the Bronx, Jamal Wallace (played by Rob Brown). Jamal has gained a sports' scholarship into a prestigious New York private school. However, his real ambition is to become a writer.

In one scene, they sit opposite each other both facing typewriters (yes, typewriters – no computers here). Forrester starts typing rapidly.

Forrester:	Go ahead
Jamal:	Go ahead and what?
Forrester:	Write!
Jamal:	What are you doing?
Forrester:	I'm writing ... like you'll be when you start punching those keys ... (pause) ... Is there a problem?
Jamal:	No, no ... I'm thinking.
Forrester:	No ... no thinking! That comes later. You write your first draft from your heart. Then you re-write from your head. The first key to writing is to ... write ... not think.

The point of this exchange is that often we just need the impetus to start writing. In the accompanying scenes, Jamal slowly moves from typing nonsense into forming complex sentences and ideas. A storyline evolves on the paper before him.

The movie might be fiction but there is, however, a substantial merit in this technique. If you have difficulty either starting or continuing, just start typing. Just get words and your thoughts down on paper – you can always edit sections later. You might be surprised how many books have been started this way.

● The purpose and value of feedback

During your time at university, you will receive feedback on your various assessments. This feedback should not be ignored; nor should it be considered in isolation.

Instead, each piece of feedback is a valuable resource towards helping you to develop your subject understanding and knowledge. You are therefore encouraged to make active use of the feedback to improve and develop your work for subsequent assessments.

You will usually receive feedback on your submitted assignments. This feedback usually takes the form of:

Comments within the main body of text – This usually highlights both the positive and negative aspects of your assignments. For example, querying the level of evidence presented to substantiate your recommendations and /or conclusions.

Feedback coversheet – This should encapsulate the various points made by the examiner within the main body of your assignment. These can be stated under various headings such as:

- What you did well – This highlights the positive elements of your assignment. However, it is very easy to become complacent, especially if you have achieved a high grade. Look at what you have done well and see if you can improve upon it for the next assignment. For example, your tutor might comment on your range of sources. For your next assignment, you might want to seek out a wider range of sources that you can both validate and triangulate to strengthen the quality of your recommendations. Increasing the quality of your work step-by-step helps you to gain higher marks in the future. Moreover, it opens your mind to exploring the subject area, both in terms of depth and breath.
- Where you can improve your assignments in the future – These are the issues or areas that perhaps let you down in the assignment and reduced your marks. Consider how you could improve these areas of your work before you tackle the next assignment.
- Critical issues – These are issues that you need to resolve before you undertake another assignment. For example, this could be the quality of your referencing within the main body of your assignments. If you do not tackle this critical issue, you could either fail your next assignment or be accused of plagiarism.

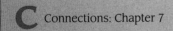

C Connections: Chapter 7

● **Using feedback effectively**

Collating your feedback

It is advisable to collate all your feedback into one folder – ideally, a ring bound folder. This will help you focus on the areas that you need to improve, as well as develop your strengths even further. You might find the two feedback logs presented in Examples 9.3 (Portfolio Log 1) and 9.4 (Portfolio Log 2) useful in collating your feedback.

Example 9.3   Student feedback portfolio: log 1

Student name:
Student number:
Module:
Semester:
Date:

What you did well	Action proposed	Date	Outcome	Date
What you need to do to improve	Action proposed	Date	Outcome	Date
Critical issues	Action proposed	Date	Outcome	Date

The three key areas that you need to consider. The most important issues being those designated as critical. These must be addressed before you tackle your next assignment. This could mean the difference between passing or failing the module.

It is one thing to note what needs to be done. This is a passive action. You need to be pro-active and propose realistic and feasible actions.

Once the proposed action is stated, there needs to be a date by which the task(s) are completed. If you do not place a specific time limit on the action, then you may become complacent and not take any action at all.

Taking action is only one part of the exercise. You need to consider the outcome of your actions. So if, for example, you revised your approach to referencing, you will need to check whether or not it was successful. In other words you will need to benchmark your work. Also, you should note the date of the outcomes (for example, feedback from your next assignment). This allows you to keep an on-going record, so that you can benchmark further changes. The objective is to continually improve the level of your work and, thus, your grades.

· Transfer the key points from your assignment feedback onto the log presented in Example 9.3, then decide on the course of action that you propose to take in each of the categories:

- What you did well
  Can you improve your skills, for example in the areas of research, synthesis and evaluation?
- What you need to improve
  Developing your skills, knowledge and understanding to a higher level.
- Critical issues.
  These are issues that you must address as a matter of urgency prior to the next assessment. For example, this might be the use of referencing within the main body of text.

It is all well and good stating your proposed actions or intentions. However, you need to consider how you are going to measure your performance through implementation. In the section marked 'Outcome', state what happened after you completed your proposed action. Did you exceed your proposed actions? Did the situation remain the same? Or, did you miss your target? If the latter, you will need to examine why? Then, consider what course of action you will take to improve for next time.

Portfolio Log 2
This is for critical issues that keep recurring and that result in consistently lower than average marks/grades. Critical issues can include problems associated with:

- Using resources to gather data and information.
- The evaluation of data.
- The application of models/theories.
- Critically analyzing ideas and concepts.
- Presenting recommendations and conclusions.
- Referencing, both within the main body of text and at the end of the assignment.
- Structure of report or assignment.
- Grammar and spelling.

Identify the critical issues within your feedback and transfer them onto Portfolio Log 2 given in Example 9.4. As with Portfolio Log 1, state your proposed action against each of the critical issues. Again, you will need to measure the success of your actions in the outcomes section of the log.

Your approach
The successful development of these logs comes from:

- Being honest with yourself – If a tutor has indicated a weakness, accept the comment and consider ways to improve and develop your skills and understanding.
- Being realistic – Whilst you need to propose an action plan, you also need to be realistic as to what can be achieved within the designated time frame (that is, by

Example 9.4   Students feedback portfolio: log 2

Recurring critical issues

Issues	Action proposed	Date	Outcomes	Date

the next assessment deadline). Of course, this cannot be used as an excuse for undertaking no action or very little. That will not improve your marks/grades. After all, the fundamental rationale for the exercise is to improve and develop your skills to acquire higher marks and grades.

● Doing it! – It would be easy just to file the blank logs attached and forget about them. However, completing them increases your opportunity for success. But, ultimately, the decision is yours!

● Making deadlines work for you

Every assignment will have a fixed deadline. There are various DOs and DON'Ts associated with deadlines that you must bear in mind. Table 9.1 will help you to plan your assignments effectively.

ACTIONS	DOs	DON'Ts
START	Start researching your assignment on the day that you receive it. This will help to focus your attention on the task. It will also highlight to you the potential scale of the task. For instance, some of the information that you need to meet the assignment requirements might not be that easy to access. So, starting early helps you to detect your possible weak areas. Thus, you have time to rectify the problems before they become insurmountable.	Leaving your assignment to the 'last minute' is a recipe for disaster. It is unlikely that you will have been able to undertake all the necessary research, let alone answer the question to a standard to get you a pass grade. This is a very high-risk strategy, especially if you are undertaking assignments/a module that counts towards your degree classification.
STUDY PLAN	Create a time plan (see Chapter 4). You will need to develop a time plan in relation to your other obligations on your degree programme (for instance, timing of other assignments and revision for in-class tests). Work backwards from the deadline and allocate time for research, writing one or two drafts, peer review sessions (if scheduled), final revisions, printing out and delivery.	Approach the timing of research and writing in an unstructured fashion. Again you risk the non-completion of the assignment by the due deadline. There are several reasons why you should not leave the printing of your assignment to the day of the deadline: 1 You might not be the only student attempting to gain access to the university's computers to print out the assignment. Imagine how you will feel as the time ticks by and there are still 20 or more students in front of you trying to print out assignments. 2 You might never have had a problem with your computer before – but this is probably the time when you do! The laws of statistical probability are set to thwart you. Most universities do not allow 'computer failure – disk failure – printer failure' as an excuse for late delivery. As well as your computer disk failing, you might be looking at a failing grade simply because you did not get your work in on time.

Table 9.1 The DOs and DON'Ts of deadlines

ACTIONS	DOs	DON'Ts
FOLLOW INSTRUCTIONS	The instructions are typically set out in module workbooks or assessment documents. If, for example, you are required to seek out specific types of publications/information (say, a marketing research report or a journal article), then you must do so. Missing these elements of the assignment brief can severely hamper your marks. There might also be specific presentation guidelines (see later example).	The instructions are set out to: 1 Meet certain teaching and learning objectives for the module – for instance, developing your research skills by requesting you to seek out specific information (say, from a commercial market report). 2 Help you to plan for the task. 3 Help you to present the assignment to a required standard – both in terms of analysis and visual presentation. For example, you might be asked to staple the assignment in the top left hand corner only and not place it in a plastic wallet. Now, you might think that a plastic wallet is a neater alternative. However, imagine if you are the marker of, say, 70 assignments and you have to empty each one from a plastic wallet! It can be very frustrating. Therefore, do not ignore the instructions as they have a real purpose.
HAND-IN	Check the deadline and how you are supposed to submit the final work. Key points to recognize: 1 How many students are handing their assignment on the 'final' hand-in day? If there are large numbers of students and they are all handing in 'on the button' of the deadline, then there is risk of a log-jam.	Never leave handing in an assignment to the very last minute. This is a high-risk strategy and could lead you having marks deducted for a late submission.

	2 Where and how is it being handed in? Is it being handed in at the beginning or the end of the session or is it being handed in at a particular office – for instance, the undergraduate office? 3 Make sure that it is handed in BEFORE the deadline. This might actually mean handing it in a day early (if that is possible).	1 Fail to collect your assignment and/or 2 Ignore the feedback. It is devised to help you in your future studies. If you fail to collect your assignment and review the feedback, then you are only reducing your chances of gaining a degree and/or a better classification of degree. However, it is surprising how many students do not review their feedback and continue to make the same mistakes over and over again. In some cases, they actually fail to graduate as a result.
FEEDBACK	Once marked and available for collection (if not handed out in class), collect your work and read the comments. Do not focus solely on the mark (whether good or bad) – review the comments. Consider what you did well, what you need to improve on and what are the real critical issues. Whether you like the grade you have received or not, there is very little that you can do about that. What you can do is look forward and see what you need to do to improve/ develop your standard of work in the future.	

Table 9.1 Continued

Reflection zone

Here are a few key summary points for you to reflect upon:

- Appreciate the merits of different types of assignments and how they are used within the assessment process.
- Consider how reports are structured and how enhancing your report writing skills will prepare you for the business world.
- Consider how to examine and analyze a case study in order to produce viable recommendations.
- Understand the value gained from undertaking peer reviews.
- Appreciate the value (both short- and longer-term) of submitting professional looking assignments.
- Understanding the purpose and value of tutor feedback and how to use such feedback to enhance your work.
- Consider techniques and approaches to make deadlines work for you.

Further reading

Greetham, B. (2008) *How to Write Better Essays* (2nd edn), Basingstoke: Palgrave Macmillan.

Peck, J. and Coyle, M. (2005) *Write it Right*, Basingstoke: Palgrave Macmillan.

Peck, J. and Coyle, M. (2005) *The Student's Guide to Writing* (2nd edn), Basingstoke: Palgrave Macmillan.

10 Team Working

'Coming together is a beginning.
Keeping together is progress.
Working together is success.'

Henry Ford, 1863–1947,
American entrepreneur and industrialist

Contents

► Introduction
► Why is team working often integrated into business programmes?
► Why is team working important to your future?
► Necessary skill development
► Creating a team work agreement
► Reflection zone

Introduction

There are many professions and vocations where team working is a vital ingredient. It is often the glue that holds a project together. If the team working function is weak, then failure often ensues. Just consider, for one moment, the following examples of team working:

- Formula One racing
  During a race, Formula 1 racing cars will have four wheels changed and additional fuel taken onboard within a mere ten seconds. This operation is often undertaken two or three times during a particular race. There are three men at the corner of each car. One with a wheel gun (to remove and replace the wheel nut), another to remove the wheel and a third to attach the replacement wheel. There is one mechanic who operates the front car-jack, while another operates the rear jack. Two men hold the fuel pipe and another holds the stop/go sign in front of the racing car. That makes 17 men, plus a fire crew on alert just in case the unthinkable happens and fuel is splashed across the hot engine and ignites (there are safety cut-off valves – but systems do fail!). Each of these men knows exactly what to do and works in concert to make the pit stop a highly efficient example of team working.

  In Formula One racing, an extra (unwanted) second at the pit stop can mean the difference between first and second place. This, in turn, can result in winning or losing the overall championship and is reflected in the value of sponsorship gained the following year. It might be a sport to broadcast television viewers such as you and me; however, in reality, it is a multi-million dollar business.

- Musicians
  Whether in a group or a symphony orchestra, all are dependent upon each other to produce a coherent performance. While several takes can be recorded in a studio environment, in a stadium or a concert hall the performance has to be seamless – right first time.

- Movies
  If it were not for effective and efficient team working, some of the most successful movies of all time – indeed, perhaps your own favourite movie – would not
  have achieved such accolades. Indeed, it would be what is elegantly considered in
  the movie business as a 'dud' or a 'turkey'!

The same is applicable in any form of business, whether you become an entrepreneur,
building a web-based business, or an executive at a major retail chain, team working
could make or break your business. Team working, as you will see, is about applying the
management skills that are integral to your programme. This is very much 'learning on
the job' and why, as stated previously, you need to integrate or link other modules within
your programme to such activities as team working.

Why is team working often integrated into business programmes?

There are several answers to this question:

- Team working, within an academic environment, helps to prepare you for both
  the positive and negative aspects of the real business world. Moreover, it is a
  safe, and to some extent controlled, environment: there are no organizational
  repercussions, as there might be in a commercial environment. This means that
  if a colleague is not contributing effectively, there can be tutor intervention. This
  can be used to protect the marks of those who have taken the team-working
  project seriously and sought to produce a realistic contribution. In the real
  world, there might be no external intervention to protect the team. In other
  words, it might be simply down to the team to impose safeguards or,
  indeed, sanctions to afford itself collective protection. At least, within the academic environment, there is an understanding of the issues that can confront a
  team. It has to be realized that not everyone, for whatever reason, is a team
  player.
- Team working allows you to understand and appreciate the various forms of
  dynamics that pervade a team. In the course of your studies, you will read and
  discuss the ideas of such researchers and practitioners as Meredith Belbin and
  his work on team types. Indeed, you will probably be asked to analyze your own
  team type personality. Of course, in reality, you might not be placed alongside
  those people with whom you would integrate perfectly. This is the reality of life
  outside university. However, your understanding of such typing will help you
  appreciate how to work with individuals, whether they are on your programme
  of study or, indeed, within an organizational environment.
- Leadership experience can be gained. Teams need leaders – some will be
  effective and others will not. However, the academic environment provides the
  opportunity for individuals to test out their abilities and, hopefully, learn from

both their successes and failures. The university and college environment is generally forgiving of errors or misjudgements on the part of team leaders – the real world is often less forgiving. Indeed, leadership errors in business might well cost you your job. While nothing can better on-the-job experience, leading a team within a university/college assessment environment can illustrate some of the real-world pressures. These include time pressures, working with the diversity of the human spirit and understanding your own strengths and weaknesses.

- Team working provides a forum for debate. With an individual piece of assessment (for example, an assignment based on a case study) you are being challenged to research information and analyze a problem by yourself. Here, you have the opportunity to debate the issues with colleagues. This debate will encompass everything from who is going to be team leader down to the tools or techniques that are going to be used to analyze the assignment problem. Once again, there is the opportunity to use a range of interpersonal skills from presentations to negotiating.

- So far, you might think that team working is a chore that you have to endure to complete your module. That is not necessarily the case. You can have great fun (as well as learn a great deal) from team working. First, you can come to understand people better and why they react in certain ways. Second, you can build on current friendships and develop new ones – these might be for life. As stated earlier, within business degree programmes there is the opportunity to develop networks that will stand you in good stead for the future.

- Team working can help enrich individual knowledge: it might often involve the complete analysis of a particular business/industry problem. This analysis can be reported back (as a piece of assessment) either as a business report and/or presentation. Often, the team leader sets individuals tasks to complete – for example, Student X might undertake an internal environmental analysis of the company while Student Z reviews the external environmental analysis. When this information is brought together (along with other issues), it helps all those involved to share and understand the complexity that surrounds business. Effective team working is synergistic. In other words, as individual pieces of work they have a value. However, when truly combined and analyzed the individual parts bring another dimension, a much deeper understanding.

- Team working can be used as an effective form of assessment. Within business and management modules, it can be used as a mode of assessment for several reasons, mainly to:
  - ○ Examine whether students have integrated knowledge learnt from other modules, such as organizational behaviour and how people interact within group situation.
  - ○ Provide the practical experience of students working together on an assignment task. This helps to prepare you for the external organizational environment.
  - ○ Provide an opportunity to develop – enhance interpersonal skills such as negotiation and presentations. There might be four fellow students in

your team. Four of you are meeting regularly and researching your individual areas (as per the assignment brief). However, you never hear from the fifth member of the group. The four of you are working very hard on the assignment and, if all of you will receive the same grade, then you are carrying the fifth member of the team. So, what are you and your fellow students going to do about it? Such issues arise in real working environments and you need to utilize practical solutions.

○ Team working enables you to learn from each other. Groups might comprise people of different skill sets and nationalities. Their experiences might be very different to your own – thus, there is an opportunity to enrich your own knowledge base.

● Why is team working important to your future?

One of the major complaints from students about team working on assessed assignments is the performance of the other team members. For instance, a particularly strong student might find themselves within a team of students who, for one reason or another, are not high achievers. This can be particularly frustrating for the high achiever, who might be in line for a First Class Honours degree. They might feel that their degree classification might be in jeopardy from the abilities and skill levels of the other team members.

Universities might create safeguards to protect high achievers from losing such a classification grade. However, as indicated earlier, within an organizational context you might be placed within a team of variable skills and knowledge. Therefore, you will have to employ your organizational and interpersonal skills to find the best solution possible. This experience can be beneficial to you when you pursue your future career.

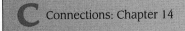

C Connections: Chapter 14

Your *CV*

When you come to prepare your *curriculum vitae*, you can include team working as part of your own skill development. This will demonstrate a practical skill that the vast majority of organizations today believe is essential for the future prosperity of both the individual and organization.

The job interview

Unless you are a mature student, you will probably have had very little actual commercial experience. Therefore, an interviewer will often focus on sections of your *CV*, for instance:

● *What skills you feel you have developed over the past three/four years?* You might respond by stating you were involved in various team-working assessments.

● *Can you provide me with an example of a difficulty within the team and how this difficulty was overcome?*

You might respond by stating that one team member was being uncooperative (perhaps missing meetings and not submitting work on time) and how you and the rest of the team were able to change or modify this person's behaviour. You could use this as a way of demonstrating your understanding of the issues that might affect group working and suggest possible solutions.

The work environment is a highly competitive marketplace. You will not be the only business graduate seeking a position. Therefore, you have to demonstrate, beyond your degree classification, that you have skills that place you above the other candidates. Group or team working might have inherent difficulties. However it might just provide you with the edge over other job candidates.

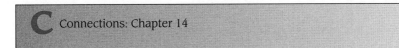

Connections: Chapter 14

● Necessary skill development

Working in teams provides opportunities to develop skills in the following areas:

Interpersonal skills

How do you react to (and with) people on both an individual and a group basis? This also encompasses negotiation, selling (we all sell ideas as well as products and services) and presentation skills (how you convey your ideas to a wider audience).

Project management

Just as in your whole degree programme, you will have to project manage individual pieces of work. Then, while it is your own individual piece of assessment, it is very much down to you to meet the deadline. It is a different issue when you are working with several other people. Individually and collectively, they must meet deadlines in order to produce the final piece of work for submission. Therefore the project must be carefully managed in order to achieve the ideal outcome.

Time management

As the Roman poet Virgil (*Publius Vergilius Maro*) (70–19 BCE) stated, '*Sed fugit interea, fugit inreparabile tempus*' (But meanwhile it is flying, irretrievable time is flying – *Georgics*, nos 3, 1.284). This is an appropriate quote, as you will usually be faced with a tight deadline, especially if the tutors want to create a deadline that is as realistic as possible. Let's say that your tutors have given your team a problem that focuses on a company in severe financial difficulties (perhaps through no fault of its own) and you have been asked (as a team) to formulate a rescue plan. Time is of the essence. If you do not create an effective rescue strategy in time, the company will be liquidated at the cost of several thousand jobs and the resultant devastation of a local community. While you might have access to significant material resources within the real world, time will still be problematic. Therefore, understanding the issues surrounding time management in all its disguises will be of benefit to you within the real business world.

Exploration

As with anything linked to business and management, you need to explore the wider world and issues. If you take a myopic view (Levitt, 1960). you will not grasp the wider issues facing business (both for-profit and not-for-profit) in the 21st century. As stated earlier in this book, you need to have an open mind and explore.

● Creating a team work agreement

While everyone in a group should be striving for the same outcomes and goals, sadly this is not always the case. Some team members might invest more effort and energy than others. Some tutors will, as a matter of routine, provide you with some form of agreement document. However, if they do not you might want to use the one provided in Example 10.1.

The following example illustrates why it is vital that working as a group is taken seriously:

- 50% of the marks are allocated to group work.
- 50% of the marks are allocated to two individual assignments. One comprises a reflective analysis of the group work experience; the other, a presentation of recommendations based on the group's analysis of a specific set of problems or issues.
- A significant amount of the overall learning experience involves working within the same group for two semesters.

Bearing these factors in mind, it is valuable for the groups to sign up to an agreement to work effectively and efficiently together. Example 10.1 gives a format that you and your colleagues can use as an agreement between all parties.

Activity log

When working together, it might be useful for you to keep an activity log. This log might include:

- Times and dates of meetings and who attended and who did not. Did the members of the team who did not attend inform anyone in advance of their non-attendance?

Example 10.1   Student group working agreement

Module number:

Module title:

Group name:

Group number:

Academic year:

> You may want to devise a name for your group. For example, you might suggest 'Stealth' or 'Matrix'. Group work can be fun too!

We, the undersigned members of this group, undertake to be bound by the following conditions:

- To attend all meetings on time, except where a prior agreement has been made with the other group members, or where documented evidence can be provided (for example, a medical certificate).
- To be well prepared for each meeting, ensuring that all relevant material is adequately researched and presented.
- To participate actively in both the preparatory and the formal group meetings.
- To contribute actively to the research, drafting and final preparation and submission of the report/project by the due deadlines.
- To respect the views of all members of the group, and to support and encourage others to actively participate.

> These are the 'rules' by which each member of the team agrees to operate. Hopefully, there will be no problems – however, if a member of the team does not participate then action can be taken to preserve the marks of those who have done the work.

We agree that if a group member breaches this agreement, then the group has the right to request a reduction in the individual student's group mark. These marks would then be subsequently distributed equally amongst the remaining members of the group. In the eventuality of such a request, we realize that the module leader will seek, in writing, both the reasons and evidence to support such a request. We accept that the decision of the module leader is final in such matters and that such a request may be declined.

	Last name	First name	Student no.	Signature	Date
1					
2					
3					
4					
5					

Please note:

- Each member of the group **must** keep a copy of the completed form.
- A completed copy **must** also be submitted to the module leader.

- A decision on the method of working – what tasks will be undertaken by whom and by what time. In other words, the provision of a schedule of activities for each member of the group, with timeframes.
- Notes on any problems encountered and how they will be overcome.

The aim of a student group working agreement is fourfold:

1 To help you become familiar with the concept of a contract. Throughout your business life you will engage in activities through contracts. These can either be straightforward or immensely complex in form. This will depend on the nature of the activity. You will already have contracts for your mobile phone, bank account, credit card and accommodation, and also with the institution. However, you might not have looked upon them in the business sense but have perceived them more in terms of lifestyle.

2 A working agreement helps define responsibilities, both for the group and the individuals within the group.

3 To help build collegiality. In other words, 'we are all in this together' and so let's make it work and have fun while doing it.

4 A working agreement seeks to prevent 'social loafing'. As indicated earlier, some students worry about assessments that have a group work component. Their concern is whether or not their grades will suffer if the team becomes dysfunctional. Social loafing is where a student opts out of taking any responsibility for doing any work in the belief that the others will do it to protect their grades. Therefore, the social loafer gets a free ride. However, penalty systems can reduce the risk of social loafing and, thus, the free ride. If a student does not actively participate, then their marks can be used to support those who have worked.

Reflection zone

Here are a few key summary points for you to reflect upon:

- Appreciate the added value of effective and efficient team working to an organization.
- Appreciate the use of team or group working within a business degree as a way of enhancing your interpersonal skills for future employment.
- Consider how team-working agreements can add value to the smooth operation of a team.

11 Presentation Skills

'There are always three speeches, for every one you actually gave. The one you practiced, the one you gave, and the one you wish you gave.'

Dale Carnegie, 1888–1955,
American writer and educator

Contents

► Introduction
► Developing your mindset
► Organization of your materials
► Creating a format
► Creating visuals
► Prompts or cues
► You!
► Issues for your next presentation
► Reflection zone

● Introduction

Throughout your undergraduate studies, you will be asked (both as an individual and as part of a team) to undertake a presentation. For many students, this is the scariest time at university, for you are up there in front of an audience that can range from 20 to over 100 of your contemporaries, not including your tutors. Whether you are alone or with others, this can be a very daunting task. It might or might not alleviate the stress to know that most CEOs often consider presenting in front of such large audiences a daunting task. However, it does not always have to be so!

The purpose of this chapter is to help you prepare for presentations, so that they are not as stressful as they might be. Each of the stages is designed to help you develop your presentation skills – not only for university life, but also for your business career.

● Developing your mindset

There are three important steps to consider when developing your mindset:

- Be positive. If you are negative about your presentation, then it will be negative. The best approach is to look forward to the experience. It is important to be positive throughout the process.
- It is about your development. You are working in the relatively safe environment of a university. If you make a mistake in your presentation, it will not be the end of the world! Therefore, use your university experience as a means of developing and enhancing your skills for the much more pressured external world.
- Learn from your performance. Make a critical evaluation of your own presentation, considering what worked and what did not. Then compare and contrast with any other feedback, whether it is from your tutors and/ or peer group. Build upon your successes and seek to overcome any difficulties.

● Organization of your materials

It is important that you have a firm starting point in order to determine:

- Your subject: What overall subject and linked topics are being considered?
- The purpose of the actual presentation: The purpose will depend on the setting of the presentation. For instance, is it part of normal coursework where 10% is allocated to the presentation? In the business world, it might be a pitch presentation that might (or might not) win you a major business account.
- The audience who will see and hear the presentation: In an academic setting, this will normally be your peers and the tutors who will be assessing your work. However, they might be asked to assume particular roles, such as potential clients. Therefore, your presentation should address them within their role-play characters. Moreover, you might find that in some modules the tutors will enlist the support of business people to comment on the presentations.

In order to achieve validated responses, link those questions to the following:

- What do you want to say about the topic? Now, you might be presenting as an individual or as part of a group. If the latter, then you will have to balance your expectations with the other members of the group. As long as there is fair apportionment of sub-topics, you have to agree that individuals do not always 'get' what they want to do in a group presentation.
- Why do you want to say it? In other words, what value does it add to the overall presentation? If it does not add anything to the presentation, then you need to question whether or not it should be included.
- Who do I want to hear it? Your knowledge of the audience should assist you in determining what to include and what to exclude. It will also help you to identify particularly 'persuasive' data. In other words, forms of evidence that your audience will find convincing. For example, let's say that your presentation covers the acquisition of one business by another. Clearly and succinctly stating how the advantages will overcome the disadvantages (of such an acquisition), will help build a stronger case.

● Creating a format

Formats do vary and, indeed, you might be instructed to follow a particular format. If not, the following might be useful:

Issues

What are the issues or problems under discussion? Are you being asked to make a critical evaluation of a model or an idea? Are you being asked to role-play being consultants and pitch for a business account?

Viewpoint or perspective

You might wish (or, indeed, be encouraged) to express a particular viewpoint or perspective on the issue. For example, you might believe that a particular business model is a great theory. However, you might feel that it has very little relevance to the real and dynamic world in which business operates.

Evidence to support your viewpoint or perspective

It is very easy to say that you either agree or disagree with something. However, it is much harder to provide evidence to support your views. Nevertheless, that is what you have to do in order to make a viable presentation. You will need to provide facts through statistics and expert opinion (texts, journal articles and interviews) to support your case. It is important that you make the connection between the evidence and the issue being supported or dislodged by the evidence. Think of it in terms of the two lawyers in a courtroom. One is attempting to provide evidence that the person charged is guilty, while the other is attempting to provide evidence that they are innocent. Often, the outcome of the trial is dependent on the weight of substantial evidence provided.

Conclusion/summary

At the end of the presentation, summarize the key points and, where necessary, provide recommendations.

● Creating visuals

Approximately 85% of the information that is stored in our brains is received visually. Usually, information that we see is more likely to be remembered than information that we hear. Perhaps a *caveat* to that is music, which is generally only heard – yet many of us can remember scores in extraordinary detail.

If, as suggested, so much information is gained from the visual, then we must plan our visual presentations carefully. Your aim is to create visuals that will help reinforce, support and illustrate your perspectives and conclusion. Usually, today, most people use Microsoft's Powerpoint® presentation system rather than OHPs, although they are always useful should the technology let you down (more on that later).

DOs and DON'Ts of presentations

In this section, we will consider the various DOs and DON'Ts as a way of helping you to construct a viable presentation.

- Consider very carefully the background that you are going to choose for your slides. There are many structured and colourful slide backgrounds. However, you have to consider that a background that is too fussy might: (a) detract audience attention; and (b) not work well with the text size, font and colour that you have chosen.

Strategy – Definitions

'A set of related actions that managers take to
    increase their company's performance'. Hill &
    Jones (2007).

'The *direction* and *scope* of an organisation over
    the *long term* which achieves *advantage* in a
    changing *environment* through its configuration
    of *resources* and competences with the aim
    of fulfilling *stakeholder expectations.'*
    Johnson *et al.* (2005).

This is a very simple
design over a white
background. The
typeface is clear and
functional.

Figure 11.1   Clear and functional slides

- Consider very carefully the type, size and colour of your font. This relates to the point above. Fonts and backgrounds can clash, making it very difficult for the audience to read the slides. Figure 11.1 presents a clear and functional slide.
- Try not to overcrowd your slides with too much information, keep it simple. Usually, depending on length, keep each slides to a few bullet points. It will be your role to develop the points highlighted on the screen. Figure 11.2 illustrates an overcrowded slide; Figure 11.3 shows a readable one.
- Statistical information is often difficult for an audience to absorb if shown as a standard numerical table. However, a chart (bar, pie, graph) can create a greater meaning for numbers. This is especially so if your audience is not numerically focused. Moreover, graphs and charts convert numbers (often abstract quantities) into a visual shape – thus enhancing the presentation.
- Think of using shapes or images to enhance your presentation. These also either replace or break up the text. This is illustrated in Figure 11.4.
- As stated throughout this text, be prepared to challenge the theories and models. If you are asked to review a particular model or theory, then look at it objectively and note the criticisms. This will also demonstrate that (a) you have read around the subject area; and (b) that you are able to compare and contrast issues. Figure 11.5 demonstrates how to achieve this.

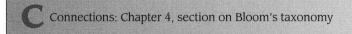

C   Connections: Chapter 4, section on Bloom's taxonomy

- If you have referred to sources within your presentation, then you must attach a final slide that lists your references, as demonstrated in Figure 11.6. If you are also providing a written document to support your presentation (this might

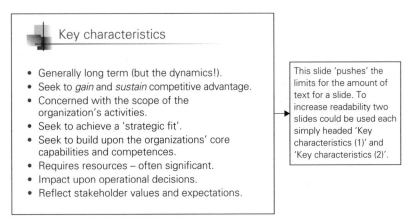

Figure 11.2 Cluttered slide presentation

Figure 11.3 Readable slide presentation

be part of the assessment requirements), make sure that the document reflects the sources used.

- If you are presenting written documentation to support your presentation, then seek to use the same font where possible, or something similar. This helps to demonstrate a unity between the two activities.

Prompts or cues

- Avoid reading out a presentation from sheets of paper. This will demonstrate a lack of knowledge about: (a) your presentation; and (b) the subject of the

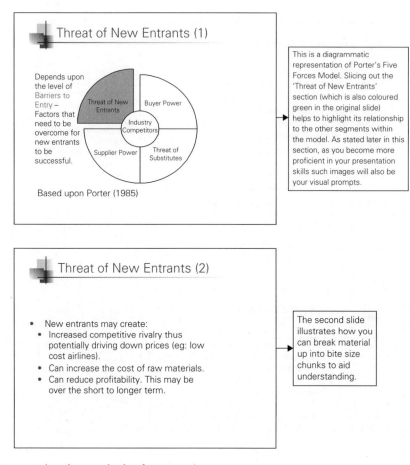

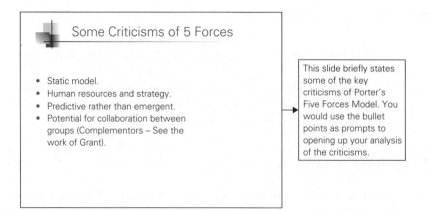

Figure 11.4 Clear methods of presentation

Figure 11.5 Critical review

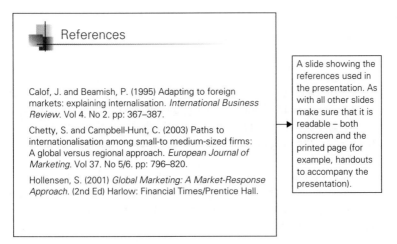

Figure 11.6 Referencing

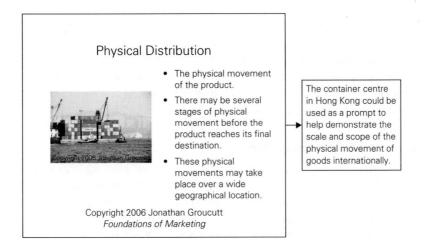

Figure 11.7 Images as prompts

presentation. Moreover, if you continually look down to read from a page of script, then your voice is automatically lowered. It might become muffled and, thus, inaudible.

- Use cue cards with bullet points on them or, ideally, use the bullet points on the screen as your prompt. If you use the latter technique, then make sure that you are facing the audience when you speak.
- As you become more skilled in presenting, you might use images as your prompt. See, for example, Figure 11.7.

You!

Here are some basic techniques to help you as an individual during your presentation.

Stature

How you stand is a crucial factor in the style of your presentation for the following reasons:

- You need to create a presence (an authority) within the room. If you slouch, then it might convey to the audience that you really do not care about this presentation. It might communicate a 'so what' attitude. Now, that might not actually be what you are thinking or feeling. However, your body language is saying something different.
- By being physically straight – but relaxed – you are able to channel energy through your body. This often results in expressive gestures that heighten and enliven the presentation. You become engaged in your presentation, and thus you will demonstrate this to your audience.

Eye contact

Try to maintain eye contact with people. As they say in the theatre – 'work the room'. Usually, by maintaining eye contact for a few seconds you are (a) helping yourself to focus on the issues; and (b) engaging with the audience – getting them involved in what you have to say. However, there is a *caveat* here. As with physical proximity to people, the level of eye contact permissible does vary from culture to culture, so you will have to bear that in mind. One thing that you should try to avoid is staring at someone. After all, you do not want to make anyone in your audience feel uncomfortable.

Turning your back on the audience

Although TV weather forecasters tend to do this on a regular basis, try to avoid it as much as possible. Yes, you might have to move over to the screen to point to a particular issue. However, at this point stop talking. Make the move and then, once facing the audience again, restart the presentation.

When you first try this it might seem 'staged' and awkward. However, as you 'practice by doing' presentations, you will gain confidence and your actions will become more fluid.

Dress sense

In a university or student environment this is, generally, not important. However, consider very carefully how dress and dress sense communicates who you are. What does it say about you? Do you look the part of a young executive? This is something to consider seriously when you go for your first career interviews.

If your group presentation is assessed, I would strongly recommend that you 'dress for the part'. This demonstrates to the assessors that you are taking it seriously. Moreover, think back to earlier chapters of this book where I have stressed the need to approach your degree programme from a business perspective. This can help drive your mindset for the future. Dressing for the part (as any actor will tell you) helps you to take on that role. Dress business and think business.

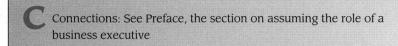

Connections: See Preface, the section on assuming the role of a business executive

Rehearse

A rehearsal will help you to:

- Practice your presentation – the more practice that you can get, the better honed will be your final presentation.
- If you are working in a group, it will also help you to focus on making the group gel together. This is relevant in terms of both content and delivery. The worst situation to be in is when one member of the group says one thing and another, a few moments later, totally contradicts what has been said. This demonstrates that the group is dysfunctional.
- Time your presentation. Many assessed presentations are usually only 15–20 minutes, with a 5–10 minute Q&A session following. You need to make sure that you are able to stay within the timeframe allotted to you. If a strict time limit is imposed and you are about to overrun, your session might be stopped. As a result, you might have missed the opportunity to deliver a key part of your presentation, as well as provide a summary. Make sure that you are able to keep to the time limits.

Issues for your next presentation

Once you have completed your presentation (group or individual), do the following:

- Consider any feedback from the assessors. Pay particular attention to any comments regarding content and your analysis of that content.
- As an individual or as part of a group, consider any thoughts that you have regarding the presentation. Consider what you felt went right and what did not work (and why)? What could you do in the future to rectify anything that went wrong?
- Collate this feedback under the following headings:
  - Critical issues – Things that you must change now. This could, for example, be the level of analysis employed or the range of background reading undertaken.
  - Issues to develop – These are not critical issues; however, they are things that you need to work on. For example, aspects of your delivery.
  - Positive points to enhance further – We can always do more to enhance our performance. You might be told, for example, that you did particularly well in terms of your delivery of the facts. If so, see how you could improve it further – building on the success.

Reflection zone

Here are a few key summary points for you to reflect upon:

- Understand how undertaking presentations, within your business degree, can enhance your interpersonal skills and employability.
- Consider how you can effectively and efficiently organize your materials to enhance your presentations.
- Consider how format and the use of visuals can enhance presentations.
- Appreciate how your personal appearance and actions affect presentation effectiveness.
- Consider how to use feedback (both from tutors and peers) to develop your presentations.

12 Examinations

'Nothing in life is to be feared. It is only to be understood.'

Marie Curie, 1867–1934, physicist and chemist

Introduction

An examination is an assessment technique to discover your level of understanding/knowledge of a particular subject area. It is not an attempt to catch you out nor is it purely a memory test. So, if you have come from an educational environment where you had to remember a set of facts, then you will have to reappraise your approach to studying for a business degree. Remembering a series of facts directly from a textbook or a lecture is unlikely to be a successful strategy. While you will have to know the various theories and concepts, studying for a business degree relies on your abilities to *apply* your knowledge.

The following is to help you prepare for and undertake examinations. Please consider each section carefully. Long-term revision, as well as the immediacy of examinations, must be taken equally seriously. Moreover, it is important that you continue to attend lectures. By not attending lectures, you risk losing valuable insight and understanding of key issues (which might be in the examination!).

Contents

- ► Introduction
- ► Why examinations?
- ► Types of examinations
- ► Planning your revision
- ► Examination week
- ► What to do the night before the examinations
- ► The day of the examination
- ► Examinations – frequently asked questions
- ► Common examination mistakes
- ► What makes a good answer?
- ► Post-examination
- ► What should I do if I fail?
- ► Reflection zone
- ► Further information

Why examinations?

This question is often asked in relation to business degrees, both at undergraduate and postgraduate level. The perspective is that you do not undertake examinations within a business setting, so why for the degree? The rationale is this:

- Examinations are a means of gauging your level of understanding of a particular topic or module at a particular point in time. This might be mid-term (often used in US universities) and/or at the end of the module.
- Business is often about making decisions under pressure and in short time scales. In an examination, you are often asked to analyze an issue or problem and make recommendations that are supported by a rationale. An examination, to some extent, replicates the business environment.

Types of examinations

There are various types of examinations that can be set to test your level of knowledge and understanding. Moreover, in terms of short-answer, essay-styled and case study responses, your objective is to also demonstrate your ability to analyze, synthesize and evaluate.

Connections: Chapter 2

Short answer responses

As the name suggests, you are being asked to provide short, succinct responses. You might find that you use a combination of short paragraphs and extended bullet points to answer the questions. Extended bullet points are a means of succinctly adding information to, usually, a one- or two-word bullet point. This helps clarify issues. For example, you could use extended bullet points to explain, for example, PESTLE factors or the key elements of a model, such as Porter's Five Forces or Schwartz's two-dimensional model of motivational values.

Essay-styled responses

This is the more traditional form of examination answer. You are expected to provide a relatively detailed answer in written essay format. Typically, this would comprise:

- An opening introductory section
  This is the scene setter, where you explain the approach that you are taking. For example, you might state the models that you are going to use to solve the question and why you have chosen these models.
- Main section
  Here, you will explore, analyze, synthesize and evaluate the various issues posed in the question.
- Conclusion
  This is where you draw together the key issues and form a supported conclusion. The support for your conclusion will emanate from the points discussed within the main body of your answer. For example, 'Company X should avoid entering market Z due to the current high entry barriers as shown in the Five Forces analysis . . .'

As tutors seek detailed responses in essay-styled answers, there is usually a balance between the number of questions you are required to answer and the time available. For instance, if it is a two-hour paper, then you might be required to answer two questions only. This should provide you with sufficient time both to plan your answer and to respond in the required level of detail.

As stated later in this chapter, it is advisable to plan your answers prior to writing anything. This helps you to structure your answers. This will, in turn, aid:

- The logical arrangement of your ideas, points of view and supporting evidence.

- The flow of your writing and, therefore, the readability of your answer. Clarity of thought improves the flow of writing, thereby providing a better chance of you expressing what you really mean. Thus, the marker does not have to hunt through the answer to detect whether or not you truly understand the issues.

Multiple-choice (also known as 'multiple-guess') responses

This is where you have a choice of four or five possible answers and you have to choose the one that best answers the question. The structure of multiple-choice papers does vary. However, often the potential answers follow a particular pattern – the correct answer, an answer that could be deemed close to the correct answer (but is wrong), one/two answers near the topic (but also wrong) and one that is usually far removed from the correct answer. There is also the catch-all answer 'all of the above', which might, or might not, be the correct one.

Multiple-choice examination papers are usually used in the first year of study. The aim is to help you to understand key concepts and make basic links across different disciplines. For example, this might help you to appreciate how to link key writers on leadership to their various models and theories.

Sometimes you will lose marks for a wrong answer. Therefore, contrary to the 'multiple-guess' title, guessing is not really an ideal approach to take. The situation is one of either knowing the answer (thus further emphasizing the importance of revision) or calculating the answer. In other words, using reason to eliminate the alternatives presented to you on the paper.

Here is an approach to reasoning an answer to a question about which you are not sure:

Step 1:

As with any examination paper, carefully read all the questions first. Indeed, in many colleges and universities there is a set reading time (usually 10–15 minutes) before you can do any writing. Use this time wisely.

Step 2:

Tackle the questions where you are clearly sure of the answer.

Step 3:

Look at the questions where you are not sure of the answer. Then look at the ones you have just completed. Compare and contrast the questions and possible answers. Can you see any links? Are there any similarities? If, say, you have 40 questions on management to answer, there is most likely to be some overlap or connection between the questions. By a process of elimination and rational thinking, you might be able to answer the questions you first thought were impossible.

Step 4:

Make sure that you have time to re-read all the questions and your answers before the end of the examination. Check that you have clearly indicated your chosen answer. (Remember, large multiple-choice papers are usually machine read so it has to be able to read a clear impression of your pencil mark.)

Case study questions

As demonstrated in the earlier chapter on assignments, case studies can be valuable in understanding the relationship between theory and practice. Usually, you will be presented with the case study several weeks prior to the examination (in Example 12.1, some 12 weeks).

The case study provides the platform upon which you can build your knowledge and understanding of the key issues prior to the examination. The examination itself provides the vehicle for:

- Synthesizing that knowledge and understanding.
- The critical evaluation of the issues or situations faced by organizations.
- The application of ideas and approaches.
- The drawing of conclusions supported with reliable evidence.

Example 12.1   Case study: Crisis in the European Airline Industry (in Brennan _et al._ 2003)

Extracts from student module guide

In the examination you will need to:

- Demonstrate that you have read beyond this case study.
- Demonstrate that you understand the implications for major 'traditional' carriers of the introduction (and development) of the low-cost carriers.
- Provide evidence to support your views and opinions.
- Be able to evaluate critically the issues rather than purely describing events.

The two questions within two hours should provide you with the time to:

- Produce answers that display depth and quality of analysis.
- Demonstrate a clear understanding of the critical strategic marketing issues facing major traditional airlines operating within Europe.
- Produce answers that have clarity of expression demonstrating your knowledge acquired not only on this module but also in previous modules.

Question 1

Clearly, there are dynamic macro and micro changes occurring within the European airline industry. National carriers, for instance, continue to face difficult times ahead. Assume that you are the strategic marketing director of a major national European airline, such as British Airways, Air France or KLM. Formulate a marketing strategy that could stimulate consumer demand, thus assisting in your airline in gaining and sustaining a competitive advantage.
Remember to justify your approach.

[_Here the students are examining the formulation of a marketing strategy._]

Question 2

Low-cost and no-frills airlines have gained a significant share of the European airline market as a result of deregulation. You have been called in to advise a brand new company on formulating their marketing strategy. What would you advise them to do and why?

[_The student's response could vary from not entering an already overcrowded market to finding ways of differentiating the airline from other low-cost carriers._]

The case study given in Example 12.1 was used for final year undergraduate students and was contained within the core textbook for the module. This case study formed the basis (or platform) of the research that the students needed to undertake. They were expected, as part of their studies, to update this case. The updating and development of the case was important, as the European Airline industry is a particularly dynamic one. The aim, as you will see from the questions, was to encourage the students to think like business people.

Combinations

In such cases, the examination paper is divided into two or more sections. Section 1 might take the form of a series of multiple-choice questions as outlined above. Section 2 might comprise one or more short-answer styled questions. You might be asked to complete one compulsory question and have to choose one/two questions from a selection. If there is a compulsory question, it is advisable that you complete that prior to starting the other short-answer styled questions.

● Planning your revision

When should I start revising?

Planned revision is necessary in order to pass your examinations successfully. Please do not leave your revision until the night before the examination – it is most unlikely that you will receive a good grade or, indeed, even a pass!

When the course started, you should have begun reading around the subject. Independent study is an important element in gaining an academic qualification, as not everything relevant can be contained within a lecture/seminar or a few pages of hand-outs. This is especially true on a fast-track programme. In some countries, degree programmes can be undertaken within two rather than over three or fours years. These are intensive programmes that require significant levels of language and academic ability, as well as commitment.

During the first half of the module, you should prepare a series of additional topic notes. As you move into the second half of the module, these can help form the basis of your revision.

It is important that you start revising the subject as soon as possible. Please do not leave it to the very last moment – this is a very risky strategy.

A question of attitude

Our mental attitude towards a task often affects the outcome. If we consider revision/studying boring, a chore, too difficult – then it will be. However, if we consider it a challenge, an opportunity to develop ourselves and to progress, then we might approach it differently. Therefore, revision becomes something that we look forward to, no matter how difficult we first perceive the task.

Revising for examinations is like a sports personality preparing for the Olympic Games. If they go into an event with a negative mental attitude, then their chances of winning that Gold Medal will surely elude them.

Think positively throughout the examination period.

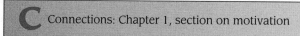

Connections: Chapter 1, section on motivation

Creating a revision timetable

Prepare a timetable of topic areas that you intend to revise. This will allow you to cover all the key areas. Put variety into your timetabling. It is advisable not to spend a whole day, or a revision session, on only one topic area. Create variety by spending time on, say, a management topic, followed by a marketing problem and then a human resource issue. Variety in your planning also helps to keep you refreshed.

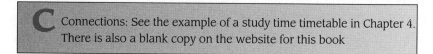

Connections: See the example of a study time timetable in Chapter 4. There is also a blank copy on the website for this book

Time management

The French general and politician Napoléon I (1769–1821) is alleged to have said that *he could always replace generals but that he could never replace lost time.* Time is perhaps our most precious commodity. Therefore, we must use it wisely. Your objective is to maximize your available time – effectively and efficiently.

However, studying or revising for long periods without a break does not increase your understanding of the subject matter. Moreover, it can adversely affect your health and, thus, your overall performance. It is therefore necessary to take breaks in order to refresh yourself and your interest in the subject/topic.

Ideally, you should revise/study for a maximum of 50 minutes – then take a 10-minute break (walk around, do a few stretching exercises, go outside and get some fresh air). These actions will help prevent you becoming physically tired and bored with the subject/topic, allowing you to comeback to the matter refreshed.

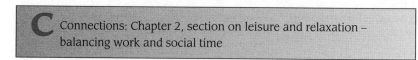

Connections: Chapter 2, section on leisure and relaxation – balancing work and social time

An appropriate place to revise

It is important to find a suitable place to revise – one that suits your temperament, your emotions; if you need absolute quiet, then you might find an empty classroom ideal.

Revision notes

As stated in Chapter 4, there are various forms of note taking. Ideally you collate your various lecture and study notes (session by session or topic by topic). If this is undertaken on an ongoing basis, it will be easier to reflect upon the core issues of the subject. There are additional techniques that you can use to assist your revision – revision cards and a Dictaphone. However, these will only be of value if you have undertaken the necessary work over the length of the module.

Revision cards

Study cards or record/index cards can be purchased from most newsagents and stationery suppliers. They come in a range of sizes and colours to suit individual tastes. However, perhaps the 6 × 4 (15 cm × 10 cm) is the ideal size in terms of providing sufficient space to note key pieces of information.

Record cards can be utilized when, for example, you are travelling on a bus, coach, train or even in a friend's car.

They can be used in several different ways, for example:

- On one side of the card, write down a question, for example: What do you consider to be the core competences of automotive company Honda?
- On the other side, write a response to the question. This can either be a paragraph or a list of extended bullet or key points.

  or

- You can note on one side of the card a particular point of view; for example, that globalization is good.
- On the other side of the card, you could note down another point of view that suggests the opposite. Such an approach allows you to reflect upon the differing views of both academics and practitioners. It is particularly important (as stated elsewhere) that within your degree programme you consider different perspectives.

These record cards, of course, will only provide a snapshot of information. However, they will help to keep your memory refreshed on the key issues/terminologies.

Using a Dictaphone or MP3 player for revision

A small Dictaphone or MP3 player can be useful for recording and playing back key points. You can listen to this whilst you are travelling to/from the college.

- Prepare a brief outline of the key areas you want/need to consider.
- Gather the necessary materials together in the order that best suits you. Plan what you are going to say before you record.
- Dictate summaries/key points into the Dictaphone. Make sure that you give sufficient pauses/breaks between each of the sections.
- When recording your summaries/key points, add excitement to your voice. Engage with the words and the ideas. Sound enthused by what you are saying.

Expectations

Whether they say them or not, your friends, family and tutors will have expectations of you. As people seek to support you, you might also feel under pressure to meet their expectations of you. If these expectations start to cause too much pressure for you, then discuss them either with your supporters or someone independent. For example, you might seek out a family friend or a university counsellor. In our attempt to support people, we often, unknowingly, create additional pressures for them.

Examination week

Here are a few tips to help your overall performance during the examination week.

- Make sure that you have plenty of sleep/rest. There is sufficient evidence to suggest that, in order to be alert and perform effectively mentally, a human being needs several hours of good sleep. Catching one or two hours of sleep before an examination is unlikely to create an agile mind.
- Make sure that you eat meals regularly, and that they are nutritionally balanced – that is, no junk foods. Do not skimp on or avoid meals in favour of revision. A balanced diet helps the body and mind to function more effectively under the stressful conditions of an examination.
- Do not stay up till very late revising/cramming for the examination scheduled for the next morning. Very rarely does such action reap any form of positive reward. Getting a good night's sleep is far better preparation.
- If you have any problems regarding the examination, especially medical ones, please contact a member of staff as soon as possible. Colleges and universities operate various policies in terms of a medical re-sit (see your individual college/university regulations).
- Be careful what you eat. You might want to avoid shellfish, cold seafood or that burger from the all-night takeaway. It is not worth the potential food poisoning risk prior to an exam.

What to do the night before the examinations

Rather than cramming for the examination, you are better off preparing your examination equipment and relaxing.

- Make sure that you have plenty of working pens and pencils. There have been cases where students have entered an examination room with only one pen. It is usually in that situation that the pen stops functioning, much to the embarrassment of the student.

● Make sure that you have a ruler. Diagrams can add significant value to your examination answer. However, they must be clearly presented and annotated for the marker to understand both their meaning and value.

Relax

Relax . . . yes, that is easy to say. However, reading pages of notes will not help. If, over the previous weeks, you have revised the topic areas, then you should be prepared to undertake the examination. Therefore, it is better to relax, read a general book, a magazine or indeed watch something light and enjoyable on television.

However, you still need to think positively about the outcome. Research in the United States and elsewhere indicates that if a person goes to sleep thinking positively about an event the next day, then they will wake up more refreshed and positive. This is because, whilst you are asleep, the subconscious memory actively works towards a positive outcome. (This research includes the work of sports psychologist Dr James E. Loehr. Example: Loehr, J.E. (1990) *Training to Achieve and Command the Ideal Performance State,* New York: Nightingale Conant.)

● The day of the examination   .

● Remain positive and relaxed
Throughout the period of the examinations think positively about the outcomes. Remain focused on what you want to achieve.
● Clothing
If you are going to sit in an examination room for, say, two to three hours, then you need to feel comfortable. Therefore, think about the type of clothes that you will be comfortable wearing. Make allowances for cold/heat, as examination rooms can get quite warm, especially if there are hundreds of students taking the examination on a summer's day.
● Arrival time
Make sure that you get to your college/university in plenty of time. It is better to leave earlier than normal in order to avoid potential delays on the trains, buses and/or road system.
    If you arrive in plenty of time, there is an improved opportunity to relax before the examination. If you arrive at the very last minute, you will not be in a relaxed state and it will take valuable minutes in order for you to relax. In an examination, you must use every minute wisely.
● Food
It is advisable to eat light snacks prior to an examination. If you consume a large, heavy meal the stomach will need more oxygen to commence the digestion process. This additional oxygen demand will be taken from all areas of the body, including the brain. This is the reason you might sometimes feel tired after a large evening meal or weekend lunch. During an examination, you need

to maximize your energy and oxygen levels. In terms of foods, sports scientists, often recommend fruit as a means of increasing energy levels.

In the examination room

The physicality of the examination room

It is best to arrive early at the examination room in order to be one of the first to enter. This is for several reasons:

- You might be able to choose where you sit. This might not be the policy in some universities and colleges where a seat number is allocated. However, if you can choose where to sit, then you can place yourself in a spot where you will feel comfortable. For some people, the best position, psychologically, is in the centre of the examination room. This might be because the individual feels surrounded, protected and, thus, comfortable. For others this might not be the ideal, inducing, instead, a feeling of being enclosed and thus, for them, a position on the edge of the seating area might be more ideal. However, as stated earlier you might not have much choice.

- You can check your table and chair to see if they are comfortable or not. It is not the ideal situation to be in if you have a rocky table. If you are in the examination room early, you can either move (if allowed to) or ask the invigilator either to replace the table or correct the rocking by placing a wedge underneath one of the legs. The advice is not do this yourself: (a) it is the college/university's responsibility to provide you with appropriate seating arrangements; and (b) never have a piece of unofficial paper in your hands within the examination room. There is always the risk of being accused of unprofessional conduct.

- Being early or on time allows you time to unpack from your bag the items that you will need for the examination – for example, pens, pencil, ruler and calculator. Moreover, it provides you with the opportunity to pack the items that you must not have on your desk – for example, mobile phone and/or language translator. (You will need to check this prior to the examination. However, many universities, especially in the UK, now consider it a disciplinary offence if you have a mobile phone with you during the examination, even if it is switched off.) Therefore, it is vital that you check beforehand what is required for actually undertaking your examination. Moreover, as stated later in this section, listen carefully to the instructions of the head invigilator.

- Refreshments (This will be subject to individual institutional regulations). Some universities and colleges will allow you to have bottled water only and nothing else on your table. If water is allowed, then do make sure that you have a bottle on the table. The UK's Food Standards Agency suggests that you should drink a regular intake of water per day, usually 1.2 litres or more if it is particularly hot weather (FSA, 2007). If it is hot weather and you are in a non-air conditioned examination room (this is probably the majority of examination rooms in the world!), then water is important in reducing dehydration. If you are thirsty, you are already showing signs of dehydration. Apart from the potential risk to your health (for example, kidney stones) dehydration can lead to headaches, lethargy, a loss of concentration and, indeed, fainting. According to the European Food Information Council 'even a small reduction in hydration can affect mental performance' (EUFIC, 2007). Therefore, it is important to keep your body hydrated before, during and after your examinations.

The role of the invigilator – instructions

It is most likely that you have come across invigilators at your school or at the college where you gained your qualifications for university. Perhaps, in many cases, you actually knew the invigilators, as they were your teachers. At university, it will be unlikely that you will have met the invigilators beforehand. They will usually be staff from the examinations department and/or ancillary services. They will not know you as an individual. Their role is clear: 'to enable an efficient and effective examination process that is fair and equitable to all candidates'. Therefore, their role and responsibility is to make sure that examination operates within the university's procedures and regulations.

Your role in this process is:

- To listen carefully to any statement that an invigilator makes, either to the whole group or to you.
- Follow all instructions stated fully, otherwise an innocent action could result in a disciplinary outcome. For example, if the regulation states that you must leave your mobile phone (switched off) in your bag at the front of the room then do so. Do not leave it in your pocket, thinking that it will not matter. If you are spotted, even leaving the examination room, with your mobile phone in your hand, you could find that your examination paper becomes null and void. DO NOT TAKE THE RISK.
- Read the instructions on the examination paper very carefully. Make sure that you are fulfilling **all** your obligations. Make sure that you write your name, unit number, unit title and the numbers of the questions attempted **clearly** on the first page of the examination book.

Reading time

At some universities, there is an amount of time set aside, prior to commencing the examination, for reading the examination paper. This does not (usually) mean that you can make any rough notes. It is purely for you to read through the paper – both instructions and the questions. Wisely use this time by focusing on the question paper in front of you. Read all the questions carefully. See whether there are any links between questions that will help you decide on the approach that you will undertake..

If, on reading through the questions, you initially feel that you cannot answer any of them you need to:

- Sit back and relax for a few seconds. Yes, that is easier said than done. However, you need to clear the clutter of your mind and refocus.
- Then read through them again, slowly and carefully. Try to see the connections or issues raised within the questions. If there is one question where you feel you have some understanding of the issues being asked, then start brainstorming the answer.

BUT

- **Never** walk out of an examination room before the end of the examination. The only person who loses out is **you**. Stay calm and remain positive about the outcome of the examination.

 Connections: Chapter 1 – Reflect back to your part within the learning process. There, I said that you have ownership of your own destiny. By staying in the examination room you are taking control of your own future. Stay with it and you have a greater chance of success.

Planning your answers

Allocate sufficient time for each question. It is important that you meet the examiner's requirements. If you need to answer three questions, plan your time to meet those requirements.

Assume, for example, that three questions must be completed within an allocated three-hour timeframe. Figure 12.1 is an example of how the timings might break down. However, you must plan your examination timetable to suit your individual needs. But do make sure that you have planned sufficient time to answer all necessary questions.

- Read all the examination questions very carefully. Again, make sure that you understand what is being asked of you.
- Where choice exists, ensure that the right choice is selected, so that maximum marks are obtained. Do not disregard a question out of hand.
- When you read through an examination question, focus on the **key words** within the question. Underline them for clarity. Keep thinking – 'What am I being asked to do?' It is **essential** that you answer the question as stated. Do not merely repeat course notes – they must be repackaged and developed to suit the question.
- Once you have chosen a question, spend some time brainstorming the answer by writing down relevant key phrases/words. Allocate time for this function. Once you have completed the brainstorming process, enumerate the

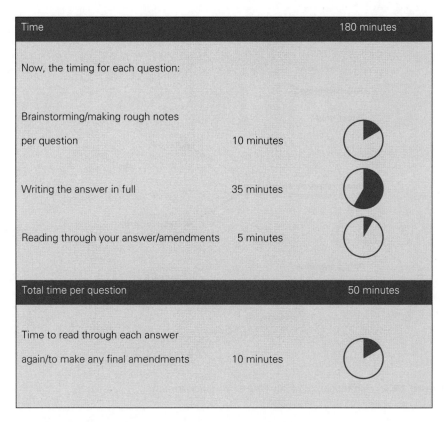

Figure 12.1   Example timing break-down of an examination

phrases/key words. The enumeration helps you to decide the order in which to discuss the key issues – in essence, this provides you with a structure. (See Figure 12.2 for an example.)

Enumerating the various points helps to create an order to your answer. Then the various points/issues can be fully developed with supporting information and evidence.

When you have finished with your brainstormed points draw a diagonal line through them. This shows to the examiner that these are your rough notes, and are not to be marked. Think through your answer before you write it.

- Conclusions – It is important to bring your various thoughts/points together in an effective conclusion. Final impressions can be as important to the examiner as the first.
- Commence each question on a new page. This is for two reasons:
  - ○ It marks a clear distinction, for the examiner, between your answer to one question, and the subsequent one.

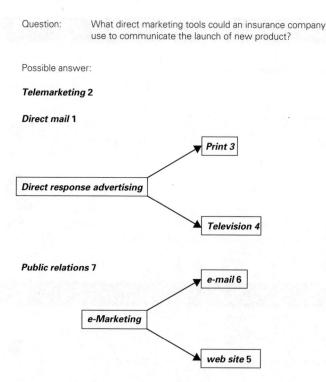

Question: What direct marketing tools could an insurance company
                use to communicate the launch of new product?

Possible answer:

Telemarketing 2

Direct mail 1

Figure 12.2   Identification of key issues by brainstorming

○ Having clear space between one answer and another allows you to add more information to the previous answer, if required. For example: let's say that in the examination you tackled Questions 1, 2, and 3. On your final read-through, you remember a key point that you have not raised in Question 1. You can make use of the valuable space between Questions 1 and 2 to write down the point that you did not raise earlier. In such circumstances, even if it is written down as a brief bullet point, it might help you to gain more marks or credit for knowledge gained, and used.

● Please do not use highlighters or marker pens to underline/highlight sections of texts. As well as wasting your time, the highlighted text can be difficult for the examiner to read.

● Spelling and grammar
Although examiners make allowances for both spelling and grammar under examination conditions, this does not mean that spelling and grammar should be ignored. Part of the rationale for making rough notes (see above) is to help you in your sentence construction. Moreover, taking care in the construction of your sentences will help you improve the communication of your message to the examiner. Your message is your ability to demonstrate to the examiner that you clearly understand the issues and can evaluate them critically.

If grammar is a particular weakness, then it is best to seek advice prior to undertaking any examinations (this is equally applicable to assignments and dissertations). Poor grammar will most likely severely affect your overall performance on your programme.

- Legible handwriting

The legibility of your handwriting is absolutely vital. As stated in Chapter 5, an examiner might have anywhere between 20 and 100 examination scripts to mark within a relatively short timeframe. While many markers will try to read difficult handwriting, they too are under time pressures and, thus, might be forced to turn the page and focus on your next answer.

Many students, in an attempt to write down all the issues/thoughts quickly, often let the quality of their handwriting suffer. You might be making a valid point only to lose marks because the examiner cannot read and understand your illegible handwriting. If your handwriting becomes illegible, then stop and pause for a minute or two. It is better to do that and have the examiner be able to read your writing (and, thus, the valuable point that you are making) than not at all.

- Effective use of diagrams

Diagrams can be a very useful in presenting functions and theories. However, they must be clearly drawn and labelled and, where possible, referenced. Moreover, it is vital that you link the diagram to the main body of your answer. Link the diagram and say why you are using it and what it reflects.

- People around you

During the examination, focus your attention on **your** work. Do not consider or, indeed, worry about what others might be doing. A colleague might be busily writing as you are jotting down rough notes. However, your rough notes might produce a significantly more valuable output. The **quality** of the answer is the key to gaining higher marks.

● Examinations – frequently asked questions

The purpose of this section is to answer questions that are generally asked by students. While it might not be an exhaustive list, it should nonetheless provide you with additional insight. Equally, you should be able to ask your tutors when they undertake examination revision with you.

Q: Do I need to remember exact quotes from journal articles and textbooks?

A: It is most unlikely that you will remember exact quotes. The purpose of university education is not for you to remember points word-for-word and just repeat them. This is called learning by rote. University is about understanding and application. The key is your understanding of the theoretical perspective and its relevance to real-world situations. For example, Michael Porter created the Five-Forces Model. However, there is great debate as to whether or not this model is applicable to all real-world situations. That understanding and application is far more important than being able to quote Michael Porter word-for-word from an article in the *Harvard Business Review*. All that does is demonstrate that you have good memory skills – it does not demonstrate knowledge and understanding.

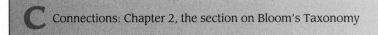

Connections: Chapter 2, the section on Bloom's Taxonomy

Q: Are all theories applicable to real-world situations?

A: Theories might or might not be applicable to real-world situations. They might have a universal appeal or be limited to very specific areas or spheres of influence. Equally, the theory itself might be challenged in terms of its rigour, even though it might have no direct real-world application. Just think of how many scientific theories remain, currently, just theories and how the scientific community challenges them. The same is applicable to business, management and marketing theories. Porter (1980, 1985 and 1990) and Levitt (1983) have both written about globalization. However, for example, Rugman (2001) and others have challenged the very notion of globalization. It is a hotly disputed area. Do global companies really exist? Various perspectives can be put forward both to support and to challenge the concept. You might have your own views. Your views will be dependent upon your own experiences and your reading around the subject areas.

Q: What is the expected length of an answer?

A: It is really an issue of the quality of response rather than exact quantity of words. Of course, if your response happens to be a few short paragraphs, then it is unlikely that you have debated and analyzed the question sufficiently enough to have passed. That is perhaps obvious. Equally, you might write copious amounts of words – but not focus on the question, or focus only on one part of the question. This, too, reduces your opportunity to obtain a pass mark on that question.

Q: How important are seminar activities in helping to answer examination questions?

A: Seminar activities, as lectures, are important in contributing ideas that are valuable to passing examinations. Active debates within seminars help generate disagreements and provide additional perspectives. They bring together other people's experiences and knowledge (both tutors and students), thus helping to provide real case examples. These examples can help either to challenge or to support some of the more theoretical perspectives.

● Common examination mistakes

Here is a list (not exhaustive) of the most common mistakes made by students during examinations.

When reading through these, reflect back to the examination techniques above. This will help you avoid such mistakes.

- Make sure that you answer the question as written on the examination paper. Unfortunately, some students read an examination question and focus on one or two key words only – they do not look at the question as a whole. The result is that they only partially answer the question. Whilst that part of the question might be well answered, the examiner cannot award high marks.
- Some questions have two or more parts. Again, some students only answer one part. When reading through the questions at the beginning of the examination, make sure that you can answer all parts of the question.
- The answer is not planned and the result is confusing to read. It is important to plan your answer. Answers need to be structured with a brief introduction, the main issues and then a conclusion. Answers that are not planned tend not to address the key issues and are often confusing to read.
- Some answers, both at undergraduate and postgraduate level, show a lack of depth and analysis. This often reflects the student's poor level of understanding of the subject material. Students need to demonstrate that they understand the subject/topic area by answering the question fully. This includes, where appropriate, analyzing the issues, comparing theory with practice, discussing various critical perspectives and developing their own viewpoint (with supportive information).
- Handwriting, as stated earlier, must be legible. Handwriting that is illegible is often difficult to read and decipher. Whilst you might have written a valuable comment/statement, if an examiner cannot read your writing you might miss out on additional marks.
- Diagrams can be very useful in describing functions and theories. However, diagrams need to be clearly drawn and labelled – so often they are not. Additionally, you will need to link them into the text. It is important to say why you are using the diagram and what it reflects.
- It is vital that you allocate sufficient time to answer the required number of questions. Often, students spend a great deal of time on two questions then only provide brief notes for their third question. Whilst the two answers might be of high quality, the lack of attention on the third question will deliver a low mark. It might even be a fail.

What makes a good answer?

The objective of this section is to place in some context the requirements for a range of answers. Examples are used to offer *broad* illustration of the different levels of responses. While only brief extracts can be provided, they should, nonetheless, illustrate examples of basic and good practice. Each is followed by a brief commentary.

As stated in Chapter 2, you will need to demonstrate different levels of knowledge and skill (see Bloom's Taxonomy). The examples below illustrate some of these different levels.

Depth and breadth of knowledge – knowledge and comprehension
Good responses
Example 1

'Strategy is about winning – Grant. If we agree with Grant's definition of strategy, then survival is the key. Ansoff's classical approach to strategy in this case becomes slightly obsolete due to the dynamics of the environment. Mintzberg is a believer of the Learning School's Strategy Theory. He is of the belief that strategies emerge and that organizations should therefore be recipients of this idea. This is probably the best chain of thought.'

Commentary

In this example, the student illustrates that they have read around the subject and is able to link the authors.

Example 2

'Argyris and Schen developed the ideas of learning within the strategic organization by explaining how the processes within the firms alter within given levels of knowledge. It is important to note here that knowledge-based learning is what the proponents of the literature emphasized. Strategy development can take place through knowledge organizations via a single loop in which individuals notice discrepancies and rectify them without disturbing the underlying thinking and values in use. This can prove to be repetitive, as not at all correction is recorded or registered in the organization. The interaction is on the individual level. However, with double loop learning the organization witnesses changes to the existing processes and symptoms within the organization. Thus, problems are identified in a deeper vein and (traced) to alterations acquired to the systems and values in use.'

Commentary

Again, the student demonstrates a depth and breadth of knowledge. They have clearly set out all three learning loop principles.

Example 3

'Thomas Friedman in *The Lexus and the Olive Tree*: understanding globalization attempts to make sense of the new world in which countries, industries and individual businesses are now operating. The effect of the Internet and how people now are able to respond to in what he terms the "electronic herd" without their support . . .'

Commentary

The student has read beyond the standard sources. This demonstrates an interest in and the ability to explore the topic.

Basic responses

Example 1

'The airline industry has some of the same common characteristics. Most of the airline companies are owned by the governments or somehow linked to their state government. Most of them are so-called national airlines that carry their national flag and indirectly represent their country. The bulk of the airlines are protected by the local rules and regulations that are, most of the time, in favour of the state airline. The airlines are also heavily subsidized by the government and are inefficient and ineffective in their operations.'

Commentary

This is a series of broad generalizations. The airline industry is much more complex in its structure than is communicated here. Thus, we do not get a feel for this complexity. In some cases, local regulations do favour home country airlines. However, this is not necessarily the case once they cross their national borders. For instance, consider the impact of US and European Union regulations in terms of mergers and acquisitions.

Example 2

'Products have a life cycle in different stages.

1   In introduction stage, the duct is developed and early introduction to the market. It needs money for promotion, the sales is little, as it is not yet well known to customers.
2   In second stage (growth), the sales are as it is well known to the customer.
3   In mature stage, the sales are stable.
4   The decline stage, the sales drop significantly.'

Commentary

This is a very superficial view of the product life cycle. For example, it assumes that there is only one type of curve (bell-shaped). However, there can be numerous variants depending upon, for example, the type of product and the influence of fashion. Equally, some products can be rejuvenated through, for instance, repackaging or repositioning within the market(s). The example above only considers 'sales' – here, again, many more factors have a strategic impact or relationship to the product life cycle.

Thinking critically – evaluation

As discussed earlier, a business degree is not about repeating theories, models and concepts. It relates to thinking, considering their worth and their perceived and real value within a real-world context. The questions themselves will help set the direction with such words and phrases as: 'critically analyze', 'critically evaluate', 'explore and debate'.

Being critical can be defined as 'probing the theory or application to discover where problems or issues might or might not occur'. If you like, it is seeking to discover and explain the weaknesses within the theory, concept or application.

Being analytical can be defined as 'in-depth or penetrating questioning'. Here, a logical, methodological systematic approach is required.

Challenging the point of view and not taking theory as a given is partly what a degree programme is all about. Theories, models and perspectives are all there to be challenged – never be scared of disagreeing! However, the key is bringing together the evidence to make the re-evaluation and challenge effective.

There might not be a right or wrong answer in the traditional sense. The response to the question might depend on how the theory is applied, and the subsequent outcomes. Therefore, it is vital to have more than a basic understanding (the 'just repeating' approach) of the theory or concept. Consideration must be given to applicability and the use of, for example, real case study organizations.

Good response

Example 1

[Discussing macro environmental factors] 'Whichever approach is adopted, they are striving to attain a list of things that are likely to affect the industry and organizations within it, they are just grouped differently. None of these approaches attempts to illustrate clearly how the relative importance of each factor is ranked or, indeed, how likely any one is to change. A further critique of such models is their inability to look at the future. They are snapshots of time in which the analysis is conducted.'

Commentary

Elements of this can be debated. For example, there can be a link between models and scenario planning to consider the 'potential' future. However, this example does illustrate an attempt to think critically about the issues.

Example 2

'Combining the product life cycle with other tools such as the Boston Consulting Group matrix, as I mentioned earlier, might suggest a better grounding for decision making. However, other tools have their shortcomings too. The BCG matrix, for instance, relies on an ability to identify cash flows for each product and this is not always practicable, especially where two or more products share factors of production. It can be seen here that combining two tools with shortcomings could serve to compound the inappropriateness of the strategic choice.'

Commentary

Here, the student is prepared to start being critical, briefly identifying that decision-making tools have their shortcomings. Thus, they cannot be taken for granted. Even so, the student ventures that the combination of decision-making tools, shortcomings included, might be of value. This is often, though not always, the view taken in the course of real business activity.

Basic response

Example 1

'Until 9/11 the demand for all types of travel was growing. 9/11 changed this, demand fell sharply. Companies had been gearing up capacity that was not required, orders were delayed. The numerous rail crashes in the UK have a negative demand on rail travel.'

Commentary

Apart from the abrupt sentence structure, there are several assumptions made within this paragraph. First, that, prior to the 9/11 tragedy, all types of travel was growing. Second, that this growth was global insofar as no location determinants were included. Third, that demand fell sharply after 9/11 and, fourth, that this drop was a global occurrence.

The student has not been sufficiently analytical here. The growth and/or decline varied across the range of transport systems in different countries prior to and subsequent to 9/11. For example, in some the airline business was expanding or contracting (at various rates) prior to 9/11. It was very dependent upon other micro and macro factors. In a few cases – for example, Swissair – they were already in financial difficulties prior to 9/11. Subsequent to that time, the reduction in passenger numbers severely impacted upon the already debt-laden business. This eventually pushed it into insolvency. For some airlines, post 9/11 witnessed growth rather than decline – an example here would be the European low-cost carrier easyJet.

Providing evidence – application

Challenging a theory or perspective is more than saying 'It will not work in my country.' You need to say more – for instance, why it does not work in your country. You need to be specific as possible.

Good responses

Example 1

'An internal knowledge management intranet – perhaps called a "knowledge network" – would be a great source of feeding innovation and moving the organization to becoming a leading a "learning organization". Ideas from employees based on experience – a key component for strategic success in Stacey's writings about chaos theory – and ideas from the public and learning institutions, as well as others involved with "families, kids and fun" could all be sourced through such a network. This is important for "visualizing a future", I believe, because looking at best practice and past activities stifles creativity and innovation and prevents people from thinking "outside the box".

If they really "visualize a future", the possibilities are endless. These move beyond employers helping remove inefficiencies through suggestions around improving customer satisfaction and displaying ideas for increased sales. Markets within "kids, family and fun" areas could include a new family-friendly healthy restaurant, toy design promotions/competitions in schools and universities, ways to involve the community, learning classes for children and, perhaps, even reviewing the US strategic asset of real estate to invest in solar power to utilize in the future and reduce energy costs. Toys 'R' Us could benefit significantly by tapping into ideas and helping promote them through the use of knowledge networks, think tanks, increasing communication with alliance partners and networks.'

Commentary

Although these perspectives can be debated, the student has provided evidence as to why they believe a 'knowledge network' could benefit the company. It is more than just saying that the company needs one.

Example 2

'As China, the emerging market, has opened its door to the world, Japanese companies are forced to make radical changes to stay competitive or, in fact, in business. To remain competitive, many Japanese companies have either to close non-performing operations or sell them to a third party. Operating as a conglomerate with loss-making operations will result in overall loss and the loss of confidence of the investors. Many Japanese companies are forced to consolidate among themselves or to seek strategic alliances with others in order to operate profitably or maintain a market share.'

Commentary

While slightly convoluted in its structure, the student has attempted to say 'why?' However, more could have been stated – for example, the linkage to the economy, recession and increased competition.

Basic responses

Example 1

'With technology, there would be a tendency to manufacture large aircraft that can carry over 600 passengers like the Airbus A380. This would be profitable for large companies in the USA and Europe because of the number of travelling passengers.'

Commentary

This is a very generalized statement that does not develop the case for the Airbus A380. Many aviation economists, for instance, have doubts about the viability of the project. Some airlines placed advanced orders, while airlines of similar stature have not. Airbus's rival Boeing is not planning to develop, at this time, aircraft with a capacity of 747. Their current alternative is a smaller, faster long-range aircraft (the Dreamliner) that will fly from an increased number of global hubs. In this example, there is an assumption that the large aircraft bought by large companies will be profitable. Numerous other factors need to be taken into account such as passenger number predictions, routes and airline operating efficiency.

The real world – application

Much of your evidence will probably be derived from real-world cases. Indeed, you might be asked to analyze an organization of your choice as part of the question. The examples can come from any aspect of your studies or experience (textbooks, journals, business magazines/newspapers, television, radio, the Internet or organizations that you have worked for). Of course, they must be relevant to the question.

Good responses

Example 1

'Hamel and Pralahad put learning as a key component, a "core" competency to getting to the future first. I believe that if you adhere to their philosophy, then this is the area in which Toys 'R' Us has the most room to maintain significant market share, to increase innovation and to build on their core competencies as per the resource-based view of gaining strategic advantage.

Questions have arisen over whether organizations themselves learn or whether individuals learn. I believe that individuals learn but that it is possible to improve the ability of an organization to turn tacit knowledge into explicit knowledge, and to build an architecture around this to improve learning. Knowledge management theorists talk about the "art" of knowledge; acquisition, retention and transfer. If Toys 'R' Us can improve their knowledge management processes, then a successful strategy is potentially more likely to "emerge" from within the company.'

Commentary

Here, the student has made a link between academic perspectives and a real-world example. Equally, they have imbued this with their own thoughts. It is important to be able to relate to real-world cases, for it can be a means of testing theories or concepts on many levels. Equally, organizations are not the same, they might display certain commonalities but that does not mean that what works for one company will work for another. There are numerous micro and macro factors to take into consideration.

Example 2

'Writers about learning organizations include Argyris and Schen, who write about single and double feedback loops. Learning to learn is becoming increasingly important and Toys 'R' Us appear to realize this. Symbolism such as renaming their toy designers "toyologists" promotes their importance and sends a message of commitment from senior management. Senge also writes about learning organizations; he claims that mental models, personal mystery, a shared vision, group learning and systems thinking to integrate all these things are vital for success. Toys 'R' Us are clearly on the right path, as shown with the project named 'Mission Possible' as the way to clearly define shared vision'.

Commentary

Although this is a brief extract, and some of the language is slightly convoluted, it still demonstrates that the student is tying together academic views with a real-world example.

Basic responses

Example 1

'Companies can consider introducing number of ways to cut down the cost. It might consider to offer more value-added services to customers such as free email services etc. Consider branching out to related sectors such as pick up services from the airport. From travel companies to offer to offering travel services to the customer.

'Competition – Join existing strategic alliances. Co-operate on those routes that the airline is strong at.'

Commentary

Firstly, there are a couple of general issues with this extract. The language is either convoluted or over simplified. There is also a contradiction. The student talks about cost cutting and then embarks on discussing added-value services, which have a financial cost. The student could have suggested, for instance, a reduction of costs in one area to help finance the development of value added services, which would become self-funding in the future.

In terms of real world examples, the student does not proffer any examples. Various airlines, for example, have embarked on strategic alliances. Perhaps the two most notable are One World (lead by British Airways and American) and the Star Alliance (lead by United Airlines and Lufthansa). Equally, airlines have embarked on relationships with companies such as Hertz car rentals and the Hilton Hotel chain to provide value-added services to both business and leisure passengers. It is always helpful if you can link ideas and concepts to real-world examples.

Linking ideas – synthesis

It is important to link issues and ideas. As stated elsewhere in this book, it is important to 'think outside the box'. We tend to compartmentalize issues, usually within functional areas (see Chapters 2 and 4). For example, we talk about marketing often at the expense of including operations, finance and human resource management. Yet, all these are interlinked in one way or another.

Good response

Example 1

The Japanese economy

'Obtaining consensus on all decisions of strategic importance is time consuming and therefore increasingly market opportunities were lost. The debt/equity structure of the country also made them extremely susceptible to interest rate movements. This resulted in a crisis situation. Inability to reduce numbers of employees because of socially acceptable lifetime employment pressures was driving costs up and losing companies large amounts of capital. Forced with decisions to cut staff, Japanese managers were creating overseas operations with lower-cost employees rather than engaging higher-cost employees locally.

The alliance between Nissan and Renault took the CEO of Renault to significantly reduce employees of Nissan to avoid bankruptcy and turn the company around.'

Commentary

Although there are some convoluted and confusing sentences in parts, the student has made an attempt to link various issues. These range from politics, economics, unemployment, tradition (what might be socially acceptable issues) and finance. The student has demonstrated that there are links across a broad range of subject areas, many of which impact upon each other.

Basic response

Example 2

'In summary, strategic alliances will lead the future. Those companies that can fully utilize the benefits of strategic alliances will continue to prosper and survive. Strategic alliances have helped the right companies to better compete than those without such alliances. But we must remember that before deciding to form an alliance, the companies need to look at all the factors that might affect the success of the alliance.'

Commentary

There are two basic underlying assumptions here: that (1) strategic alliances will lead the future; and (2) those companies that fully utilize the benefits of alliances will 'continue to prosper and survive'. True, it might increase their opportunities. However, there are numerous micro and macro factors that could, to a greater or lesser extent, impact upon (or influence) the strategic alliance. These factors might not be known in advance – for example, changes in legislation as a result of political changes. While the companies might utilize the benefits of the alliance, other factors might, in the longer term, hamper its success, even its survival. The student needed to further explore the links.

● Post-examination

It is not advisable to discuss your examination answers with your friends and colleagues. This is because, during the examination, you and your friends might have tackled the question from different perspectives. Therefore, you might needlessly worry about who is right and who is wrong. This adds additional stress and distracts you from concentrating on your next examination. Once you have left an examination room, there is nothing you can do to change the outcome – that is only possible whilst you are still writing your answers.

When one examination is over, you must focus all your attention on the next examination paper – give that your undivided attention.

When they are all over – **relax!**

● What should I do if I fail?

Do **not** give up!

No one likes to fail. However, it probably happens to everyone at sometime in his or her life. Failure goes hand-in-hand with success. We often learn more from our mistakes. You might want to reflect back to the Thomas Edison quote in Chapter 8 and how he approached life when experiments or ideas failed.

Of course, there is peer and family pressure to succeed, and that can lead to stress during assessment, and extra stress if you fail.

If you fail an element or a subject, it is not the end. There are usually further opportunities (please refer to your college/university programme regulations for specific details).

1 What you must do is focus on the resubmission and/or resit.
2 Look to the future. Do not think of the failure – only the future and success.
3 Look at the element/subject again.
   Assignments: The top sheet of the assignment will have been handed back to you. Your tutors aim to make these detailed to: (a) show you where errors have been made; and (b) show where improvements can be made.
   Examinations: Did you answer all the questions? Did you allow sufficient time? These are just two areas. Please re-read the section on common examination mistakes.
4 Re-read this study guide. Reflect upon the points in this guide. Consider how you can use them to your best advantage.
5 Allocate sufficient time to prepare for the completion of the new assignment/revision for the resit. Planning your time effectively is vital.
6 Remain self-confident and focused on what you need to achieve.

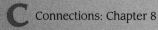

C Connections: Chapter 8

Reflection zone

Here are a few key summary points for you to reflect upon:

- Consider the merits of the different types of examinations that can be used for assessment.
- Review your approach to examination revision. Consider how you can enhance your skills.
- Reflect on how you will prepare yourself for examination week. This will include planning to arrive at the examination room ahead of the start time.
- Consider how you might approach planning your answers – for example, in terms of time management and brainstorming.
- Overall, consider how to maximize the opportunity for a positive outcome through planning, revision and a positive mental attitude.

● Further information

There is also additional information on 'Eating for Exams' on the UK's Food Standard's Agency website: www.eatwell.gov.uk

13 Managing Dissertations

'Nothing exists except atoms and empty space; everything else is opinion.'

Democritus, c. 460–370 BCE, Greek philosopher

Contents

► Introduction
► Using previous experiences
► What is a dissertation?
► Structure of a dissertation
► Opportunities presented by dissertations
► A few thoughts to help your approach
► Working with your supervisor
► Your dissertation proposal
► Feedback and progress logs
► Reflection zone
► Additional resource

● Introduction

The above quote from the Greek philosopher Democritus has merit when discussing dissertations and other related projects. Such extended pieces of work are normally undertaken towards the end of your studies – the culmination of your college/university experience. Through your taught sessions and your own exploration of the subject areas, you should have drawn your opinions and thoughts. Although you will have critically examined case studies and the work of academics, now you have the opportunity, within an extended assessment, to develop a truly critical approach to your work.

As Democritus suggests, everyone has opinions and here is your opportunity to express your opinions based on your own exploration of a specific topic. Of course, as has been stated earlier, you have to support your perspectives with evidence. This evidence can be derived from a combination of both primary and secondary research.

● Using previous experiences

By the time you have reached either your third or fourth year of study, you will have completed several individual and group pieces of coursework. If you have followed the guidance highlighted in Chapter 9 and logged your strengths and weaknesses, you should have honed your analytical and writing skills. You should now be ready for your major and final piece of work for your degree. It is important to remember that dissertations and other projects often accrue double the points or credits of an ordinary module. Therefore, the outcome of your dissertation can have a significant impact upon your final result.

By reviewing your previous experiences you might want to consider the following issues:

- Time keeping – scheduling – planning: Your ability to keep to a scheduled plan of activity.
  If you have written your assignments in haste at the last minute, then repeating this action is highly risky for a dissertation.

- Research skills
  Reflect upon the quality of your research skills for your previous assignments and presentations. What comments have your tutors made in terms of feedback? Are you fully aware of the different types of research skills necessary to undertake a dissertation?
- Analytical skills
  Again, reflect back on tutor comments for your previous work. What do you think you need to do to improve/enhance your analytical skills?
- Quality of your writing
  Have you been able to express yourself effectively in your writing to communicate your knowledge?

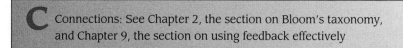

Connections: See Chapter 2, the section on Bloom's taxonomy, and Chapter 9, the section on using feedback effectively

What is a dissertation?

A dissertation can be described as an extended study of a topic (usually chosen by the student) that is related to their field of study (in this case, business). With a dissertation, a student should be able to demonstrate knowledge, the ability to comprehend, apply, critically analyze, synthesize and evaluate. Additionally, a student should be able to justify the choice of research methodology appropriate for the topic of study.

Structure of a dissertation

Dissertations are usually structured as described in this section. However, you will need to check your college/university regulations for how they wish you to present your dissertation.

Title page

This will typically comprise:

- The title of the dissertation
- Your name
- Your college/university number
- Module or course number
- Submission date.

Abstract

This should be between 150 and 250 words long. It should convey concisely the key aims of the dissertation, including an overview of the methodology used.

Declaration

Some colleges and universities ask students to sign a declaration and bind it within their dissertation. The declaration usually states that this is your own original work. Where you have referred to other people's work you have to state that this has been properly acknowledged.

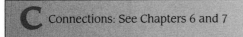
Connections: See Chapters 6 and 7

Acknowledgements

You might have received significant support in terms of time and research documentation from particular organizations. You can use this section to acknowledge their cooperation. Sometimes students want to acknowledge the support provided by their supervisor. In such cases, it is usually advisable to seek their permission first. Not all supervisors, for a variety or reasons, wish to be acknowledged.

Table of contents

This needs to present clearly the various chapter headings and relevant page numbers. In some cases, you might also list major subheadings.

List of tables

All tables need to be sequentially numbered.

List of figures

All figures need to be sequentially numbered.

Introduction

This is where you set the scene for the remainder of the dissertation, outlining the topic and why it is being examined. Here, you would also state your research objectives (see later section) and your rationale for choosing this topic.

Literature review

In a literature review, you seek to compare and contrast contemporary writings on elements of your chosen topic. For example, take the topic of the success rate of mergers and acquisitions (M&As) in Hungary. Here, you would examine the different perspectives writers have on what constitutes successful M&As. Your aim is to draw out the different points of view. Several writers might share a particular point of view; others might not agree. Does the multi-shared point of view have greater validity than the view proposed by a single author? These are issues that you can draw out and discuss.

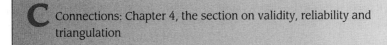
Connections: Chapter 4, the section on validity, reliability and triangulation

Methodology

This is your *justified* approach to how you researched the topic – your research strategy. For example, you might have chosen to use purely secondary sources as the foundation for your critical review. This might be perfectly valid; however, you will need to explain why you chose such a route.

You might set out with good intentions, only to find various obstacles prevent you from undertaking part of your methodology. Sometimes the problems are minor and easily resolved, other times they are not. For example, many students state that they are going to conduct primary research through employee questionnaires and interviews. This might be a valid approach supported with good intentions. However, the company might decide, for whatever reason, that they no longer want to participate in your research.

Contrary to what you might think at the time, this is not the end of your dissertation. Whether there are either minor or major difficulties, it is always advisable to have a section within your methodology chapter entitled 'Difficulties or research limitations'. While it is beneficial to state the difficulties encountered (proving that research rarely goes according to plan), you should also state how you attempted to overcome the difficulties. In the case cited above, you could revert to using company information (in the public domain), as well as other secondary sources.

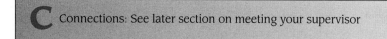

C   Connections: See later section on meeting your supervisor

Analysis and findings

This is where you will use various models and theories to examine the problem or issue under investigation. It is important that you also refer to the different perspectives stated in your literature review, linking them to your analysis. As a result of your analysis, you will have various results or findings. These need to be stated clearly and linked back to your overall research question.

Recommendations

As a result of your analysis, you might see the opportunity to present various recommendations. This can be a worthwhile approach. However, you will need to support your recommendations with evidence (typically drawn from your analysis and literature review). Evidential support provides a strong case for your recommendations.

Conclusions

This draws the work to a close, providing you with the opportunity to link various issues together. Furthermore, it allows you to state whether or not the research objectives have been met. It is advisable to provide a rationale if a research objective has either not been met or has only partly been met. Again, this will demonstrate that you are thinking about the limitations/difficulties of undertaking a research project of this scale.

References

Your work (as with assignments) should contain appropriate referencing throughout. Furthermore, there should be a full list of references listed at the end of the dissertation.

Appendices

These should be individually numbered. Normally, appendices contain supporting material that would be inappropriate within the main body of text. For example, if you were examining a large conglomerate such as the Tata Group of India, you might list all the subsidiary companies in an appendix.

● Opportunities presented by dissertations

A dissertation provides you with the opportunity to:

- Research and write up a topic of your choice.
- Be supervised or guided by an individual who has knowledge and understanding of the topic area. Consider this in the same vein as a good manager providing advice within a business setting.
- Research and write up a lengthy document. Normally an undergraduate dissertation varies from 5,000–10,000 words, while a Master's dissertation varies from 12,000–20,000 words in length. Compare this with an assignment that might be between 1,500–4,000 words in length. In a business environment, you might be expected to research and write reports and other documents. These might vary considerably in the length and level of detail required. Therefore, your work on a dissertation can provide you with valuable experience across a range of issues, from analytical thinking to time management.
- Assemble information from a variety of sources at a variety of levels into a logical, coherent (thus, readable) written work.
- Further enhance your critical thinking and reasoning skills. In business, it is important (often vital) to be able to evaluate established thinking and opinions. Such critical ability could mean the difference between launching a successful product or an unsuccessful one.
- Communicate your opinions on various issues and established thinking. The key here is that you support your perspectives with evidence gathered from your research. It is the same in a business setting, where you will have to justify why you believe a company should undertake certain actions.
- Appreciate the potential problems associated with project management. In essence, you are managing a project where the outcome of the project (your dissertation) has to be delivered by a set date and time. As with many projects, there will gains and losses – both of which might be linked to time. One day you might be ahead of your schedule and the next week you find that you are falling behind. Such issues also occur in business, too, with projects of varying scale and scope. For example, large-scale projects can come in on time and to budget;

however, there are many cases where they do not. For example, the Wembley sports stadium in the UK (opened in 2007) was over 12 months late in completion. This led to the transfer of various events to other stadia around the country. In such cases, severe daily financial penalties can be incurred. Equally, in terms of your dissertation, you might have to forfeit marks for late submission. This could actually result in the difference in your grade point or, indeed, the difference between a pass and a fail.

A few thoughts to help your approach

Choose your topic area carefully

There are several questions that you need to consider prior to embarking on a dissertation:

- Does this topic *really* interest you?
  There is no point in undertaking a dissertation subject that does not interest you, as you will soon become bored and disinterested. Even if you take longer to decide your topic, choose one that does interest you.
- Are you *committed* to this topic area? This links to the question above. Commitment means more than spending an hour or two in the library. It could well mean examining pages of journal articles, travelling to interview executives and spending hours puzzling over contradictions in your research.
- Is it feasible?
  We might have a great idea for a dissertation – but is it a feasible project to undertake? There simply might be insufficient information available to help you develop the idea beyond a couple of hundred words.
- Are there secondary research materials available?
  You might have a great idea for a dissertation. However, you need to make sure that there is sufficient secondary information available to progress. For example, are there journal articles? What about access to management and research reports? Is there government information available? In the vast majority of cases, the material does exist.
- Can the secondary information be relatively easily accessed?
  With the use of the Internet (bare in mind the various *caveats* stated previously), online libraries and government sources, the vast majority of secondary sources can be accessed.
- How accurate are the secondary sources?
  As part of your exploration, you will need to validate and triangulate the use of secondary sources to support your analysis.
- What is likelihood of you gaining access to organizations/companies/government agencies?
  This is an area that often proves problematic. Students sometimes perceive that both company executives and government official will agree to appointments (sometimes with short notice). The level of cooperation will vary from none

whatsoever to the allocation of staff for interviews and significant amounts of documentation. However, you need to investigate whether or not you will gain the cooperation and support before you embark upon the dissertation. Moreover, you must consider that some governments are much more supportive in providing information than others.

- What research techniques will you will have to master?
  You will also need to consider the different types of techniques that you will have to understand, prior to embarking upon your research. Additionally, within a dissertation you will have to justify the research approach that you have taken. Therefore, it is vital that you read a quality book on research methodology (see the section on further reading at the end of this chapter).

Narrow your choice of topic

- You need to be sure that you are defining a real problem, studying a real business issue or a combination of both.
- You need to be sure that you will learn sufficient about the topic to analyze it thoroughly and draw realistic conclusions.
- You need to be sure that you can write it up convincingly and methodically.
- One problem often associated with dissertations is that of analyzing a too large, complex or ill-defined subject area. You need to be focused on a topic area that is manageable. It is very easy at the start of developing a dissertation to say that you intend to tackle this or that angle. However, is it realistic within the timeframe that you will be given?

Definition and questions

- Can you define the problem or issue in a single sentence/paragraph? What is it that you are trying to achieve/analyze?
  This will help you to formulate the topic that you want to study. Once you have done that, can you turn it into a question?
- For example, your idea might be 'A study of mergers and acquisitions in Hungary'. This is a particularly large topic area. By focusing and changing it into a question, the topic can become more manageable – for example: 'What were the positive and negative aspects of M&A in Hungary between 1990–2000?' Yes, this is still a large topic – however, it is focused on a ten-year period and will examine both the positive and negative aspects of such M&As.
- If you construct a question for your title, you can keep returning to it and check whether or not you are answering the question.
  Such an approach will help keep you focused on the topic. When you are writing a dissertation of between 10,000 and 20,000 words, it is very easy to become distracted and venture off course.

Supplementary research objectives

- Once you have formulated your topic question, you will need to formulate a series of research objectives. In other words, what are you attempting to investigate? So, if we take the research question stated above ('What were the positive and negative aspects of M&A in Hungary between 1990–2000?'), the research objectives could be to:

- Assess the degree of success of M&As within Hungary during the period 1990–2000.
- Ascertain the key factors for successful M&As in Hungary.
- Determine the reasons for the failure of certain M&As in Hungary.
- Make recommendations for companies considering M&A activity in Hungary.
- It is advisable to keep the number of research objectives to a manageable size – say, four or five.
- You will refer to these (to a greater or lesser degree) throughout your dissertation. However, when you come to preparing your conclusion you should refer to them directly. It is usually in your conclusion that you would 'answer' the research objectives.

Scheduling

- It is vital that you *allocate* sufficient time to this project. Occasionally, students underestimate the level of resources (especially in time and energy) required to complete a dissertation. Furthermore, assumptions are often made that 'nothing will go wrong', that everything will be straightforward. What has to be considered is that problems occur beyond the realms of the dissertation itself – for example, personal illness and your computer crashing. Therefore, it is advisable to incorporate time for the unexpected problems that just might occur along the way.
- To assist you, it is recommended that you create a research/study timetable. This is an effective means of time management. Your supervisor will normally discuss this with you.

> **C** Connections: Chapter 4

- The key is to start early. There is no reason why you should not be thinking of a topic in your second year of study. Focus on the areas that you enjoy exploring, try to achieve a sense of a particular area that would sustain your interest (and enjoyment).
- The following are some of the time issues that you will need to build into your plan:

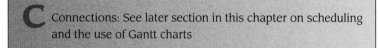

> **C** Connections: See later section in this chapter on scheduling and the use of Gantt charts

○ Reading around the topic area
   You will need to explore a range of sources, not all of which will be in your university library or online.

○ Travel time
   If you are either conducting primary research or visiting other libraries, you will need to build travel time into your schedule.

○ Questionnaires/surveys
   These take time to design. Although your supervisor will normally provide some guidance on these, you should really test them out first. You will need time for the testing and examination of the results, restructuring of the questionnaires/survey (if required), conducting the real questionnaires/surveys, the analysis and writing up.

○ Interviews
   If you are interviewing people and taping the conversations, you will need to allocate time for transcription. Never underestimate how long it takes to transcribe a single hour of taped interviews. It might well take you some four hours or more to transcribe one single hour.

○ Writing up
   In allocating time for the writing up, include allowances for:
   – Computer and machine failure
      Machines are not perfect and nor are we perfect operators. It is better to assume that something will go wrong rather than hope that it does not.
   – The physical typing
      If you have not been trained as a typist, then it will take you longer (no matter how fast you might be using two fingers). Also bear in mind that, until now, you have only had to type up between 1,500 and 4,000 (at maximum) for your assignments. A dissertation is very different, in both its scale and its credit value to your degree.
   – Grammar checking
      If English is not your first language and you are not particularly strong in writing in English, then allocate more time. It is vital that you check your grammar both during your writing up and once you have finished the draft. Ask someone who is highly proficient to read through and help you correct your spelling and grammar – remember to build this time into your schedule too.
   – Meetings with your supervisor and feedback
      Your supervisor will comment on your work. As stated elsewhere in this chapter, it is important to realize the value of this feedback and incorporate any necessary changes. This might also mean seeking out additional literature to evaluate.
   – Final read through
      Once you have completed your final draft, read through it once more as a final check. This gives you the opportunity to correct any major error, should you find one.

– Printing and binding

If you are intending to use college or university printing facilities, bear in mind that you will not be the only student. Leaving it to the last day could be disastrous, especially if their computers crash! If the dissertation regulations state that you have to use a specific outside binder, then you will have to arrange a time when you can take your work to them. Again, you will not be the only student having their dissertation bound. If the binders are particularly busy, then they might not be able to slot you in at the last minute. Hence, your dissertation will be delayed.

– Delivery

Suggest that you deliver your bound dissertation a couple of days prior to the deadline. Then you will know it has been delivered safely and you can stop worrying about it.

Back-ups

- We are perhaps all guilty of being ever-trusting of computer hard drives, floppy disks and memory sticks. Although technology and the robustness of design/manufacture are forever improving, there are still risks. While memory sticks are a wonderful development by the very nature of their size (and they are getting smaller), they can be easily lost.
- To reduce risk of losing all your data and sheer hard work: (a) back up your files with a copy on another memory stick that is kept safe; (b) send a copy (and all your updates) to a friend via email. If either your memory sticks are lost or your computer is damaged, then you still have access to your work.
- Your supervisor and your college might be sympathetic to the loss of your data. However, many regulations state that computer problems are not ground for extensions. Therefore, you might be placed in the difficult situation of having to submit work that you know is of a lower standard.

Cheating

DON'T!

Colleges and universities have strict rules on cheating. Do not take the risk – you are most likely to get caught.

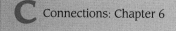

Connections: Chapter 6

● Working with your supervisor

Typically, a member of staff will be allocated to be your dissertation supervisor. You should meet with your supervisor on a regular basis at mutually convenient times. It is important to build trust with your supervisor, especially if you have not studied with them before – you need to be able to work with them. Later sections in this chapter will help you towards this goal.

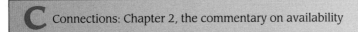

C Connections: Chapter 2, the commentary on availability

The usual role of the supervisor is to provide relevant advice. However, it must be stressed that a supervisor is only a guide or facilitator. You need to undertake the research demonstrating your knowledge and skills. The study elements on which you can normally expect support are:

- The feasibility of the research topic, based on your proposal
  Is it achievable, too narrow or too broad?
- Potential literature sources.
  Guidance on where to look – however, you will need to undertake the investigation.
- Research design and methodology.
- Analytical techniques.
- Potential validity of arguments and hypotheses (supposition made as a basis for reasoning).
- Areas for improvement, based upon either a sample chapter or a full draft of the text.

It is not the responsibility of your supervisor to:

- Undertake your literature search for you.
- Arrange interviews for you.
- Manage the project.
- Write up the research findings/report.
- Prepare the final draft.
- Correct your grammar and spelling throughout.

Pre-first meeting

Make sure that you have completed any tasks that have been previously agreed (by email or telephone). It is usual for a supervisor to request that you bring along to the first meeting an outline of the information that you have gathered to date. Moreover, you will need to be prepared to answer the following questions:

- 'Why have you chosen this particular topic?'
- 'What do you hope to gain from doing this dissertation?'

Usually, the aim here is twofold: (a) to understand the motives behind your selection; and (b) to gauge how much knowledge you already possess on the subject.

Pre-regular meetings

Make sure that you have completed any tasks agreed at the previous meeting and/or through other communication.

Prepare a list of questions. You might have a pre-arranged agreement with your supervisor that such questions must be forwarded to them prior to your meeting. This will give your supervisor an opportunity to consider them in advance of the meeting.

Forward to your supervisor (in good time) any notes that they wish to see prior to the meeting. Out of basic courtesy, do not leave forwarding of the notes to an hour or so beforehand.

The meeting

Be punctual!

Again, view this from a business perspective where punctuality (or lack of it) can influence the tone and outcome of the meeting. From the perspectives of courtesy, effectiveness and efficiency, be punctual for all business meetings. Moreover, with regard to your supervisor, he or she might have another meeting scheduled directly after yours. They will not compromise that time so, by being late, you have lost both valuable time and opportunity for discussion.

Arrive at the meeting prepared: Whatever your supervisor has asked you to prepare for that session, make sure that you are ready to present. The setting of such tasks is to help you remain on track and focused.

Take a notepad and pen with you – a combination of personal experience and discussions with supervisors across the university and college sector show it is surprising how many students overlook this point. In a business setting, you would be expected to arrive at a meeting suitably equipped with pad and pen, so keep to that business mindset. Even though your supervisor might keep a written record of your meetings (matters discussed and action points), it remains your responsibility to make appropriate notes. These notes can include:

- Your responses to your supervisor's questions.
- Your supervisor's responses to your questions.
- Ideas you might have that arise out of the discussion with your supervisor.
- Actions that your supervisor wants you to undertake (and complete) by a set date.

Be prepared to discuss your submitted questions. Often, an outcome of the discussion is a further list of questions. Again, take the opportunity to discuss these supplementary questions. Equally, you might have heard some breaking news that is relevant to your dissertation. For instance, your dissertation might be on an aspect of company mergers and acquisitions. The breaking news could refer the announcement that Corporation X is seeking a hostile takeover of Company Z. This might raise questions in your mind (and, perhaps, the supervisor's mind as well) in relation to your research. Once again, subject to time, you have an opportunity for discussion.

Be prepared to discuss issues and your progress. As stated earlier, part of your supervisor's role is that of facilitator. They will want to know:

- How you are progressing in line with your planned schedule.
- Any academic difficulties that might have arisen since the previous meeting. If so, what possible solutions have you considered? For instance, you might have stated that you sought to interview a particular CEO. A meeting had been arranged but, unfortunately, they had to cancel in order to attend a meeting at a subsidiary company overseas. They might have been very apologetic – but, understandably, they have to focus on their business. Your solution might be contacting the CEO's personal assistant to see whether another time could be arranged or whether you could submit questions in writing. The latter option permits the CEO to respond at a time convenient to them – say, when they are travelling home from a meeting (assuming that the meeting went well!). Whatever, the situation, your supervisor will want to know how you tackled the problem and the rationale behind the solution. Once again, this has a direct relationship to real-world business activities. For example:
  - At whatever level you are within an organization, you will have to work with both senior and junior colleagues. The success – or otherwise – will often depend on your level of tact and diplomacy. This particular example demonstrates how the student might seek to maintain contact with a busy CEO without antagonizing them.
  - In business, you will face various challenges and problems. While not all can be resolved, you might be measured on how you seek to solve problems and engage with the challenges.

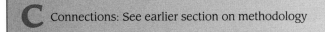

C Connections: See earlier section on methodology

Develop your active listening skills to check your understanding. It is one thing to listen to what a supervisor is saying to you; it is quite another in terms of understanding. Telford and Groucutt (1995) define active listening as a requirement by the listener 'to demonstrate, by working mentally and verbally, an understanding of what is being explained to them'. They suggest that you should 'playback' what you have heard. A playback can take the form of 'In other words, what you are saying is . . . .'

Telford and Groucutt (1995) suggest that there are three reasons for using the playback technique:

- Unlike 'parroting' back the same words, rephrasing requires you to have grasped the concept of what is being stated. When an individual hears their own concepts played back to them, in different words, they realize that you are focusing on their agenda.
- Rephrasing triggers more questions or requests for further information.

- It helps to track, summarize and reach agreement on what has been said, and ensures that you've accurately heard what has been said.

Such techniques for active listening are far from new – the Greek philosopher and teacher Socrates used the same techniques with great skill. Active listening techniques will not only be valuable while working with your supervisor, they will also be of immense value when you enter employment. Use this opportunity to build your skills in active listening.

Post-meeting

Take actions based upon the outcome of the meeting. For instance, start researching new material on a specific issue/problem. Do not leave this until the last moment prior to the next meeting. Instead, schedule it in as part of your usual planning process. It is often best to allocate time directly after the meeting to assess what needs to be achieved and within what timeframe (usually by the next meeting).

Elaborate your own notes. Check that you are clear, in your own mind, what was discussed at the meeting (this links back to active listening as stated above). If you are unclear about any issue, make a note of it and reflect upon it and/or email your supervisor (if you have agreed this between you) to gain clarification.

Feedback on your draft submissions

Students often feel that they have to produce a totally finished chapter before a supervisor will read it. More to the point, they feel that they can write a finished chapter in one attempt. Can I dispel you of this thought? Very few people, in any profession, can write anything straight off. Life is often a series of drafts before any form of committal. Therefore, we must toil at our work, honing it until it accurately reflects our views and intensions – for that is what a dissertation should do: reflect what we have investigated and believe.

Typically, a supervisor will read and comment upon drafts, usually chapter by chapter. The objective is to provide you with constructive comments and, perhaps, some direction (overall approach, potential additional reading sources and structure). However, it is your responsibility to translate these comments into actions. The submission of drafts must be in agreement with your supervisor. Do not send them an email attachment of 10,000 words and expect feedback the next day!

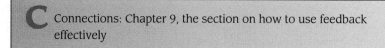

C Connections: Chapter 9, the section on how to use feedback effectively

Start preparation for the next meeting – it will come sooner than you think!

Problems

Contact your supervisor immediately if you are encountering problems, especially if they are personal problems that will (most likely) impact upon your dissertation schedule. Sadly, life rarely goes according to the plans etched within our minds. If there are personal difficulties, then it is imperative that you seek help and advice, and this includes keeping your supervisor aware of the situation. You might not wish to elaborate upon the details of the specific issue but it is best to keep the supervisor alerted to the fact that there is a personal issue that will impact upon the dissertation. If you keep the supervisor in the information loop (even with only superficial details), you will usually find them most supportive.

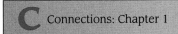

Connections: Chapter 1

Your dissertation proposal

A dissertation proposal is a document that you complete prior to meeting your supervisor and undertaking the research. It is a means of getting you to focus on what you want to do.

Example 13.1 is a generic outline of a dissertation proposal. Your college/university will have its own format for you to complete. However, this will help you to think about what you want to do, why you want to do it and how you are going to undertake it. This structure is particularly helpful if you are planning to investigate your dissertation idea early.

Example 13.1   Outline of a dissertation proposal

Proposed title

While this is most probably going to be a working title, it will still help you to focus on the topic. As stated earlier, this chapter seeks to create a question rather than a statement. Furthermore, consider the breadth and depth of the topic. Is it too broad or too narrow? Some of the questions below will also help you to address these issues.

What is the proposed dissertation about?

Outline what you believe (as you have not yet conducted detailed research) the dissertation will cover. For example, as stated earlier, a dissertation topic might be: 'The positive and negative aspects of M&A activity within Hungary between 1990–2000'.

In constructing your proposal, try to provide as much information as possible as this will: (a) help in justifying the topic; and (b) help you to think about where you might find the necessary information.

Why have you chosen this topic area?

Seek to justify your choice. Why do you want to explore this topic? What excites you about it? Are you passionate enough? Will your enthusiasm for the topic sustain you through the research and writing up?

If you are not passionate and committed, then perhaps it is the wrong topic for you? It is better to make this discovery at this stage than halfway through your dissertation, when it will be too late.

Research objectives

As stated earlier, these are the issues that you are attempting to investigate. You will probably hone these over time, especially with the support of your supervisor.

Proposed methodology

What methods are you going to use to research this topic area? To help you in this quest, it is advisable to read a text specifically on research methods – for example, Saunders, M. Lewis, P. and Thornhill, A. (2007) *Research Methods for Business Students* (4th edn) Harlow: FT/Prentice Hall.

Terminology – key words and phrases

It is useful to note down key words and phrases. The listing of terminology will help you to search for the relevant information in journals, textbooks and other sources. If we use the example of Hungarian mergers and acquisitions cited above, the key words and phrases could be:

Acquisitions
Alliances
Mergers
Mergers and acquisitions
Mergers and acquisitions in Hungary
Mergers and acquisitions in Eastern Europe

These terms can be used, for example, to search an online journals database such as Emerald. From the list retrieved, you will be able to consider which journal articles are relevant for your proposed discussion and analysis.

Possible information sources

Where will you go to gain information? Sources could include the university library, online resources (company websites, journal databases, government and NGO websites), other national and business libraries, company headquarters, government departments and so on. If you plan to start investigating your topic early, then you can test out if these sources are easily available.

Potential difficulties

You will not be able to foresee all the potential difficulties over the lifetime of a dissertation. However, sometimes just examining your topic and the resources required might indicate potential difficulties. For example, consider the following scenario:

Scenario

A student studying in the UK wants to investigate the management of the garment industry in Bangladesh. This is a worthy topic – however, it could be fraught with difficulties.

- Does the student have access (for instance, via family) to garment companies in Bangladesh?
- Will the student travel to Bangladesh to conduct the research? If so, what are the cost implications?
- While they are away, how will they communicate with their supervisor? Yes, there is email but this is not always reliable and it is difficult making extensive comments on electronic drafts.
- Are the statistics on the industry reliable?

These perceived difficulties are not insurmountable. However, you will need to have a plan that you are able to discuss with your supervisor.

● Time scales

Create a *realistic* operational plan that illustrates when you aim to undertake certain tasks. You might want to use a scheduling system such as a Gantt chart to indicate how long you intend to spend upon a particular task. Figure 13.1 shows a 12-week schedule and the various tasks to be completed within that time span. However, this is only a stylized example and you will have to devise a Gantt chart to illustrate your own particular needs and timescale.

TASK	Week 1	Week 2	Week 3	Week 4	Week 5	Week 6	Week 7	Week 8	Week 9	Week 10	Week 11	Week 12
Week commencing												
Supervisor meetings	▓	▓	▓	▓	▓	▓	▓					
Supervisor feedback	▓	▓	▓	▓	▓	▓	▓					
Reading and exploring	▓	▓	▓	▓								
Analysis				▓	▓							
Writing up						▓	▓	▓				
Taking a break *									▓			
Proof reading										▓		
Printing and binding											▓	
Submit												▓

* It is important that while working on your dissertation you take a break for at least a week. This will help you to refresh yourself and examine the dissertation in a 'fresh light'. In the example above the 'break' is taken between the end of writing up and proof reading. However, it is down to you how many breaks you take and during which period. That said, always make sure that you take some form of break, otherwise you may become too narrow in your approach and miss the wider issues, simply because you are tired. Always try and find a way of coming to your work afresh.

Figure 13.1 An Illustration of a Gantt chart

 Connections: A downloadable form is available on the website: www.palgrave.com/studyskills/groucutt

● Feedback and progress logs

As stated earlier, it is important that you keep a record of your meetings with your supervisor. Although they might annotate your work, it is often what they say in your face-to-face meetings that will aid (and drive) your progress. It is, therefore, important that you capture this information. You could tape your meetings (with your supervisor's permission) and/or create a log of the meeting (see Figure 13.2).

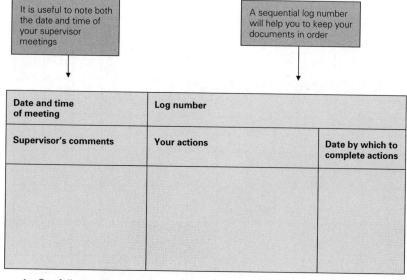

Date and time of meeting	Log number	
Supervisor's comments	Your actions	Date by which to complete actions

1 Carefully note down your supervisor's comments. Check with them that you have understood them correctly. Some of their comments will be in writing (annotation of your drafts). Add them to this log.

2 Clearly identify what you are going to do as a result of your supervisor's comments. This is particularly important if your supervisor has suggested radical changes, for example, a re-structuring of your literature review.

3 In order to keep to your proposed schedule you need to identify by which date you intend to complete the necessary changes (actions). Furthermore, your supervisor may dictate the timing of these changes (actions). They may want to see, for example, a revised chapter draft by a specific date.

Figure 13.2 Progress log

While the log captures commentary, it should not be considered a passive record. It is, rather, an action-oriented record of events. Once completing the log (both during and directly after your meeting), you should be fully aware of what you need to achieve and by when.

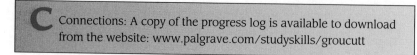

C Connections: A copy of the progress log is available to download from the website: www.palgrave.com/studyskills/groucutt

Reflection zone

Here are a few key summary points for you to reflect upon:

- The aims and purpose of a dissertation, including the opportunities presented to you.
- Consider how you will choose a dissertation topic and substantiate that choice.
- Consider the general structure of a dissertation and how you will approach the research and writing up of the work. This is particularly important in justifying your proposal.
- As with assignments, consider how you will time manage this project.
- Anticipate potential difficulties – for example, access to research data and interviewees.
- Seek a working relationship with your supervisor that is a mutually beneficial experience.

Additional resource

Saunders, M., Lewis, P. and Thornhill, A. (2007) *Research Methods for Business Students* (4th edn), Harlow: FT/Prentice Hall.

14 What's Next for You?

'Le seul rêve intéresse. Vivre sans rêve, qu'est-ce?'
(The dream, alone, is of interest. What is life, without a dream?)

La Princesse Lointaine (1895), Act 1, Sc. 4,
Edmond Rostand, 1868–1918, French playwright

Contents

▶ Introduction
▶ What do you want to do?
▶ Your *curriculum vitae*
▶ Advice on references
▶ What will business seek from you?
▶ Staying in touch – *alumni*
▶ Further reading

© Laura Furniss 2008

Introduction

Graduation is not the end – it is but only one phase in your life and career. Moreover, it could be argued that it is really just the beginning. Whatever role you undertake from now on, you will need to consider how the ideas, issues and concepts that you have learnt can be applied to the real world. Equally, you will need to contribute your own opinions supported by rational arguments.

This short chapter considers some of the 'what next' issues that you will need to consider once you have successfully completed your programme of study.

What do you want to do?

This is a far from an easy question to answer.

Some of you will already know exactly what you want to be – for example, junior manager in the family firm. Others might be thinking of further qualifications. Many of you will still be uncertain of exactly what you want to do. Perhaps there are several factors that you should consider:

- Is there a particular company that you would like to work for?
  Many companies offer graduate placement schemes, where they train and develop you in their operating styles. This period (usually six to twelve months) can provide you with an opportunity to work within a company prior to focusing upon the role that you wish to undertake.
- You might want to consider additional qualifications, whether academic or professional.
  These will range from Masters/PhD through to CIMA and ACCA qualifications for accountants. Of course, you will need to reflect on:
  - Costs
    These will vary depending upon the level of qualification, mode of study (for example, online learning) and location. In the UK, for instance, a one-year, full-time, on-campus MSc programme will cost in the region of UK£10,000–20,000.
  - Type of qualification
    You will need to reflect upon what might be the most appropriate qualification. For instance, you might have studied for a BA (Management) degree and you wish to continue with your studies, but from an international perspective. Therefore, you might consider an MSc in International Management or eBusiness.
  - Location
    If you are seeking an on-campus programme, will you stay with your current university or opt for another? In addition, will the location be in a different part of the country or, indeed, overseas? While there is clearly value in carrying on your studies within a familiar environment, it is worth appraising other institutions and finding out what they can offer. For instance, if you studied your undergraduate programme in the UK, you might want to consider an institution in, say, Australia or New Zealand. Along with the academic experience, there is also the experiencing of the culture of another country.

● Your *curriculum vitae*

Developing a *curriculum vitae* that demonstrates your worth or value to an organization can provide significant benefits. Organizations are increasing taking a holistic view of candidates – considering, for example, whether they are a well-informed and confident person. Therefore, a *CV* is more than a catalogue of qualifications and hobbies. It provides you with an opportunity to make a supporting statement about you and what you have achieved.

So, for example, if there were significant levels of group work within your programme you could outline:

- ● What you have gained from the group working experience.

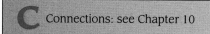
Connections: see Chapter 10

- ● How you overcame any difficulties.
  This highlights problem solving, a valuable skill in today's highly competitive marketplace.
- ● If you were the group leader what did that mean for you?
  This can also relate to handling difficult situations, for example, a team member who was not engaging in the exercise.

Additionally, you can incorporate your contribution to other activities within the college or university, for example:

- ● Membership of clubs and societies.
  Your contribution to, for example, debates, promotion and the organization of events.
- ● Being a Student Representative and your interaction between students and academic staff.
  This also provides experience of attending committee meetings and first-hand knowledge of how they operate. Such experiences can provide you with valuable insights into both the positive and negative aspects of meetings. You can use this knowledge when it comes to your attendance at meetings in the business world.

Some institutions provide the opportunity for placement or internships within organizations. Cite in your *CV*:

- ● What you believe you gained from the placement experience.
  For example, an understanding of how businesses operate, team building, mentoring, running meetings and so on.

- How you linked your studies to the placement experience and *vice versa*.
  For example, let us say you were working within the accounts department of an organization. Were you able to use your academic knowledge to understand how the accounts department linked to other operations within the organization?

Advice on references

When you come to applying – either for another academic/vocational course or for a job – you will have to supply references. You might seek these references from one or more of your tutors. Moreover, if you have undertaken a placement/internship you might want to ask your line manger for a reference.

The following is to help you understand the reference process:

- Check the institution's regulations and procedures for providing references.
  The institution might have a policy, for instance, where references must be addressed to named individuals within named organizations and not 'To whom it may concern'.
- Seek permission from the person whom you would like to act as a referee.
  This is a common courtesy. If possible, ask them face-to-face whether you can list them on the application form.
- Check the requirements of the organization to which you are applying. For example, let us say you were applying for a Master's degree. Colleges and universities often differ in the issues that they wish referees to address for such applications.
- Give your referee plenty of advanced warning.
  Do not turn up at their office and expect a reference by the end of the day. Again, it is an issue of common courtesy.

What will business seek from you?

In an increasingly competitive and global commercial environment, organizations need graduates who are:

- Self-confident – but with a realization that you do not 'know it all' and, therefore, will listen to the views of others.
- Knowledgeable – not only about their subject, but also about the wider world (that is, why it is important, as stressed throughout this book, that you remain aware of key business and current affairs issues).
- Thirsty for knowledge – wanting to soak up more information. Gaining knowledge is an ongoing quest. In today's dynamic world, situations can change in a matter of hours, so you need to be continually enhancing your knowledge base.

- Able to thinking critically and analytically – when there are several options on the table you will need to examine each option critically to determine the most suitable. Of course, choosing the wrong option could be detrimental to the future of the organization.
- Able to work with a diverse range of people, in terms of skills, temperament and attitudes.

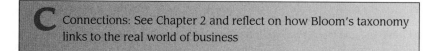

Connections: See Chapter 2 and reflect on how Bloom's taxonomy links to the real world of business

Staying in touch – *alumni*

When you graduate with your business degree, you become an *alumnus* of the college or university. Your college/university will seek to stay in touch with you, advising you of new developments and, perhaps, future opportunities.

We are all dependent on the knowledge and experience of others in order to enhance our understanding of the world. In the future, consider how you might be able to contribute to the knowledge of others. This might be through providing placement opportunities for young undergraduates and/or returning to provide guest lectures on what you have learnt through the practice of business. Through this support we help others to succeed in the future.

'All experience is an arch to build upon.'

The Education of Henry Adams (1907), ch. 6.

Henry Brooks Adams, 1838–1918. American historian and political essayist

Further reading

Littleford, D., Halstead, J. and Mulraine, C. (2004) *Career Skills: Opening Doors into the Job Market* Basingstoke: Palgrave Macmillan.

Appendix

Subject reading

The purpose of this section is to provide you with guided reading, subject by subject, for the components of a business degree. This is by no means either a definitive or exhaustive list. Subjects will vary depending on the specialism of your particular degree programme. Equally, the resources stated vary in the level of difficulty. Some are basic introductory texts that provide a broad overview of the subject, while others explore specific issues in greater depth.

The important concept to remember is that these are not merely isolated sub-categories of business. All these sub-categories are interrelated. If you view business as this interrelationship of ideas and practices, then you will have a greater appreciation of how business operates.

In addition to books, a brief selection of websites is also provided.

Accounting and finance

Arnold, G. (2005) *Corporate Financial Management* (3rd edn), Harlow: FT/Prentice Hall.

Atrill, P. (2003) *Financial Management for Non-Specialists*, Harlow: FT/Prentice Hall.

Bickerstaff, G. (ed.) (1997) *Mastering Finance*, Harlow: FT/Prentice Hall.

Drury, C. (2004) *Management and Cost Accounting* (6th edn), London: Thomson Learning.

Dyson, J.R. (2007) *Accounting for Non-Accounting Students* (7th edn), Harlow: FT/Prentice Hall.

Jones, M. (2006) *Accounting* (2nd edn), Chichester: Wiley.

Nicholson, M. (2006) *Mastering Accounting Skills* (3rd edn), Basingstoke: Palgrave Macmillan.

Owen, G., Law. J. and Hussey, R. (2005) *A Dictionary of Accounting*, Oxford: Oxford University Press.

Smullen, J. and Hand, N. (2005) *A Dictionary of Finance and Banking*, Oxford: Oxford University Press.

Sutherland, J and Canwell, D. (2004) *Key Concepts in Accounting and Finance*, Basingstoke: Palgrave Macmillan.

Business biographies (companies and individuals)

Anders, G. (2003) *Perfect Enough: Carly Fiorina and the Reinvention of Hewlett-Packard*, New York: Portfolio.

Carlzon, J. (1989) *Moments of Truth*, New York: HarperCollins.

Jones, G. (2005) *Renewing Unilever: Transformation and Tradition*, Oxford: Oxford University Press.

Malone, M.S. (2007) *Bill & Dave: How Hewlett and Packard Built the World's Greatest Company*, New York: Portfolio/Penguin.

Mantle, J. (2000) *Benetton: The Family, the Business and the Brand*, London: Warner Books.

Nathan, J. (2000) *Sony: The Private Life,* London: HarperCollins.

Schultz, H. (1998) *Pour Your Heart Into It: How Starbucks Built a Company One Cup at a Time*, New York: Hyperion.

Welch, J. and Welch, S. (2005) *Winning*, London and New York: HarperCollins.

Business (general)

Barnes, S. (2003) *Business Explained*, London: Hodder & Stoughton.

Groucutt, J. and Griseri, P. (2004) *Mastering e-Business*, Basingstoke: Palgrave Macmillan.

Klein. N. (2000) *No Logo,* London: Flamingo.

Marcouse, I. (2003) *Business Studies* (2nd edn), London: Hodder & Stoughton.

Micklethwait, J. and Wooldridge, A. (2005*) The Company: A Short History of a Revolutionary Idea,* London: Phoenix/Orion.

Pallister, J. and Law, J. (2006) *A Dictionary of Business and Management*, Oxford: Oxford University Press.

Palmer, A. and Hartkey, B. (2002) *The Business Environment* (4th edn), Maidenhead: McGraw-Hill.

Sugar, A. (2006) *The Apprentice*, London: BBC Books.

Sutherland, J. and Canwell, D. (2004) *Key Concepts in Business Practice*, Basingstoke: Palgrave Macmillan.

Vause, B. (1999*) Guide to Analysing Companies*, London: Economist Books.

Economics

Krugman, P. and Wells, R. (2006) *Economics*, Basingstoke: Palgrave Macmillan.

Mulhearn, C., Vane, H. and Eden, J. (2001) *Economics for Business*, Basingstoke: Palgrave Macmillan.

Piggott, J. and Cook, M. (2006) *International Business Economics: A European Perspective* (2nd edn), Basingstoke: Palgrave Macmillan.

Samuelson, P.A. and Nordhaus, B. (2004) *Economics* (18th edn), New York: McGraw-Hill.

Sloman, J. (2004) *The Economic Environment of Business*, Harlow: FT/Prentice Hall.

Entrepreneurship

Burns, P. (2007) *Entrepreneurship and Small Business*, Basingstoke: Palgrave Macmillan.

Ethics

Boatright, J.H. (2000) *Ethics and the Conduct of Business* (3rd edn), New Jersey: Prentice Hall.

Bowie, N.E. and Werhane, P.H. (2005) *Management Ethics*, Oxford: Blackwell Publishing.

Crane, A. and Matten, D. (2006) *Business Ethics: Managing Corporate Citizenship and Sustainability in the Age of Globalization* (2nd edn), Oxford: Oxford University Press.

Jones, C., Parkes, M. and ten Bos, R. (2005) *For Business Ethics: A Critical Approach*, Oxford: Routledge.

LaFollette, H. (ed.) (2005) *The Oxford Handbook of Practical Ethics*, Oxford: Oxford University Press.

Trevino, L.K. and Nelson, K. (2006) *Managing Business Ethics* (4th edn), Chicester: Wiley.

Hospitality and tourism

Bardi, J.A. (2006) *Hotel Front Office Management* (4th edn), Chichester: Wiley.

Goeldner, C.R. and Brent Ritchie, J.R. (2005) *Tourism: Principles, Practices, Philosophies* (10th edn), Chichester: Wiley.

Powers, T. and Barrows, C.W. (2005) *Introduction to the Hospitality Industry* (6th edn), Chichester: Wiley.

Tesone, D.V. (2005) *Hospitality Information Systems and E-Commerce*, Chichester: Wiley.

Weaver, D. and Lawton, L. (2006) *Tourism Management* (3rd edn), Chichester: Wiley.

Human resource management

Bratton, J. and Gold, J. (2003) *Human Resource Management* (3rd edn), Basingstoke: Palgrave Macmillan.

Heery, E. and Noon, M. (2001) *A Dictionary of Human Resource Management*, Oxford: Oxford University Press.

Nieto, M. (2006) *Introduction to Human Resource Management*, Basingstoke: Palgrave Macmillan.

Scullion, H. and Linehan, M. (2005) *International Human Resource Management*, Basingstoke: Palgrave Macmillan.

Tayeb, M. (2004) *International Human Resource Management: A Multinational Company Perspective*, Oxford: Oxford University Press.

Sutherland, J. and Canwell, D. (2004) *Key Concepts in Human Resource Management*, Basingstoke: Palgrave Macmillan.

Innovation

Bessant, J. and Tidd, J. (2007) *Innovation and Entrepreneurship*, Chichester: Wiley.

Conway, S. and Steward, F. (2007) *Managing Innovation*, Oxford: Oxford University Press.

Fagerberg, J., Mowery, D.C. and Nelson, R.R. (eds) (2006) *The Oxford Book of Innovation*, Oxford: Oxford University Press.

Isaken, S. and Tidd, J. (2006) *Meeting the Innovation Challenge*, Chichester: Wiley.

International business

Morrison, J. (2006) *International Business Environment: Global and Local Marketplaces in a Changing World* (2nd edn), Basingstoke: Palgrave Macmillan.

Sutherland, J. and Canwell, D. (2004) *Key Concepts in International Business*, Basingstoke: Palgrave Macmillan.

Rugman, A.M. and Brewer, T.L. (eds) (2003) *The Oxford Handbook of International Business*, Oxford: Oxford University Press.

Trompenaars, F. (2004) *Managing People Across Cultures*, London: Capstone Publishing.

Knowledge management

Burton-Jones, A. (1999) *Knowledge Capitalism*, Oxford: Oxford University Press.

Debowski, S. (2005) *Knowledge Management*, Chichester: Wiley.

Doz, Y., Santos, J. and Williamson, P. (2001) *From Global to Metanational: How Companies Win in the Knowledge Economy*, Boston: Harvard Business School Press.

Ichijo, K. and Nonaka, I. (2006) *Knowledge Creation and Management: New Challenges for Managers*, Oxford: Oxford University Press.

Law

Adams, A. (2006) *Law for Business Students* (4th edn), Harlow: Longman.

Dignam, A. and Lowry, A. (2006) *Company Law* (4th edn), Oxford: Oxford University Press.

Dine, J. (2005) *Company Law* (5th edn), Basingstoke: Palgrave Macmillan.

Judge, S. (2005) *Law for Business Students*, Basingstoke: Palgrave Macmillan.

Keenan, D. (2006) *Smith and Keenan's Law for Business* (13th edn), Harlow: Longman.

MacIntyre, E. (2007) *Business Law* (3rd edn), Harlow: Longman.

Logistics

Christopher, M. (2005) *Logistics and Supply Chain Management: Creating Value Added Networks* (3rd edn), Harlow: FT/Prentice Hall.

Farrington, B. and Lyson, K. (2005) *Purchasing and Supply Chain Management* (7th edn), Harlow: FT/Prentice Hall.

Grant, D., Lambert, D.M., Stock, J.R. and Ellram, L.M. (2005) *Fundamentals of Logistics Management*, Maidenhead: McGraw-Hill.

Hoek, R. van and Harrison, A. (2005) *Logistics Management and Strategy* (2nd edn), Harlow: FT/Prentice Hall.

Management

Boddy, D. (2002) *Management: An Introduction* (2nd edn), Harlow: FT/Prentice Hall.

Drucker, P.F. (2001) *Management Challenges of the 21st Century*, New York: HarperCollins.

Drucker, P.F. (2003) *The Essential Drucker: The Best of Sixty Years of Peter Drucker's Essential Writings on Management*, New York: HarperCollins.

Drucker, P.F. (2006) *Managing Non-Profit Organizations*, New York: HarperCollins.

Hickson, D.J. (2002) *Management Worldwide: Distinctive Styles Amid Globalization*, London: Penguin.

Linstead, S., Fulop, L. and Lilley, S. (2006) *Management and Organization: A Critical Text*, Basingstoke: Palgrave Macmillan.

Margretta, J. (2003) *What Management Is: How It Works and Why It's Everyone's Business*, London: Profile Books.

Maurik, J. van (2001) *Writers on Leadership*, London: Penguin.

Naylor, J. (2003) *Management*. (2nd edn), Harlow: FT/Prentice Hall.

Pettinger, R. (2001) *Mastering Management Skills*, Basingstoke: Palgrave Macmillan.

Pettinger, R. (2006) *Introduction to Management* (4th edn), Basingstoke: Palgrave Macmillan.

Robbins, S.P. and Coulter, M. (2006) *Management* (9th edn), New Jersey: Prentice Hall.

Schermerhorn, J.R. (2004) *Core Concepts of Management*, Chichester: Wiley.

Schermerhorn, J.R. (2006) *Exploring Management*, Chichester: Wiley.

Sutherland, J. and Canwell, D. (2004) *Key Concepts in Management*, Basingstoke: Palgrave Macmillan.

Marketing

Aaker, D.A. (1996) *Building Strong Brands*, New York: Free Press.

Brassington, F. and Pettitt, S. (2006) *Principles of Marketing* (4th edn), Harlow: FT/Prentice Hall.

Brennan, R., Baines, P. and Garneau, P. (2003) *Contemporary Strategic Marketing*, Basingstoke: Palgrave Macmillan.

Gilligan, C. and Wilson, R.M.S. (2004) *Strategic Marketing Management: Planning, Implementation and Control* (3rd edn), Oxford: Butterworth-Heinemann.

Groucutt, J. (2005) *Foundations of Marketing*, Basingstoke: Palgrave Macmillan.

Groucutt, J., Leadley, P. and Forsyth, P. (2004) *Marketing: Essential Principles, New Realities*, London: Kogan Page.

Hollensen, S. (2006) *Global Marketing: A Decision Oriented Approach* (3rd edn), Harlow: FT/Prentice Hall.

Kotler, P., Jatusripitak, S. and Maesincee, S. (1997) *The Marketing of Nations: A Strategic Approach to Building National Wealth*, New York: Free Press.

Mühlbacher, H., Dahringer, L. and Leihs, H. (2006) *International Marketing: A Global Perspective* (3rd edn), London: Thomson Business Press.

Smith, P.R. and Chaffey, D. (2005) *eMarketing eXcellence* (2nd edn), Oxford: Butterworth-Heinemann.

Sutherland, J. and Canwell, D. (2004) *Key Concepts in Marketing*, Basingstoke: Palgrave Macmillan.

Operations

Hill, T. (2004) *Operations Management* (2nd edn), Basingstoke: Palgrave Macmillan.

Looy, B. van, Gremmel, P. and Dierdonck, R. van (2003) *Service Management: An Integrated Approach* (2nd edn), Harlow: FT/Prentice Hall.

Russell, R. and Taylor, B.W. (2005) *Operations Management* (5th edn), Chichester: Wiley.

Slack, N., Chambers, S. and Johnston, R. (2004) *Service Operations Management*, Harlow: FT/Prentice Hall.

Sutherland, J. and Canwell, D. (2004) *Key Concepts in Operations Management*, Basingstoke: Palgrave Macmillan.

Walter, D. and Rainbird, M. (2006) *Strategic Operations Management: A Value Chain Approach*, Basingstoke: Palgrave Macmillan.

Organizational behaviour

Brookes, I. (2003) *Organisational Behaviour: Individuals, Groups and the Organisation*, Harlow: FT/Prentice Hall.

Buchanan, D. and Huczynski, A. (2004) *Organizational Behaviour: An Introductory Text*, Harlow: FT/Prentice Hall.

Hatch, M.J. and Cunliffe, A. (2006) *Organization Theory* (2nd edn), Oxford: Oxford University Press.

Mullins, L. (2005) *Management and Organisational Behaviour*, Harlow: FT/Prentice Hall.

Pettinger, R. (2000) *Mastering Organisational Behaviour*, Basingstoke: Palgrave Macmillan.

Robbins, S.P. and Judge, T.A. (2007) *Organizational Behavior* (12th edn), New Jersey: Prentice Hall.

Project management

Gardiner, P. (2005) *Project Management*, Basingstoke: Palgrave Macmillan.

Retail management

Jackson, T. and Shaw, D. (2000) *Mastering Fashion Buying and Merchandise Management*, Basingstoke: Palgrave Macmillan.

Randall, G. and Seth, A. (2005) *Supermarket Wars: Global Strategies for Food Retailers*, Basingstoke: Palgrave Macmillan.

Spector, R. (2005) *Category Killers: The Retail Revolution and Its Impact on Consumer Culture*, Boston, MA: Harvard Business School Press.

Statistics

Anderson, D.R., Sweeney, D.J., Williams, T.A., Freeman, J. and Shoesmith, E. (2006) *Statistics for Business and Economics*, London: Thomson.

Field, A. (2005) *Discovering Statistics Using SPSS* (2nd edn), London: Sage.

Taylor, S. (2007) *Business Statistics for Non-Mathematicians* (2nd edn), Basingstoke: Palgrave Macmillan.

Upton, G. and Cook, I. (2006) *A Dictionary of Statistics* (2nd edn), Oxford: Oxford University Press.

Strategy and strategic management

Barney, J.B. and Hesterly, W.S. (2006) *Strategic Management and Competitive Advantage: Concepts*, New Jersey: Pearson Prentice Hall.

Besanko, D., Dranove, D., Shanley, M. and Scaefer, S. (2006) *Economics of strategy* (4th edn), Chichester: Wiley.

Bovaird, T. (2006) *Strategic Management in the Public Sector*, Oxford: Oxford University Press.

Grant, R.M. (2004) *Contemporary Strategy Analysis: Concepts, Techniques, Applications* (5th edn), Oxford: Blackwell Publishing.

Grimm, C.M., Lee, H. and Smith, K.G. (2005) *Strategy As Action*, Oxford: Oxford University Press.

HBS (2002) *Harvard Business Review on Advances in Strategy*, Boston: Harvard Business School Press.

Hill, C.W.L and Jones, G.R. (2004) *Strategic Management Theory: An Integrated Approach* (6th edn), Boston and New York: Houghton Mifflin.

Johnson, G. Scholes, K. and Whittington, R. (2004) *Exploring Corporate Strategy* (7th edn), Harlow: FT/Prentice Hall.

Lasserre, P. (2002) *Global Strategic Management*, Basingstoke: Palgrave Macmillan.

Lynch, R. (2005) *Corporate Strategy* (4th edn), Harlow: FT/Prentice Hall.

Mintzberg, H., Ahlstrand, B. and Lampel, J. (1998) *Strategy Safari*, London: FT/Prentice Hall.

Moore, J.I. (2001) *Writers on Strategy and Strategic Management* (2nd edn), London: Penguin.

Pettinger, R. (2004) *Contemporary Strategic Management*, Basingstoke: Palgrave Macmillan.

Porter, M. (1980) *Competitive Strategy*, New York: Free Press.

Porter, M. (1985) *Competitive Advantage*, New York: Free Press.

Sutherland, J. and Canwell, D. (2004) *Key Concepts in Strategic Management*, Basingstoke: Palgrave Macmillan.

White, C. (2004) *Strategic Management*, Basingstoke: Palgrave Macmillan.

Whittington, R. (2000) *What is Strategy and Does it Matter?* (2nd edn), London: Thomson.

● Additional resources

English language support

The following is a selection of books that will help your English language skills, whether English is your first language or not.

Collins (2006) *Collins COBUILD Advanced Learner's English Dictionary* (5th edn), London: HarperCollins.

Collins (2006) *Collins COBUILD English Grammar* (2nd edn), London: HarperCollins.

OUP (2006) *Compact Oxford English Dictionary for University and College Students*, Oxford: Oxford University Press.

Seely, J. (2007) *Oxford A–Z Grammar and Punctuation*, Oxford: Oxford University Press.

Waite, M. (2006) *Oxford Paperback Thesaurus*, Oxford: Oxford University Press.

Research methods

Anderson, V. (2004) *Research Methods in Human Resource Management*, London: Chartered Institute of Personnel and Development.

Brown, R.B. (2006) *Doing Your Dissertation in Business and Management: The Reality of Researching and Writing*, London: SAGE.

Bryman, A. and Bell, E. (2006) *Business Research Methods*, Oxford: Oxford University Press.

Davies, M.B. (2007) *Doing a Successful Research Project*, Basingstoke: Palgrave Macmillan.

Saunders, M., Lewis, P. and Thornhill, A. (2007) *Research Methods for Business Students* (4th edn), Harlow: FT/Prentice Hall.

Smith, M. (2003) *Research Methods in Accounting*, London: Sage.

Veal, A.J. (2006) *Research Methods for Leisure and Tourism: A Practical Guide* (3rd edn), Harlow: FT/Prentice Hall.

Learning styles

Ormrod, J.E. (2007) *Human Learning* (5th edn), New Jersey: Prentice Hall.

Rice, J., Saunders, C. and O'Sullivan, T. (1996) *Successful Groupwork: A Practical Guide for Students in Further and Higher Education*, Oxford: Routledge Falmer.

Websites

Listed below is a brief selection of business-related websites that might prove useful for your studies.

Government departments

www.statistics.gov.uk

This is the official website of the UK's National office of Statistics.

Membership organizations

www.bam.ac.uk

The British Academy of Management encourages the development and sharing of knowledge about management studies. Student membership is available.

www.cipd.co.uk

Chartered Institute of Personnel and Development. This is a professional organization for those studying and working in human resource management.

www.res.org.uk

The Royal Economics Society is a professional association that promotes the study and understanding of economics.

News networks

www.bbc.co.uk

The British Broadcasting Corporation. Access to news 24 hours each day, podcasts and scheduling information. Overall this is a very detailed website.

www.bloomberg.com

This is a financial news network. Information is available via Bloomberg TV, online and in printed magazine format.

www.cnn.com

US and international broadcaster. Overall this is a very detailed website.

Non-governmental organizations

www.ifs.org.uk

This is an independent think tank that provides economic analysis of public policy in the UK.

www.weforum.org

The World Economic Forum is an independent organization based in Switzerland that seeks to bring together various leaders to help foster political and economic dialogue.
www.worldbank.org
The World Bank is actively involved in economic development. This site contains data, news and accessible reports.
www.wto.org
The World Trade Organization is responsible for negotiating trade agreements between nations.

Publications

www.world-newspapers.com
This provides a country-by-country list of newspapers and related online sites, where available.

References

Acer (2007) Acer Investor Relations (www.acer.com, accessed 19 May 2007).

Antunes, D. and Thomas, H. (2007) The competitive (dis)advantages of European business schools, *Long Range Planning*, Vol 40 No 3, June, pp: 382–404.

BAA (2006) *Fog Disruption at Heathrow Airport*, British Airports Authority Press Release, 21 December.

BBC (2007a) *Zimbabwe in Currency Devaluation*, BBC News (accessed 7 September).

BBC (2007b) *New Moves to Ease Zimbabwe Crisis*, BBC News (accessed 2 October).

Bloom, B., Englehart, M., Furst, Hill, W. and Krathwohl, D. (1956) *Taxonomy of Educational Objectives: The Classification of Educational Goals. Handbook I: Cognitive Domain*, New York: Longman, Green.

Bloom, H. (2000) *How to Read and Why*, London: Fourth Estate.

Brennan, R., Baines, P. and Garneau, P. (2003) *Contemporary Strategic Marketing*, Basingstoke: Palgrave Macmillan.

British Airways (2006a) *British Airways Cancels All Domestic Flights at Heathrow due to Fog*, British Airways Press Release, 20 December.

British Airways (2006b) *Cancellation Due to Severe Fog*, British Airways Press Release, 22 December.

Cartwright, R. (2002) *Mastering the Business Environment,* Basingstoke: Palgrave Macmillan.

Cottrell, S. (2005) *Critical Thinking Skills: Developing Effective Analysis and Argument*, Basingstoke: Palgrave Macmillan.

CSO (2007) *Inflation Statistics* Zimbabwean Central Statistical Office (www.2imstat.co.2v, accessed 19 May 2007).

EUFIC (2007) 'Food and Mental Performance', *Food Today*, European Food Information Council (www.eufic.org/article/en/page/FTARTICLE/articl/food-mental-performance, accessed 18 August).

FSA (2007) 'Eat Well, Be Well. Are You Drinking Enough?', Foods Standards Agency (www.eatwell.gov.uk/healthydiet/nutritionessentials/drinks/drinkingenough, accessed 18 August 2007).

Garrett, G. (1952) *The Wild Wheels – The World of Henry Ford*, London: The Cresset Press.

Groucutt, J. (2005) *Foundations of Marketing*, Basingstoke: Palgrave Macmillan.

Groucutt, J. and Griseri, P. (2004) *Mastering e-Business*, Basingstoke: Palgrave Macmillan.

Johnson, G., Scholes, K. and Whittington, R. (2005) *Exploring Corporate Strategy* (7th edn), Harlow: FT Prentice Hall.

Levitt, T. (1960) Marketing myopia, *Harvard Business Review*, July/August, pp: 45–56.

Levitt, T. (1983) The globalization of markets, *Harvard Business Review*, May/June, pp: 92–102.

Mark, E.L. (1881) Maturation, fecundation and segmentation of *Limax campestris*, *Bulletin of the Museum of Comparative Zoology*, Vol 6, Part 2, No 12, pp: 173–625.

Maslow, A. (1954) *Motivation and Personality*, New York: Harper & Row. (A revised 3rd edition was published in 1987 by Longman, edited and updated by Robert Frager. In addition, textbooks on organizational behaviour and management generally refer to the work of Maslow.)

McLuhan, M. and Fiore, Q. (1969) *War and Peace in the Global Village*, New York: Bantam.

Porter, M.E. (1980) *Competitive Strategy*, New York: Free Press.

Porter, M.E. (1985) *Competitive Advantage*, New York: Free Press.

Porter, M.E. (1990) *The Competitive Advantage of Nations*, London/Basingstoke: Macmillan.

RBZ (2007) *Inflation Statistics*, Reserve Bank of Zimbabwe (www.rbz.co.zw, accessed 19 May 2007).

Rugman, A. (2001) *The End of Globalisation,* London: Random House.

Saunders, M., Lewis, P. and Thornhill, A. (2007) *Research Methods for Business Students* (4th edn), Harlow: FT/Prentice Hall.

Telford, A. and Groucutt, J. (1995) *Communicating for Improved Business Performance,* Cheltenham: Stanley Thornes.

Unilever (2006) *Annual Report and Accounts*, Unilever plc.

World Bank (2006) *Doing Business in Zimbabwe.*

World Bank (2007) *Zimbabwe – Country Data Profile,* Washington, DC: The World Bank Organization (www.worldbank.org).

Index

A
Administrators   9, 43, 45, 48, 81
Alumni   198
Assessment   xiv, 33–6, 43, 51, 62–3, 69,
    79–80, 84, 88–9, 91, 101, 103, 105,
    107, 122, 125–6, 128, 133–5, 149
    175–83
Assignments   9–10, 14–16, 18, 34–7,
    39–41, 59, 62–3, 69, 71, 76, 79–80, 84–5,
    88, 91, 93, 104–30, 133–4, 152, 176, 183
  format   105, 117–19

B
Bloom's taxonomy   15–17
Business magazines   5, 9, 27, 39, 69, 93,
    110, 113
Business myths   23–6
Business newspapers   5, 8–9, 39, 72, 93,
    113
Business schools   1–4, 43–5, 102

C
Case studies   7, 27, 34, 52, 90, 110–13,
    130, 133, 149, 152–3, 168, 175
Cheating   83–92, 119, 123, 184
Connections   xv, 6, 51, 78, 141, 160
Connectivity   53–8
Contacting your tutor   46–8
Critical thinking/evaluation   3–5,
    13–15,17, 22, 33–5, 51, 58–60, 71, 78,
    91, 104, 112, 120, 125–6, 139–40, 152,
    165, 167–9, 175–6, 179
Curriculum vitae   134–5, 196–8

D
Dissertations   4, 6–7, 9, 15–16, 19, 22, 29,
    36, 45, 59–60, 69, 79–81, 84–5, 93, 99,
    119, 175–93
  proposals   189–91
Documentary folders   8–9

E
Examinations   10, 14–15, 21, 27, 35, 41, 45,
    62–3, 75–6, 79–82, 87–8, 91, 105, 149–74

Expectations   9, 43, 156
Exploration   5–6, 14–15, 26–7, 32, 40, 49,
    78, 136, 175, 180

F
Failure (including fear of)   12, 26, 80, 87,
    100–2, 129, 133, 173–4
Feedback   35, 82, 101, 103, 105, 114, 117,
    122–6, 129–30, 147–8, 183, 188, 192
Formative assignment   107–8

G
Gantt chart   191
Generalizability   70, 78, 93

H
Harvard system   94, 97–9, 112, 116
Holistic perspective/approach   4, 11, 51

I
IELTS   22
Internet   38, 63, 70, 83–5, 93, 180

J
Journals   18, 27, 36–8, 60, 68–9, 78, 80, 85,
    93–4, 97, 110, 113, 118, 128, 141, 163,
    180

L
Language   5, 21–2, 38, 116, 118, 121, 125,
    162–3, 183, 185, 205
Learning outcomes/objectives   xiii, 15, 26,
    28, 62–3, 66, 75, 128
Learning process   xiii, 10, 12, 14
Learning resources   5, 8–9, 36–40,
    49–51,60, 70–4, 93, 113
Learning styles   xiii, 41, 61, 206
Lecture notes   9, 26–7, 36, 66–8, 85, 157
Lectures   7, 12, 18, 26–7, 32, 35, 40, 42, 45,
    49, 63–4, 66–7, 71, 75, 77–8, 149, 153
Leisure and relaxation   40–2, 75, 77–8

M
Module guide/workbook   xiv, 12, 15, 27,
    62–6, 75, 78, 80, 114, 120

Modules   xiv, 4–5, 7, 10, 12, 19, 22, 35, 41, 45–6, 51, 62–6, 75, 80, 85, 88–9, 102–03, 117, 128, 140, 149, 153, 176
Motivation   10, 12, 49
Multiple choice   151, 153

N
Note taking   71–4
Numerical tests   34

O
Observation   7–9, 49

P
Peer review   113–16, 127, 130, 139–40
Physical environment   60–1, 78, 158–9
Placements   18, 21, 196
Plagiarism   62, 83, 85–8, 90–2, 94, 119, 123
Portfolio logs   123–6, 192
Positive thinking   10, 139, 153–4, 157, 160, 174
Poster presentations   34, 108
Presentations   43, 63, 107, 133, 139–48
Programme structure   19–21, 26, 63, 76, 78, 102, 153

Q
Questionnaires   178, 183

R
Referencing   93–9, 107, 112, 119, 123, 125–6, 163, 179
Regulations   36, 62, 82, 84, 114, 158–9, 176, 197
Reliability   69–70, 78, 93
Report format   109–10
Research   14, 45, 68–71, 105, 109, 120, 125, 127, 134, 175–93, 205–6
Revision   75–6, 149, 153–6, 174

S
Seminars   18, 27, 34, 45, 49, 60, 63, 110, 153
Silo thinking   51–2
Supervisor (dissertations)   45, 80, 84, 177, 182–9, 191–3
Study time   12, 35–6, 61, 63
Study timetable/plan   75–8, 182
Studying previous experience   14
Summative assignment   107–8
Surveys   49, 70, 183
Synthesis   17, 113, 121, 125, 150, 152, 172–3, 176.

T
Teamwork (group work)   58, 61–3, 106, 131–8, 147
Teamwork agreement   136–8
Textbooks   xiii–xiv, 5, 10, 14, 18, 21–2, 27, 58, 60, 64–5, 68, 70–5, 78, 85, 93–4, 97, 141, 149, 153, 163, 199–206
Triangulation   69–70, 78, 93, 104, 123, 180
Tutors   xv, 5, 10, 14, 18, 21–2, 27, 36, 43–9, 63, 66–7, 71, 79–82, 86, 88–9, 112, 117, 119, 123, 130, 132, 135, 139–40, 148–9, 163, 174, 176, 184–9

V
Validity   59, 69–70, 78, 93, 123, 180
Vancouver system   94–7, 99
Visuals   34, 141–5

W
Writer's block   119, 122
Workshops   27, 63